Drawing People

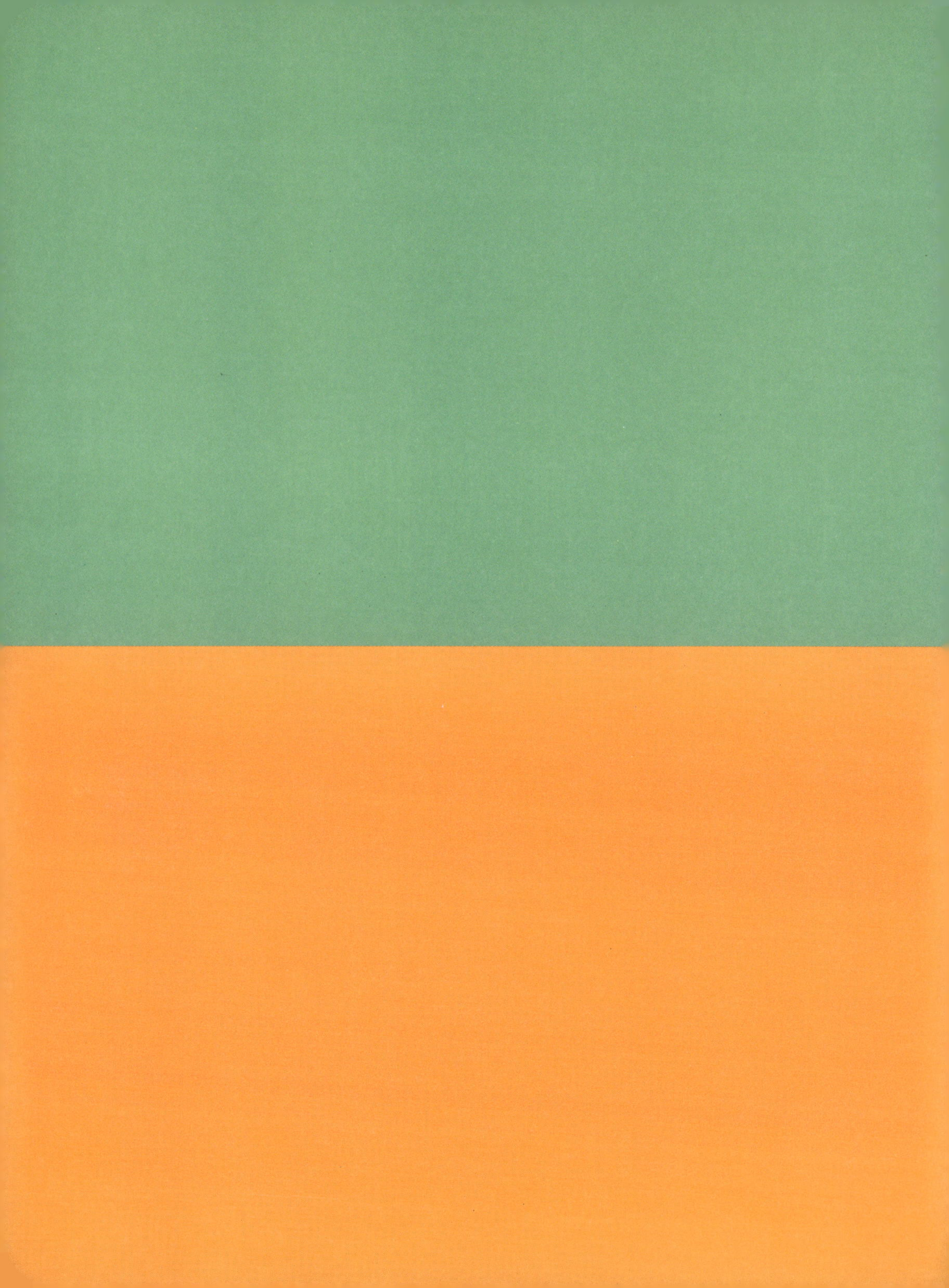

WRITTEN AND
ILLUSTRATED BY
VIKTORIJA
SEMJONOVA

Drawing People

100 Prompts, Projects & Playful Exercises

Hardie Grant

BOOKS

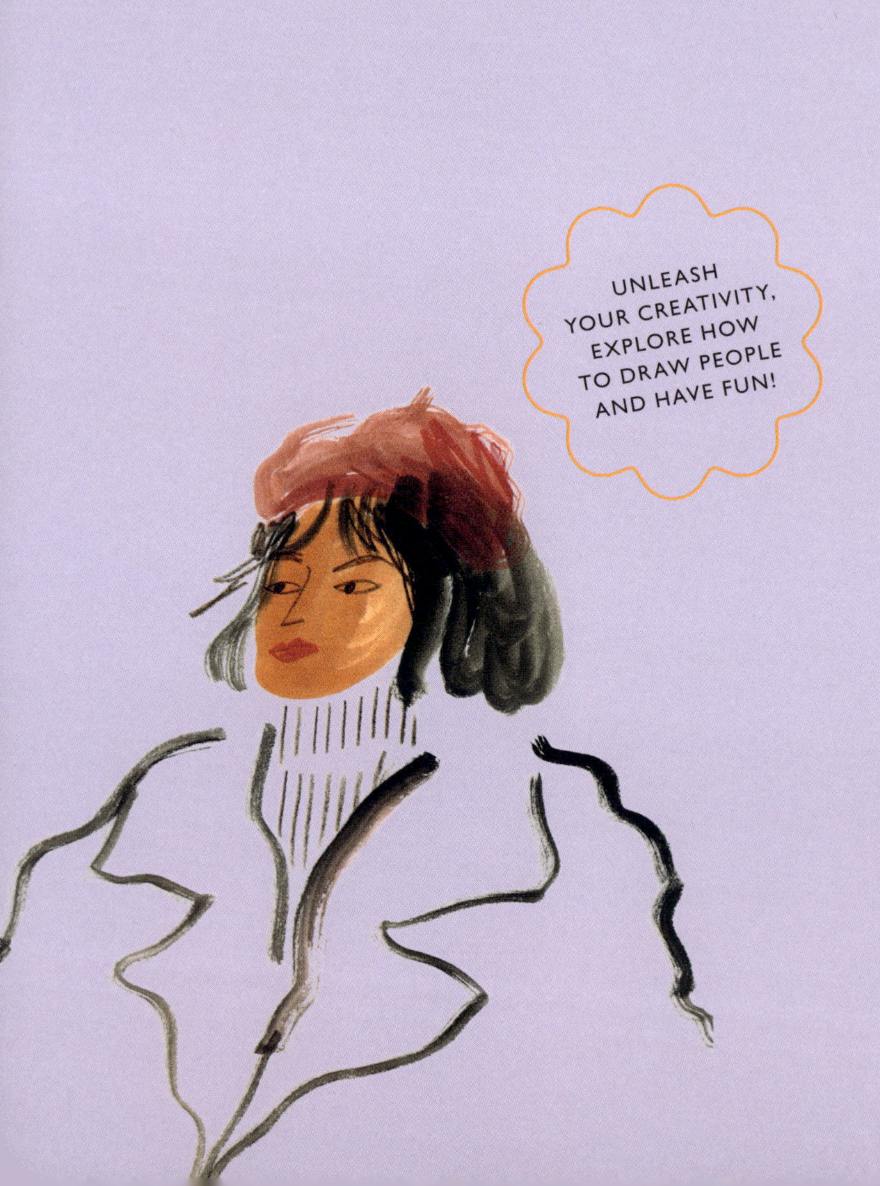

UNLEASH
YOUR CREATIVITY,
EXPLORE HOW
TO DRAW PEOPLE
AND HAVE FUN!

Contents

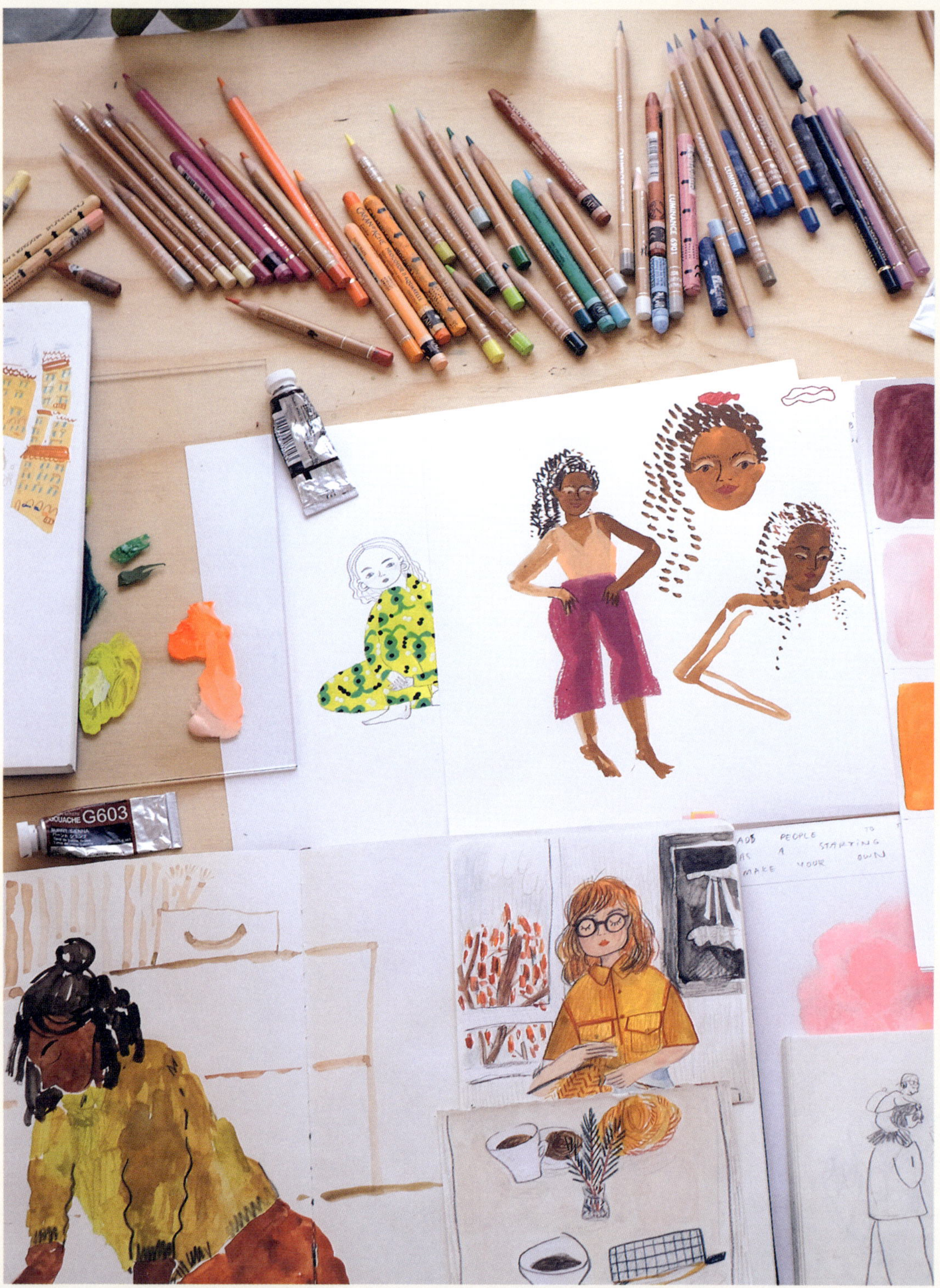
ADD PEOPLE TO
AS A STARTING
MAKE YOUR OWN

WELCOME TO
DRAWING PEOPLE

My name is Viktorija and I'm an illustrator. When people ask me what I draw, I say faces and places. I have enjoyed drawing people from an early age and the majority of my illustration work now is centred around people – I have drawn over 500 portraits at live events.

When a person sits for a portrait, I look at them and try to see what is visually unique about them. Then I ask questions to get to know the person, so I can add both emotional and visual aspects to the drawing. During sittings I often have some of the most interesting conversations. There's a special connection when you draw another human. And I try to bring this connection and curiosity to all the people I draw, whether they are imaginary, commissioned portraits or strangers on the street.

Over the years I have been asked many questions about drawing people, which inspired me to dive deeper into the subject and understand what aspiring artists are most curious about and what aspects they struggle with. These conversations, and the workshops I teach both in person and online, provided the foundation for this book.

In *Drawing People*, I have collected drawings from my sketchbooks. I have tried to include as much variety as possible in the artworks to make this book interesting and to show you that there is no right or wrong way to draw people or to be an artist!

This book is all about finding enjoyment in the process, letting go of expectations and really having fun.

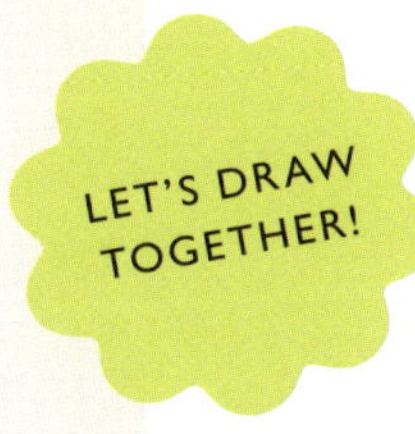

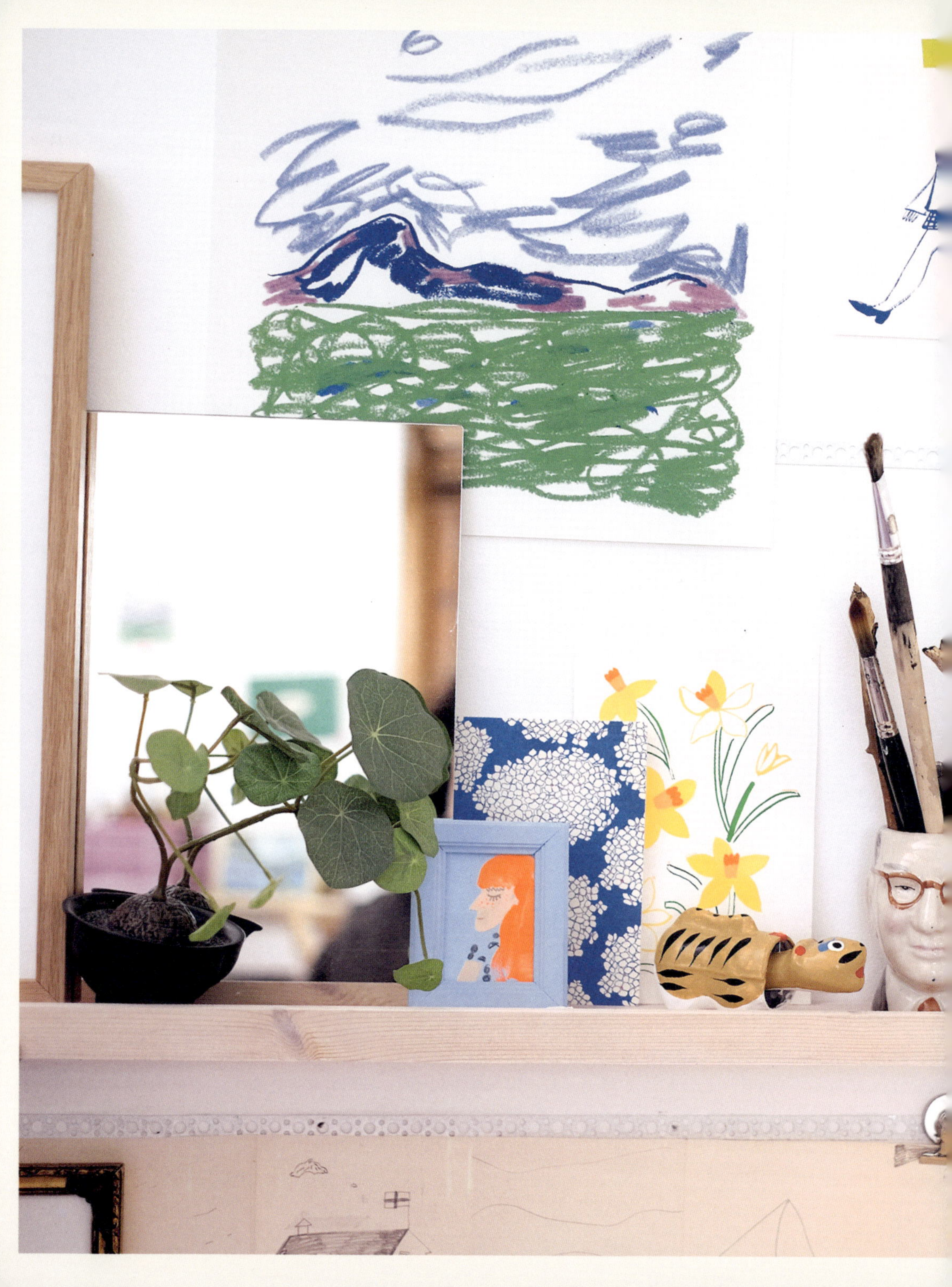

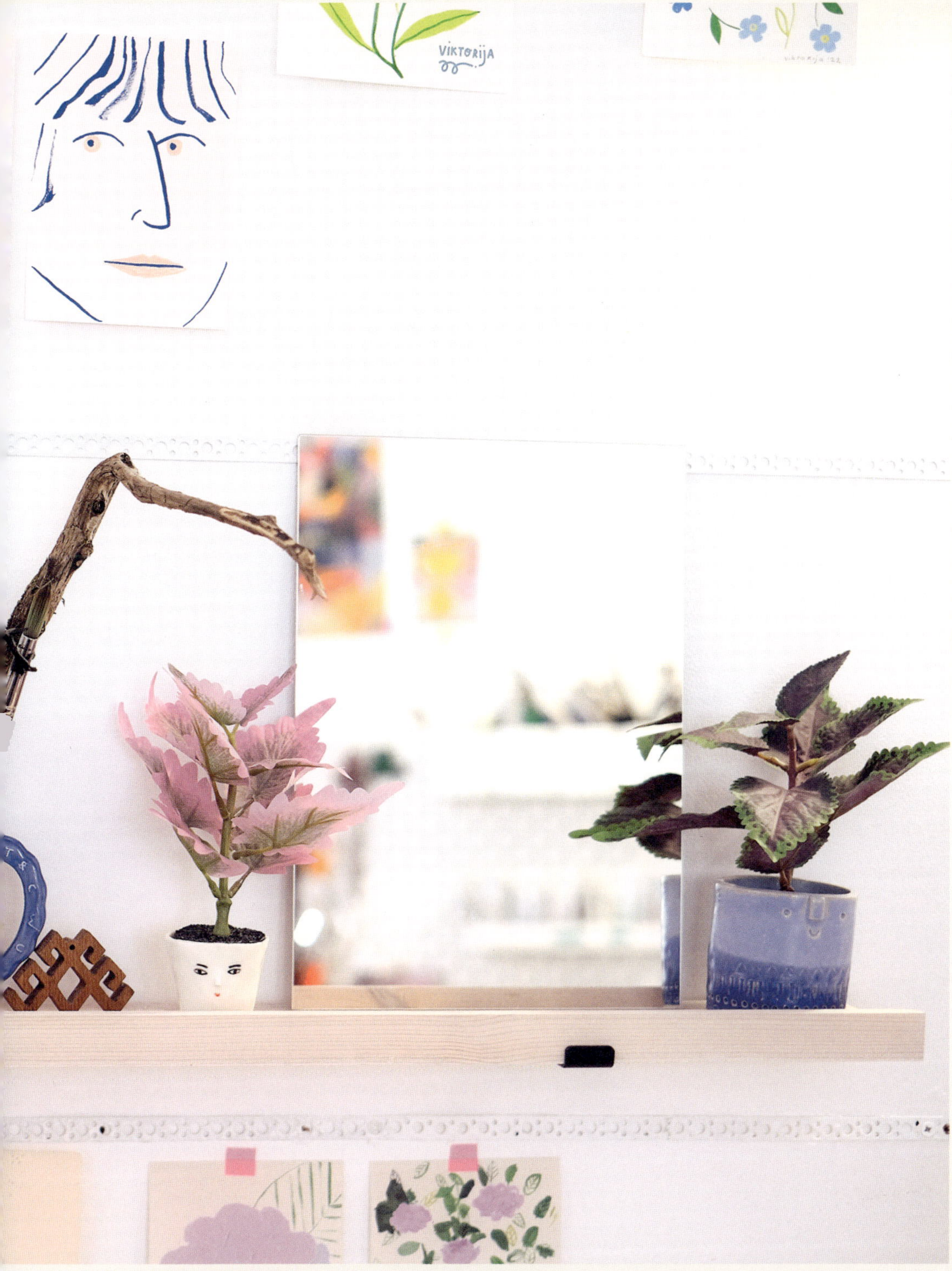

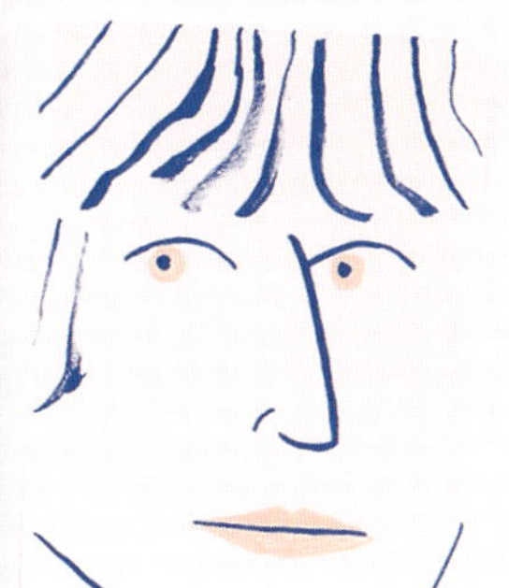
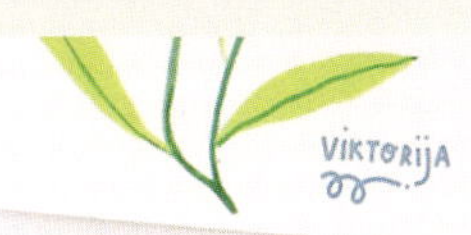

VIKTORIJA

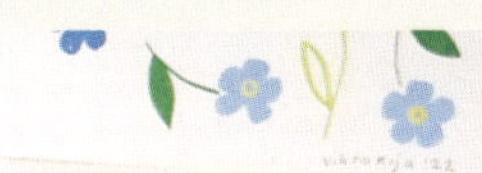

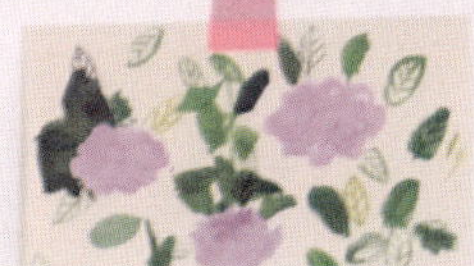

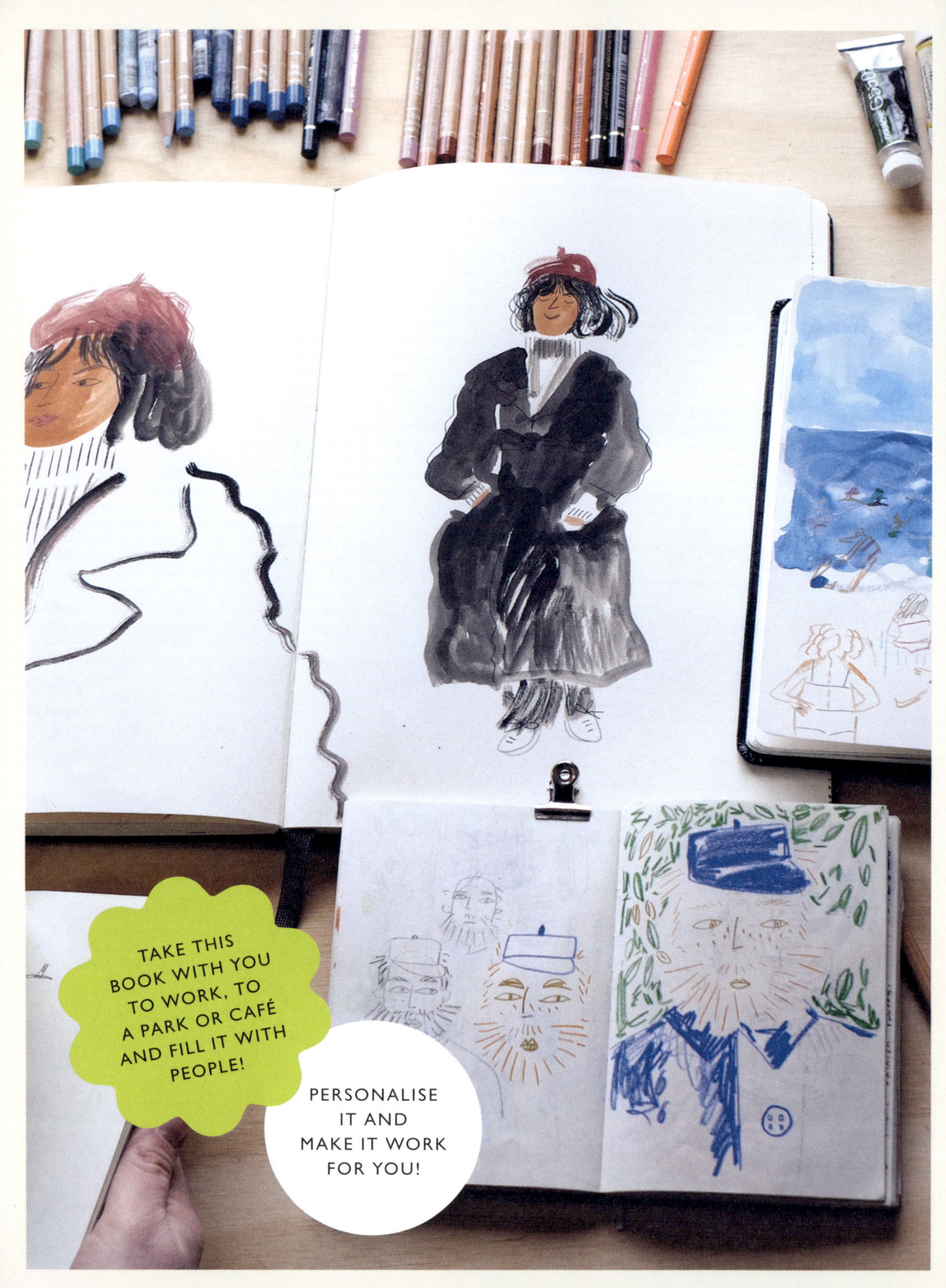
TAKE THIS
BOOK WITH YOU
TO WORK, TO
A PARK OR CAFÉ
AND FILL IT WITH
PEOPLE!

PERSONALISE
IT AND
MAKE IT WORK
FOR YOU!

PROJECT KEY:

PROJECT

PLAY

PROMPT

PROJECTS teach you how to draw by following an exercise along with Viktorija.

PLAYS are an opportunity to express yourself .

PROMPTS encourage you to try something new.

This book contains 100 projects on drawing people that differ in difficulty and type. Some focus on drawing techniques, others on anatomy and some will inspire you to think outside the box.

We'll begin with exercises that offer more guidance and are suitable for beginners. As you move through the book, the exercises allow you more freedom and independence. You can either work through the book sequentially or pick and choose depending on the mood you're in and the time and materials you have to hand.

In some exercises, you are advised to use techniques suited to certain mediums, for example, drawing with opaque pencil in a light colour over a dark background. But it's just a suggestion. Get to know your materials, understand their limitations and experiment, adjusting the exercises when you need to. Make them work for you. Change, tweak or come up with your own variations to suit the materials you are using and your working style.

You will need your own sketchbook for the four projects, as there isn't room in the book for you to draw them. If you prefer, you can keep a separate sketchbook dedicated to all 100 exercises. You can extend the exercise briefs into that sketchbook, using it to test materials, create colour palettes or play with mark making.

It is best to draw people from real life but it's not always possible. In cases where you don't have a live subject, use photos of people you have in your phone, pictures from magazines or even draw from the sofa while watching TV.

Practice makes perfect! Treat drawing as you would any other new skill and do a little every day. You will soon see results.

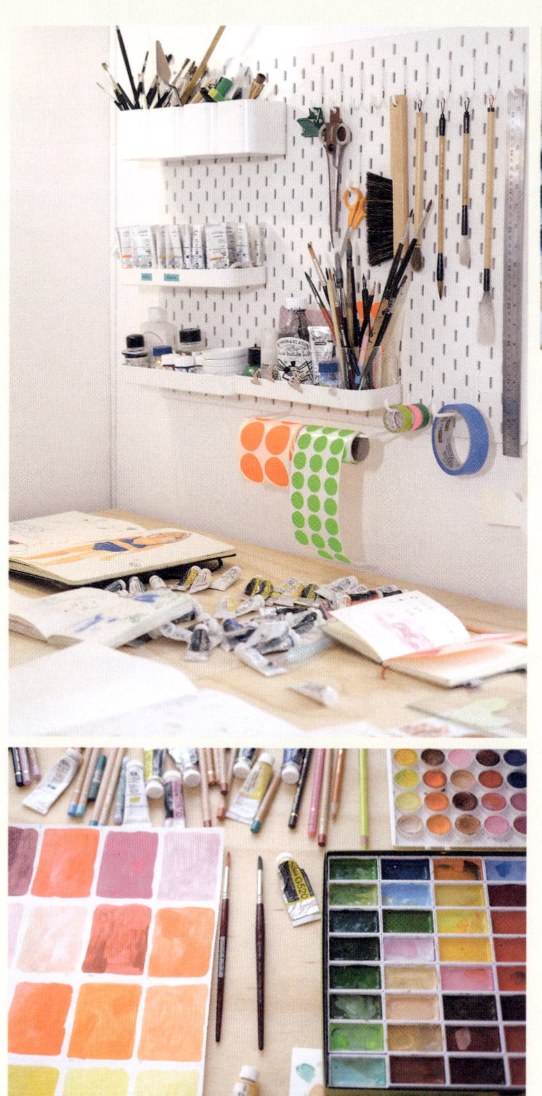

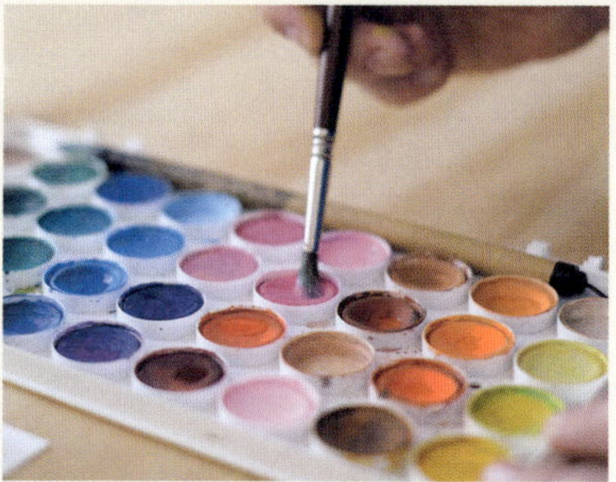

To make this book I used materials ranging in both price and quality, from supermarket gouache, to markers, pencils, pastels, ink and watercolours. I truly believe the best materials are the ones you already have and the ones that you really enjoy using. Is it markers? Cheap watercolour paints? Expensive oil pencils? It's up to you!

I love using art materials such as children's gouache for shape, and colouring pencils for lines. This is my favourite combination – something with a flowing quality and texture for shape, and another medium that can achieve quirky marks for the lines.

As well as your mediums of choice, you will need basic materials including a graphite pencil, eraser and sharpener. In some projects you will be encouraged to make a collage, so scissors and tape or glue might be useful, too.

How do you choose your preferred medium? I recommend you think about these three things!

YOU DON'T NEED ANY PARTICULAR
MATERIALS TO USE THIS BOOK, IT'S ALL
ABOUT WHAT YOU ARE COMFORTABLE
USING AS WELL AS MEDIUMS YOU
WOULD LIKE TO EXPLORE.

1/ Line and shape.

When choosing mediums, think of using one type for making
lines and another for creating shapes. For example, you can opt
for watercolours for shapes and pencils for lines. Or perhaps you
can work with colouring pencils for both line and shape. The
combinations are endless.

2/ Setting limitations.

Narrowing down your materials will make things more interesting
for you. You can always change what you are using but first, try
creating a limited selection of art materials.

3/ Working space.

Consider where you will be making art. Will it be from your sofa,
kitchen table or designated desk? You could have a more elaborate
set-up for longer projects and a portable set-up for bite-size exercises.
(Get a water brush if you want to use watercolours or gouache on the
go, then you won't need a jar and a brush. This will make the process
so much easier.)

You will be able to do all the exercises in this book with the most
limited of materials. I am certain you will be able to complete the
exercises with just one graphite pencil! I hope you will have fun
and enjoy the process, so no pressure.

Tools & Materials

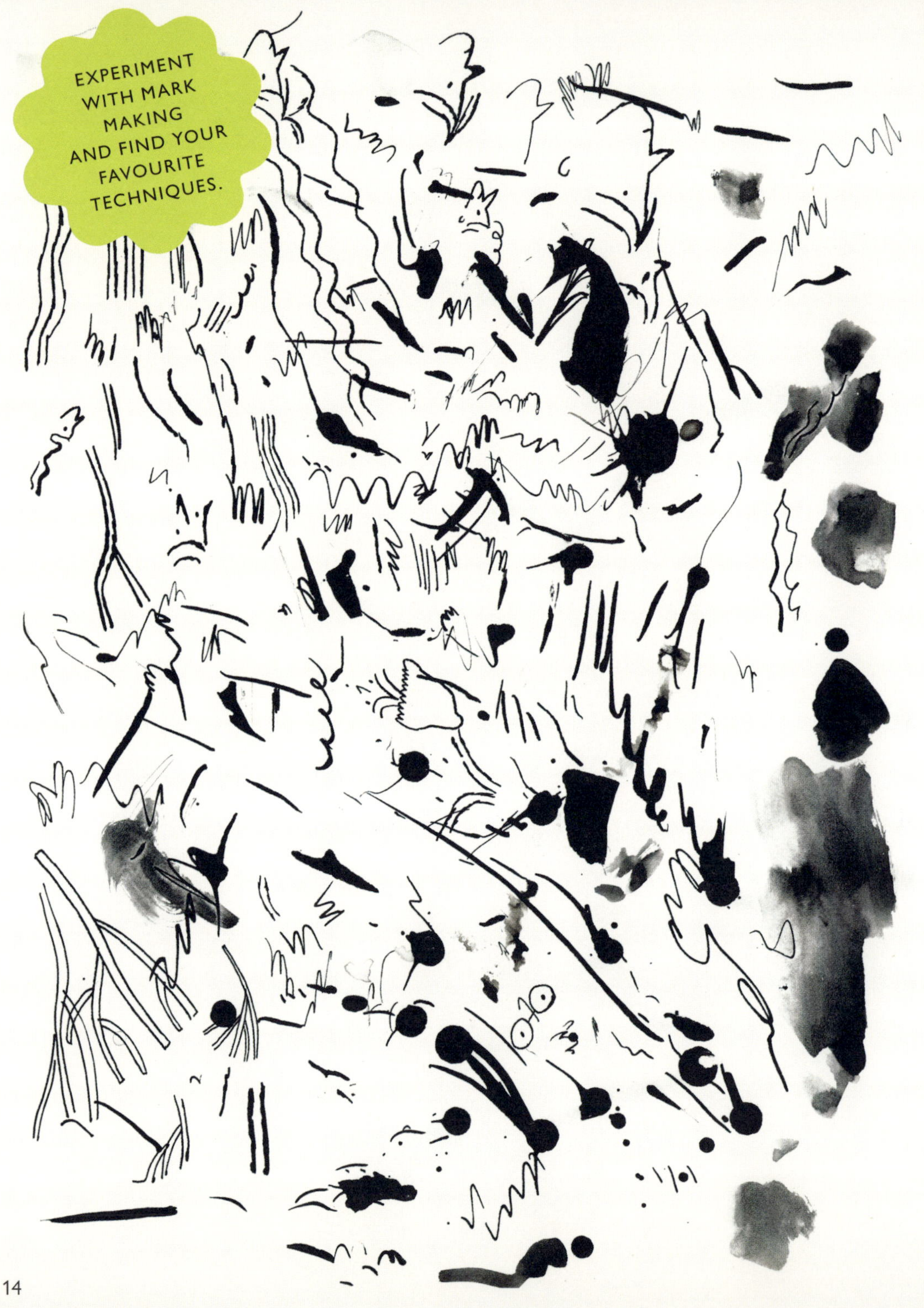

EXPERIMENT WITH MARK MAKING AND FIND YOUR FAVOURITE TECHNIQUES.

14

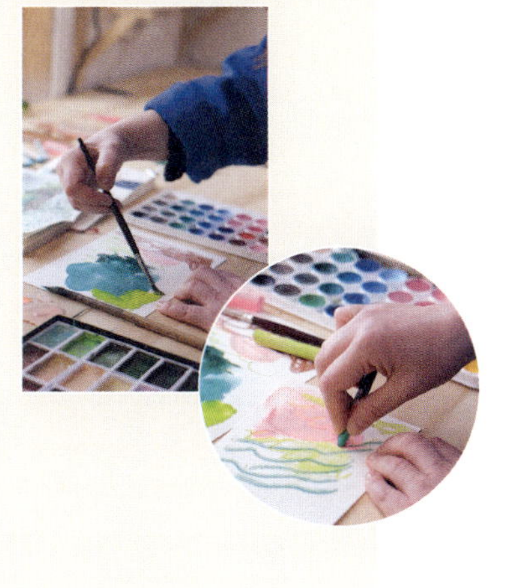

Mark Making

1/ The properties of the material.

What material are you using? Is it dry, powdery or water-soluble?
Can you add water to it, smear it or mix it? For example, if you are
using a water-soluble pencil, try drawing directly on a wet surface
as well as dipping the pencil in the water before drawing on dry
paper to see what results you yield. If you are using markers, layer
the different colours over each other, or use them to layer over
pencil. Examine the properties of each material you use and don't
be afraid to try and do something unexpected, using it in a new way.

2/ How do you apply it to the paper?

How will you make marks with your medium? For example, if you use
a marker try tapping it, creating dots or working really fast to cover
an entire area. With a paintbrush, cover an area with an even layer
of paint, make random brushstrokes or press the brush into the paper.

3/ How do you hold your medium?

When drawing with any tool, change the angle at which you hold
it as well as the thickness of the line you make. Change the speed
with which you make marks. Think fast, slow, careful and loose.

Do you notice what kind of marks you make if you are tense and
slouched versus free and open? The marks you make will always
reflect your feelings and body language.

Set time aside to play and make marks with no goal in mind.
Try unconventional materials, like using sticks to paint with ink,
to create unusual marks. Create your own library of marks that you
can refer to as you work, noticing which ones you enjoy making
the most and those you are most curious to explore.

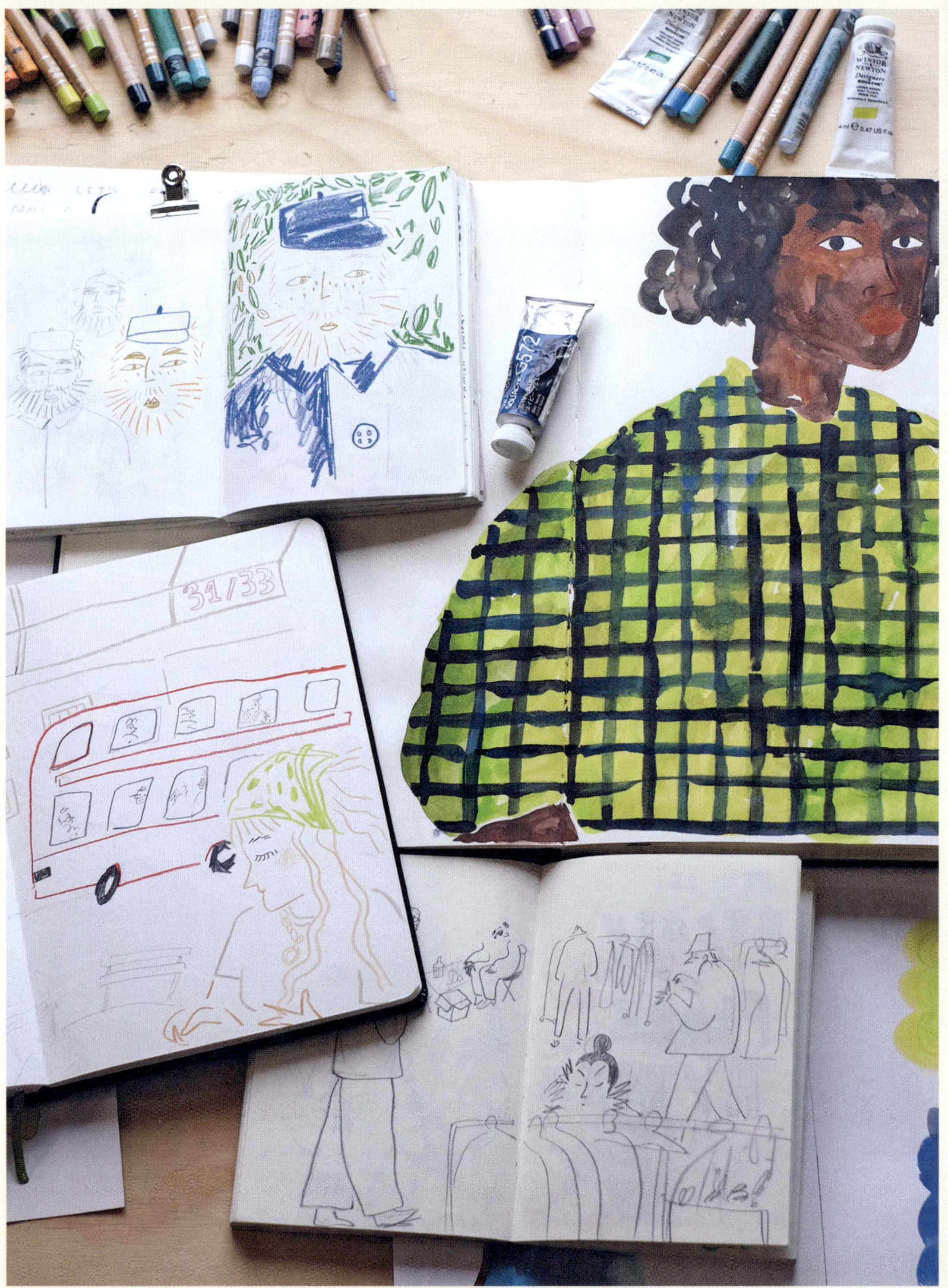

Composition

The first thing to consider is format. When drawing in this book, you will either have a whole two-page spread to work with, a page or half a page. In many cases the composition is determined for you and in others you will need to decide for yourself.

If you take your practice outside this book, you can choose your canvas, be it portrait, landscape, square, round or concertina. Once you have decided the format, you can choose the size of your artwork. Do you prefer to create bigger or smaller pieces? Often swapping the size inspires you to work in a new way!

The next aspect to consider is how you will place people in your drawing. Are they in the distance or close to the viewer? Do you see the full figure or just a portion of their body? Are they in the centre of your space or squeezed to the side, top or bottom?

Are you using the rules of linear perspective or creating a more stylised image ignoring traditional conventions? Do you draw hyperrealistic figures or bend shapes to fit your needs?

Composition is a powerful tool. Drawing someone so large that they barely fit on the page creates a very different effect compared with drawing a small figure in the middle of the page. Each will communicate a different feeling, emotion or mood.

By answering these questions before you begin your artwork, you will be able to come up with unusual and interesting compositions and solve many challenges.

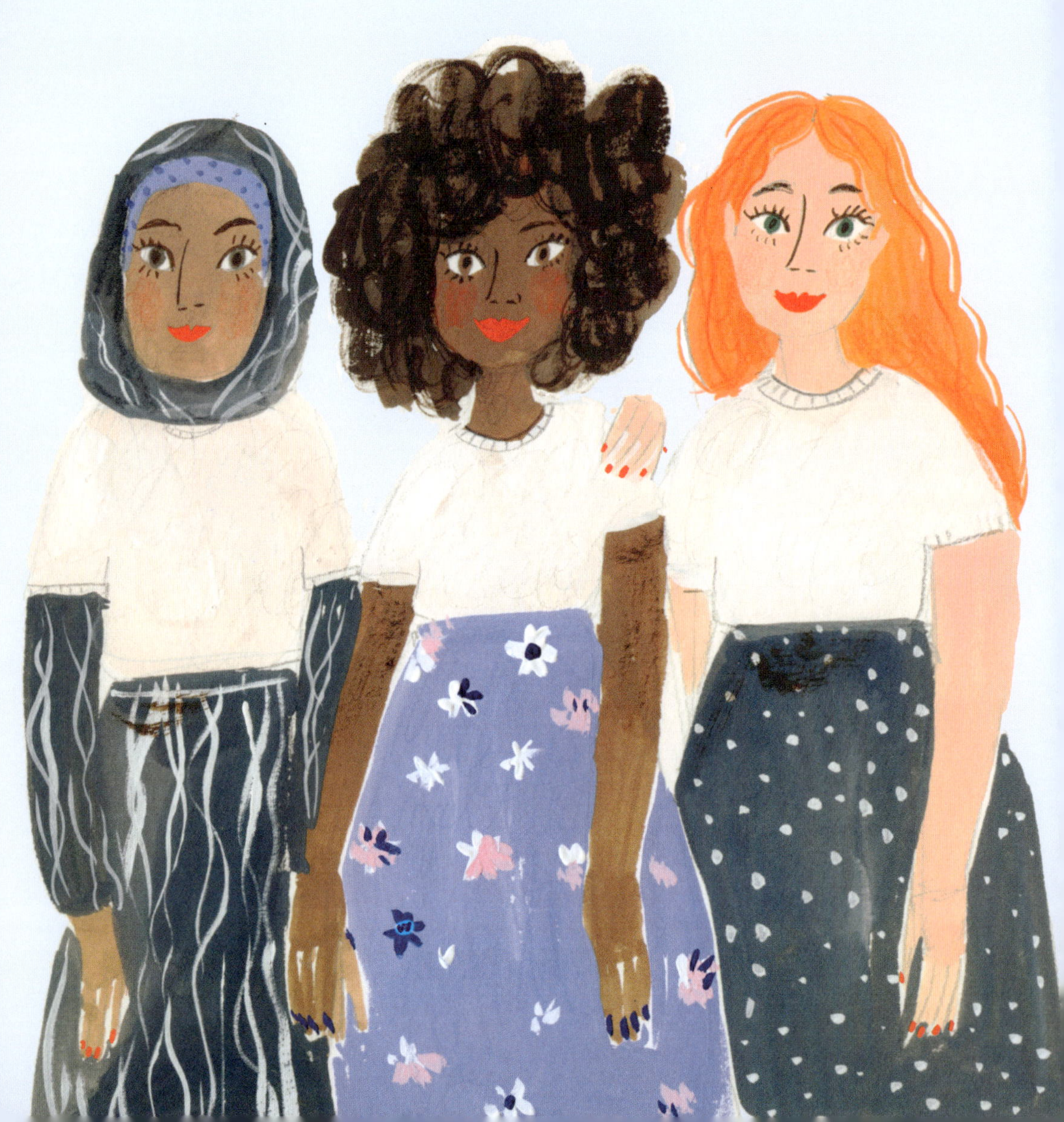

THE FIRST STEP IS TO FIND BASIC SHAPES WITHIN THE HUMAN FORM.

DRAWING PEOPLE IS EXCITING,
BUT IT CAN ALSO BE DAUNTING AS
THROUGH ONE DRAWING WE ARE
COMMUNICATING SOMEONE'S INNER
WORLD AND THEIR WHOLE IDENTITY.

Let's break down the process into bite-size elements and tackle it one step at a time. With practice, it becomes easier each time we do it. As with any new skill or muscle, the more you practise, the better you become!

To truly capture someone we need to look closely and pay attention to that person and the lines and/or shapes that make them. When you start drawing the person, ask yourself these questions: What is unique about them? What is their most striking feature? Is it their eyebrows, beautiful eyes, charismatic nose, hairstyle, lip shape, bone structure or body language? Maybe it's a facial expression or a feeling they are channelling? What mood are they in? Are they grounded, excited, sad, confused? What do you want to communicate with your drawing?

Start by drawing a person or face using geometric shapes, marking the width and the height. Add vertical and horizontal guidelines (this step is explained in detail over the page). Treat the face as any other 3D object. Which bits stand out? Which recede? Add more details and refine the sketch.

We are all unique and our noses, eyes and chins will be different from anyone else's. But there are a few proportions that are similar to everyone, and we will use them as a starting point for all our portraits. Remember that you can adjust them according to whoever you are drawing.

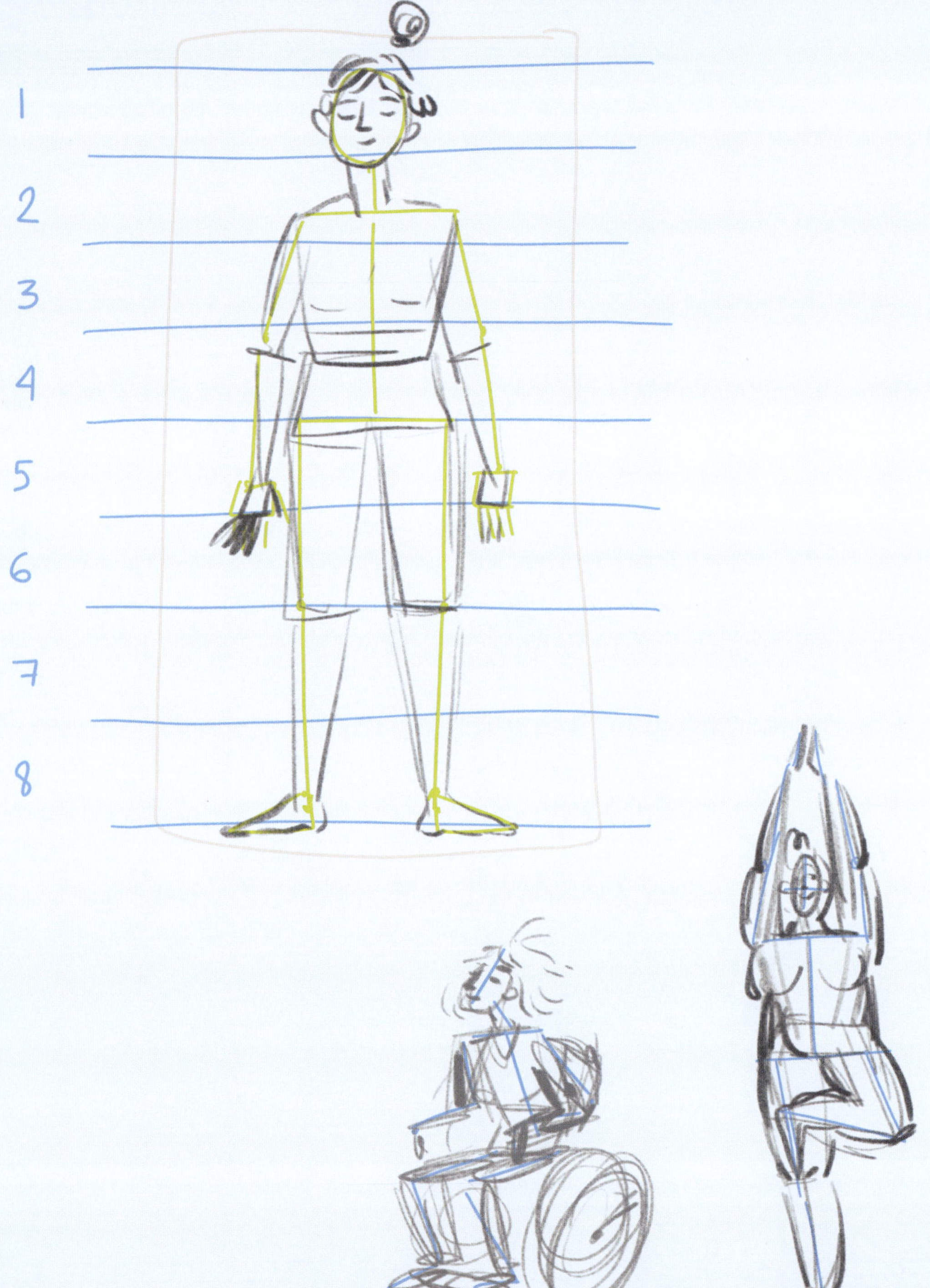

1
2
3
4
5
6
7
8

LET'S START WITH THE FULL BODY.

First sketch a rectangle and mark the width and the height of the person. Add horizontal lines to divide the height of your figure into eight equal parts. The top half is head to hips, and the bottom half is the legs.

Section 1 is where the head will go; the shoulders will be in section 2; the chest/torso will be section 3; the waist will be between section 3 and 4 and the elbows will be at the same line as the waist. You can then use this proportion to measure your arms. The upper arm will be the same length from the shoulder to the elbow as the lower arm is from the elbow to the wrist. And by measuring shoulder to waist length you can figure out the length of your arms.

Legs will start at the border between sections 4 and 5 (the length from the thigh to the knee is equal to the length from the knee to the ankle) and move through sections 6 and 7, with the feet in section 8.

Once you have mapped out where each body part will sit, draw a stick figure, pictured here in yellow, with an oval for the head and lines for the spine, shoulders, hips, waist, arms and legs. Add dots where the elbows, wrists, knees and ankles will go. This structure can help you to draw any pose – just treat the various elements as your guidelines and experiment with tilting, lifting arms, moving legs or turning around.

Once you are happy with the pose, add geometric shapes to the stick figure to add dimension and depth.

When you have finished drawing the body, add clothes and details such as hair and facial features. You can continue refining each element in the same way until you achieved the level of detail you are happy with. Then you can move on to adding colour.

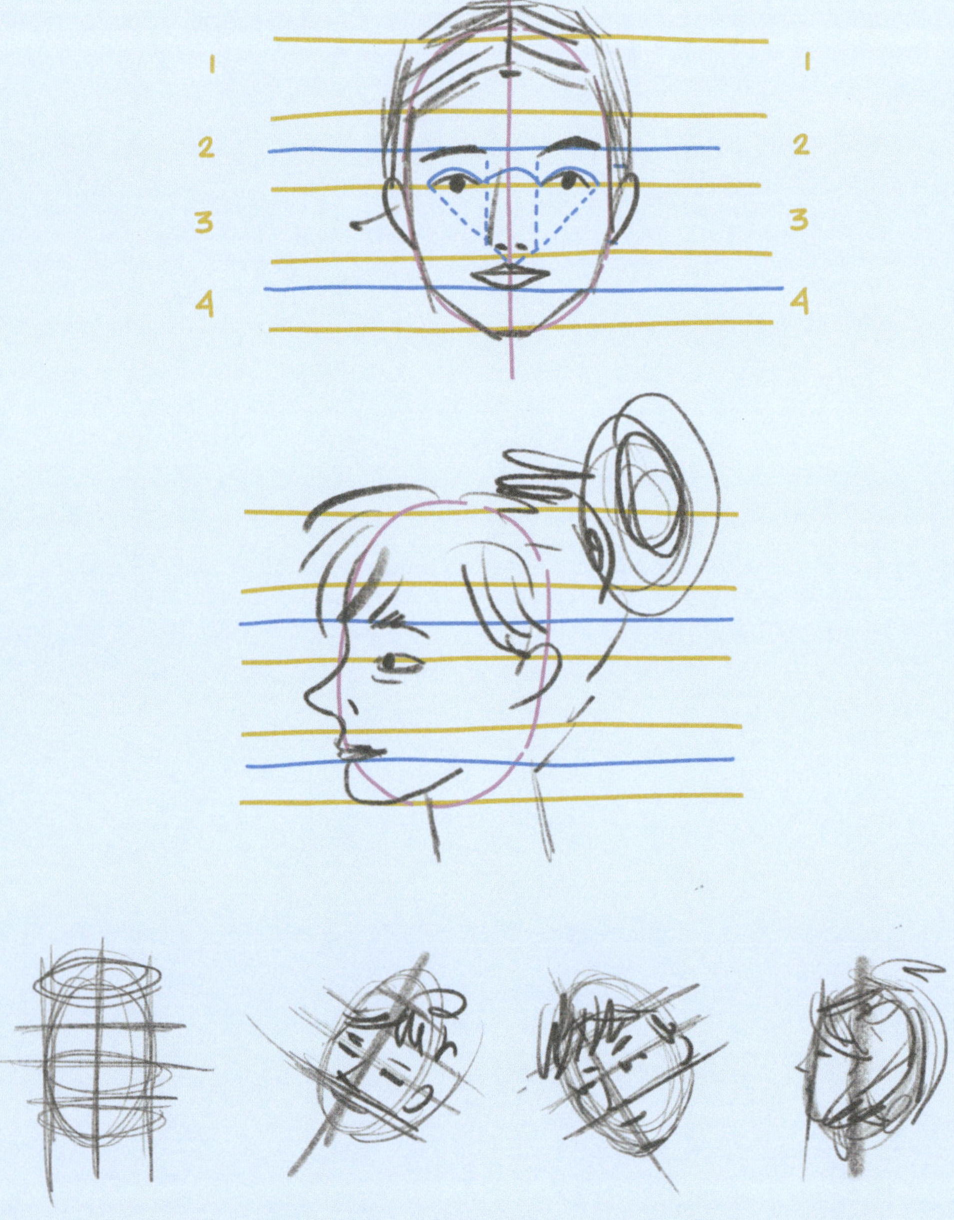

1
2
3
4
1
2
3
4

Start by drawing an oval shape and then dividing it equally with one vertical and five horizontal lines, so you have four equal parts. Divide your second and fourth quarters into halves again by adding two more horizontal lines (shown in blue opposite).

The middle line is where the eyes will go and where the nose begins. The space between the eyes is equal to the width of each eye as well as the width of the nose. Eyebrows will go around that extra line you drew in section 2. The nose will stop just above the line of the last part. And the lips will sit above the blue line in section 4. Ears are roughly the same length as your nose.

Use these proportions when you are drawing people in profile, too, and know that the width of the widest part of the head is roughly the same as the distance between the top of the head and the chin. No face is symmetrical, so neither should be your drawing.

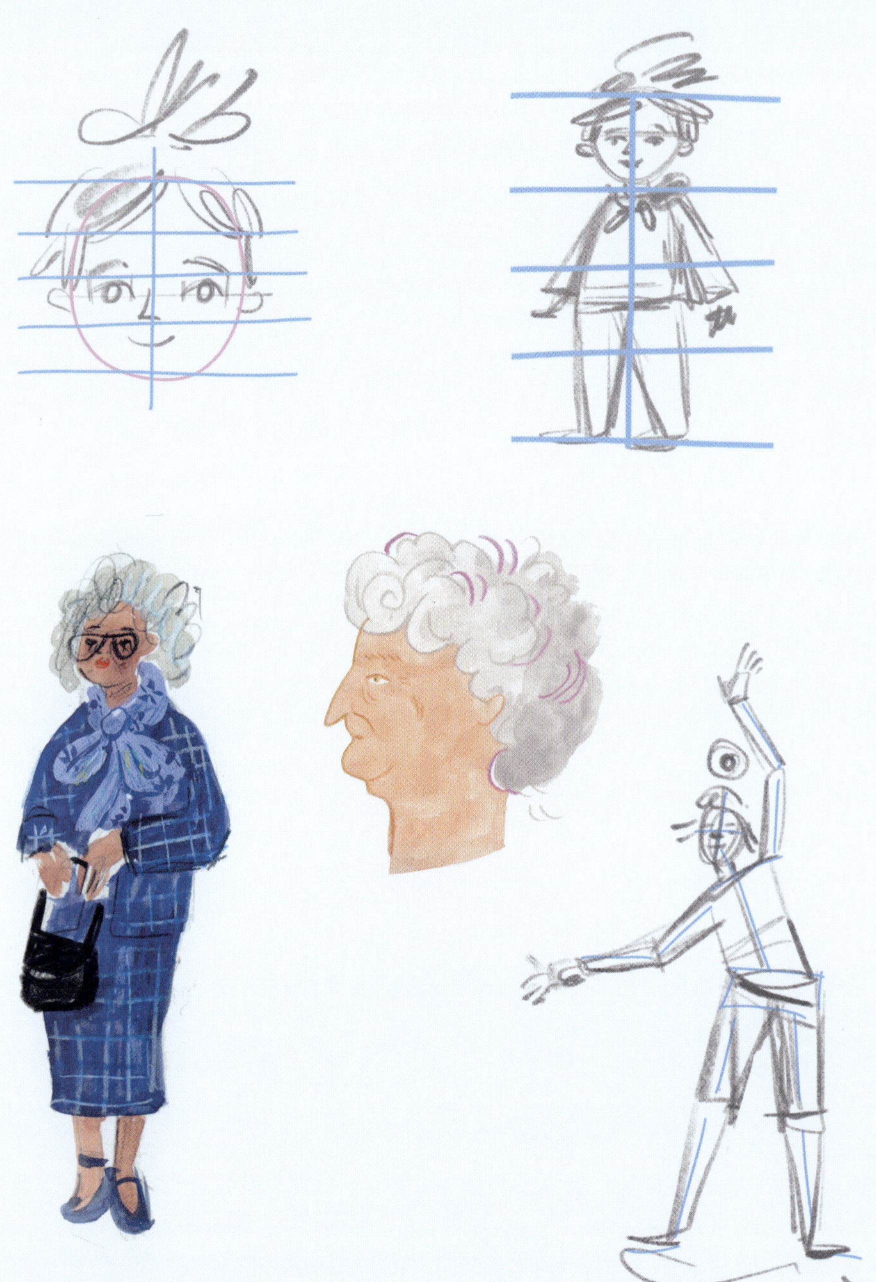

The younger your subject, the bigger their head, eyes and forehead will be, but the smaller the nose.

If you are drawing a young child, the head would be part 1 of 4 as shown opposite, with a rounder head and softer lines. Kids' arms and legs are much shorter than adults' compared to the body. The younger the child, the shorter and rounder the limbs. For example, if a toddler raises their arms, they will barely reach the top of their head (and their legs will be much, much shorter than the body).

When drawing kids in motion, pay attention to how their balance differs from adults' and how much control they have of their limbs.

Drawing older people differs, too, both in posture and face. We all age differently but in general the posture will be stiffer, maybe with a rounder back, and there may be less range of movement and shorter steps.

The older the person is, the less fat they will have in their face. We start to get wrinkles and some features change, like more visible cheekbones, more skin on the jawline, thinner lips and receding or greying hair colour.

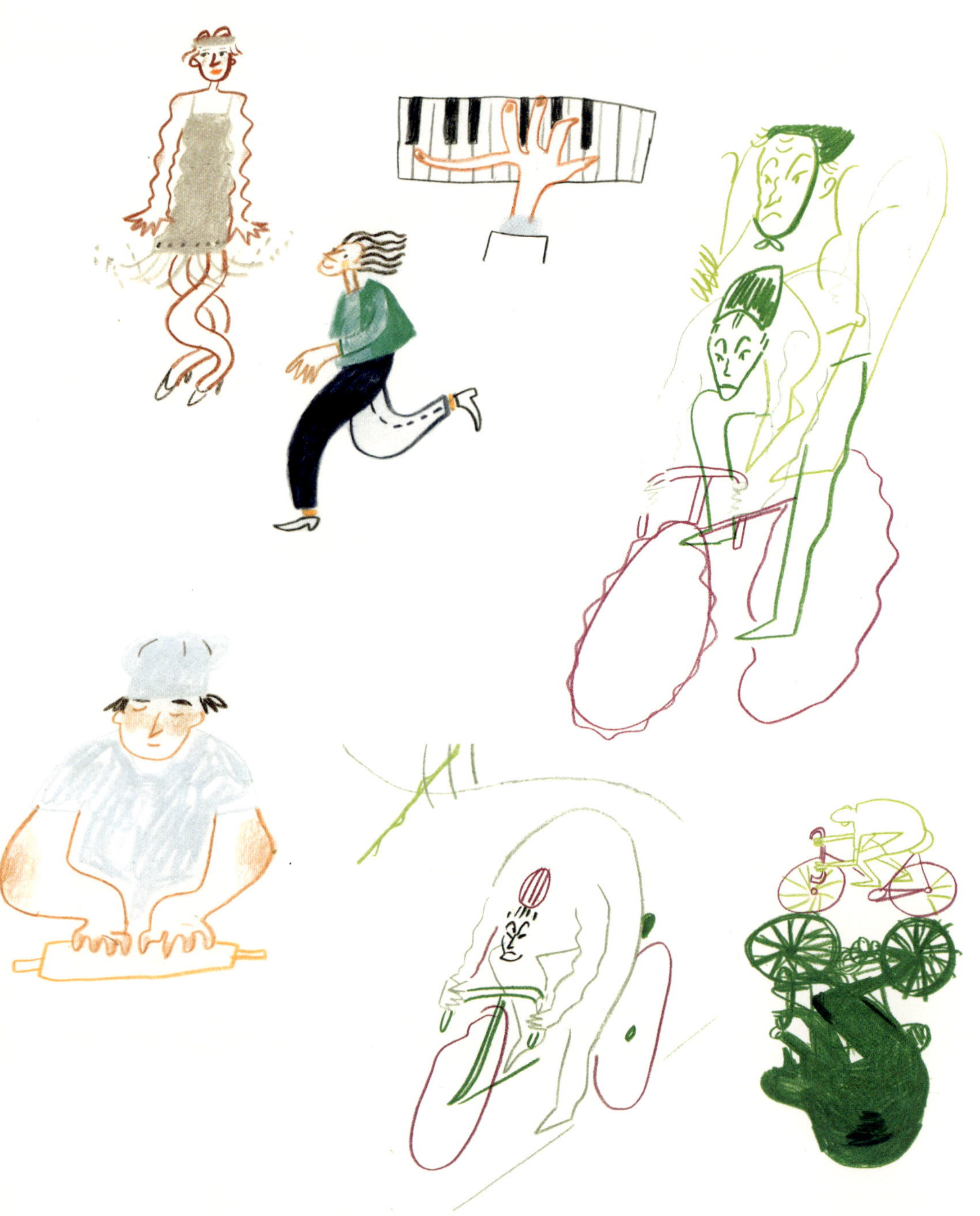

EXAGGERATION IS ONE OF THE MOST FUN PARTS OF DRAWING, AND A VERY USEFUL TOOL.

You can exaggerate a feature, movement, shape or pose. A piano player may have their little finger stretched so far to reach that low key, a baker has such big and strong arms for kneading the dough… Exaggerated features help to communicate all of these ideas in your drawing.

When drawing emotions and movement, it's better to forget about anatomical rules and start from a place of feeling. Start sketching out your feelings and don't be afraid to play with the lines and marks you make.

You can accentuate a pose, for example someone crunching over a computer, a facial feature or an emotion. The main thing to think about when using this tool is the end goal. Are you communicating emotion? Posture? Movement? Speed? Do the extra-long and thick legs or big eyes and wild hair serve the purpose?

When drawing emotions, you can add details to your mark making to help you communicate that feeling. For example, if you are drawing someone angry you can draw hair to match: messy, wild and sticking up in all directions. Pay special attention to the eyebrows, eye shape, lips and cheeks. Watch your face and notice how it changes with different expressions. And pay attention to body language. Then see if you can incorporate all these things into your drawings!

People as Symbols.

Our brains are primed to see faces in objects, and this makes it very easy to create an abstract human form that viewers will still recognise as a person. A triangle, a dot or a squiggle can easily be interpreted as a human figure. Have a go yourself and jot down some symbols that can be reworked into people.

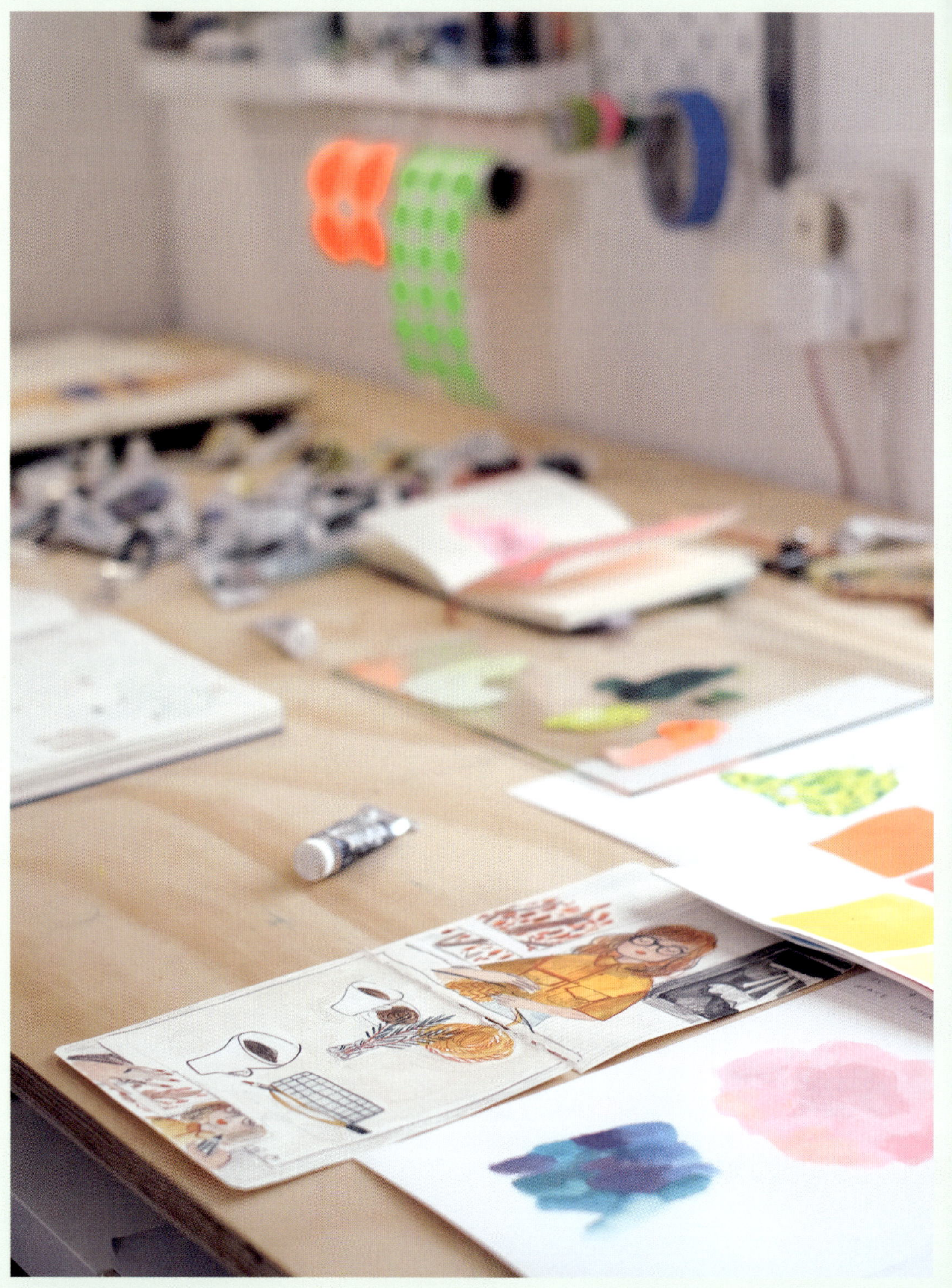

WHAT DOES IT MEAN, TO FIND YOUR VOICE IN YOUR ART?

Some people say it's style, but I really think it's something within us which makes us unique, our own visual language, our way of making art. It is something that comes from within. Think back to when you were a kid, drawing with such confidence and honesty. We didn't think 'what is art?' or worry about how things should look, we just drew.

Somewhere along the way we can get lost in other people's work, we become self-aware, shy and stop listening to that inner voice. But I believe that we all still have that very strong voice, that very distinct way of drawing within us. By nurturing it and listening to it, we are able to create work that is unmistakably ours. To let go of preconceived ideas of how you want your work to look, just draw, in a way that is natural to you. And then during this practice something happens, and you create something that never existed before, and is uniquely yours!

The way we draw changes over the years. We grow, change materials, and the final results develop, too. But as long as you make something without judgement and expectation, you are on the right path. You can set goals for your drawing but always listen to your inner voice.

How to check in with your unique voice.
- Find a reference image. Put a timer on for 3 minutes and in that time, try to create five drawings based on your reference image.
- Take a 10-minute break, before returning to your drawings. This time, put your reference image out of sight, set the timer for one minute and start sketching based on your last five drawings.
- Leave the drawings again and come back to them in a few hours or days. Choose five of your favourite drawings and ask yourself what is it you like about them. Is there a theme? Can you now describe your work with words? Next time you draw, keep these words in mind and help them guide you.

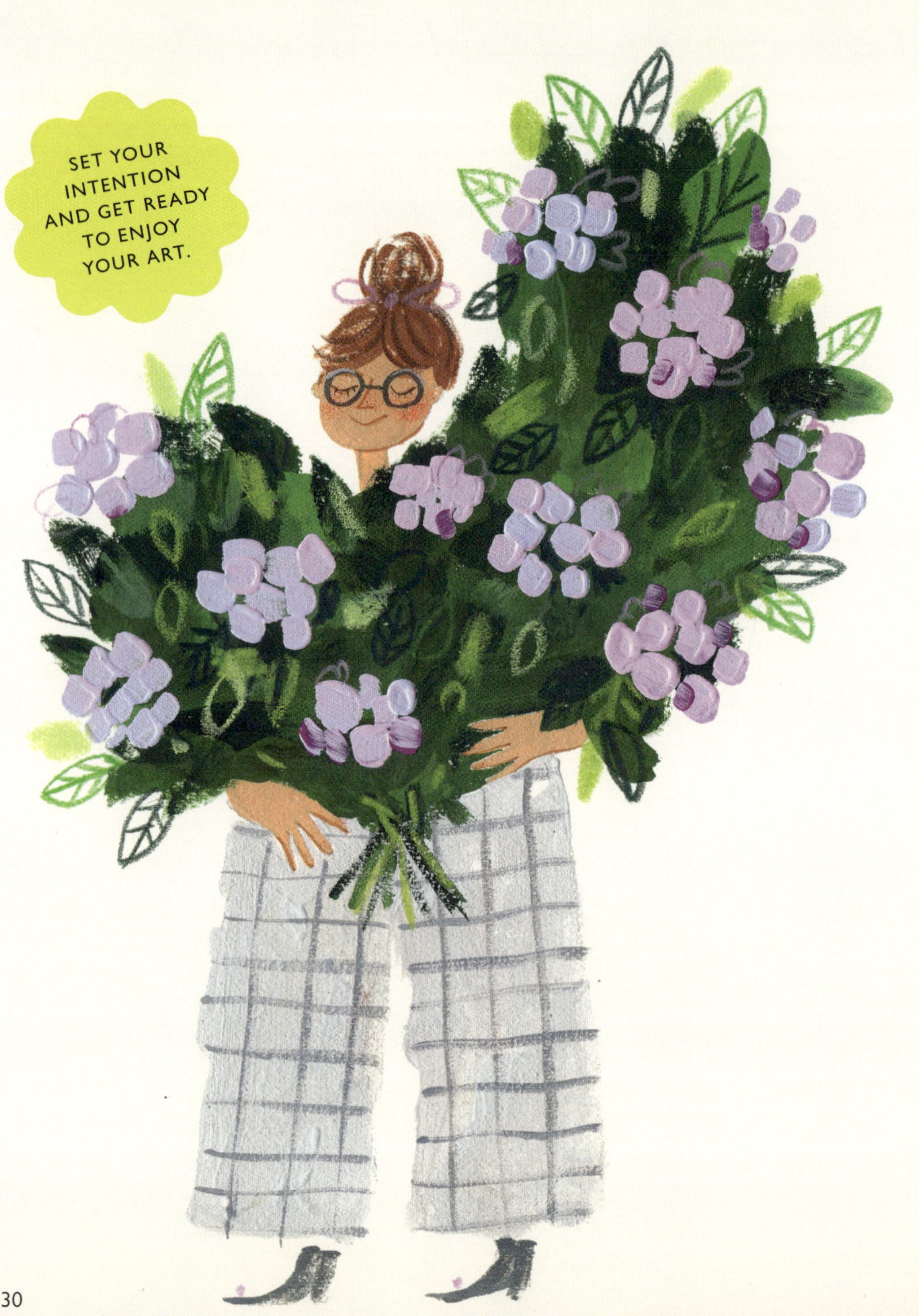

SET YOUR
INTENTION
AND GET READY
TO ENJOY
YOUR ART.

WRITE A MESSAGE FOR YOURSELF,
A PHRASE TO INSPIRE YOUR DRAWINGS
AND SET THE TONE FOR THE BOOK.

What would it be? That it's all a process and remember to relax?
Or, one day at a time? For me, it's a reminder to play and make
ugly art, because that's where I have most fun. Think about it for
a second and create a friendly reminder for yourself!

Intention

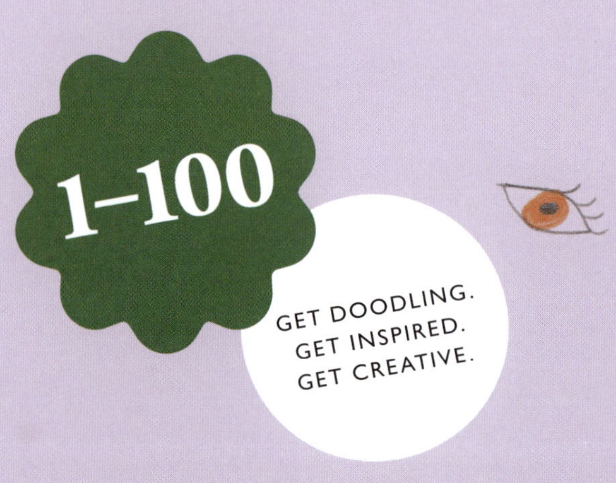
1–100
GET DOODLING.
GET INSPIRED.
GET CREATIVE.
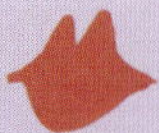

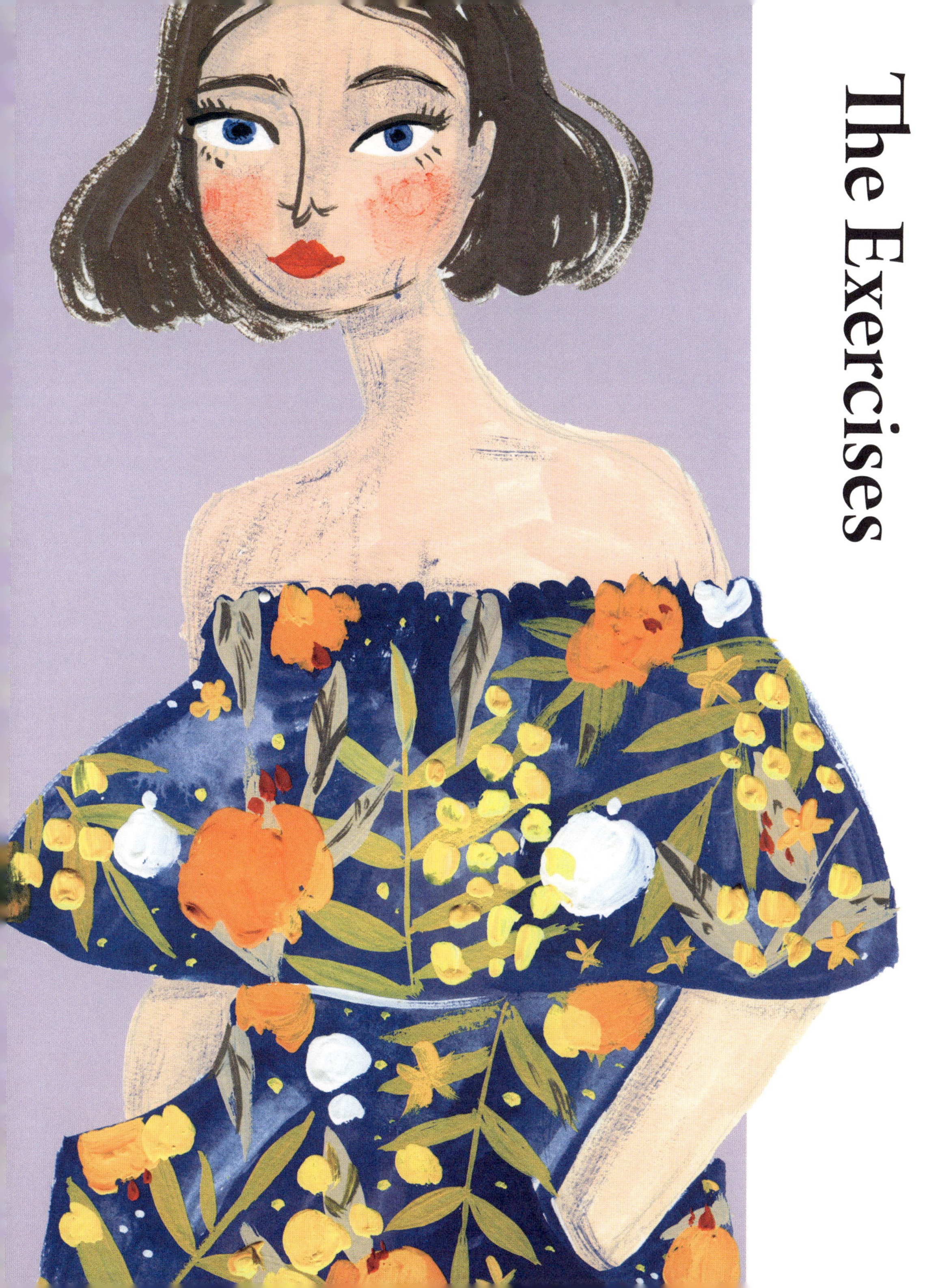
The Exercises

USING ANATOMICAL PROPORTIONS IS A GREAT STARTING POINT FOR DRAWING FACES.

Use the guidelines below to add facial features, such as eyes, nose and mouth. See pages 22 and 23 for more details.

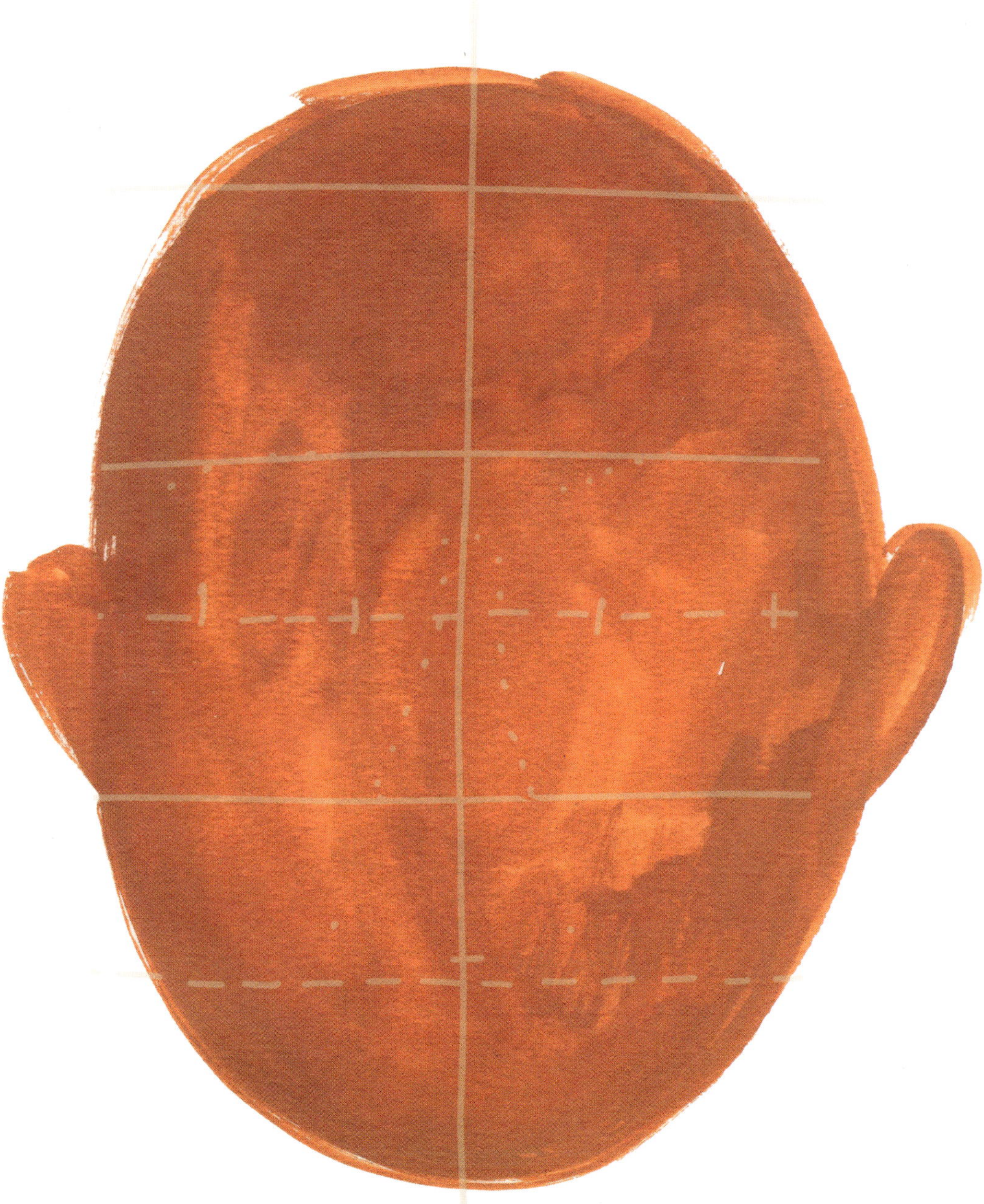

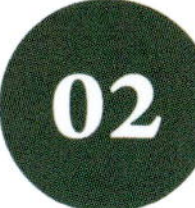 

USING ANATOMICAL PROPORTIONS IS ALSO VERY HELPFUL.
If you are drawing someone looking sideways, up or down, you can
adjust the placement of the vertical axis (the middle of the face)
to the right or left to help you adjust the various features. Add features
to the angled faces below.

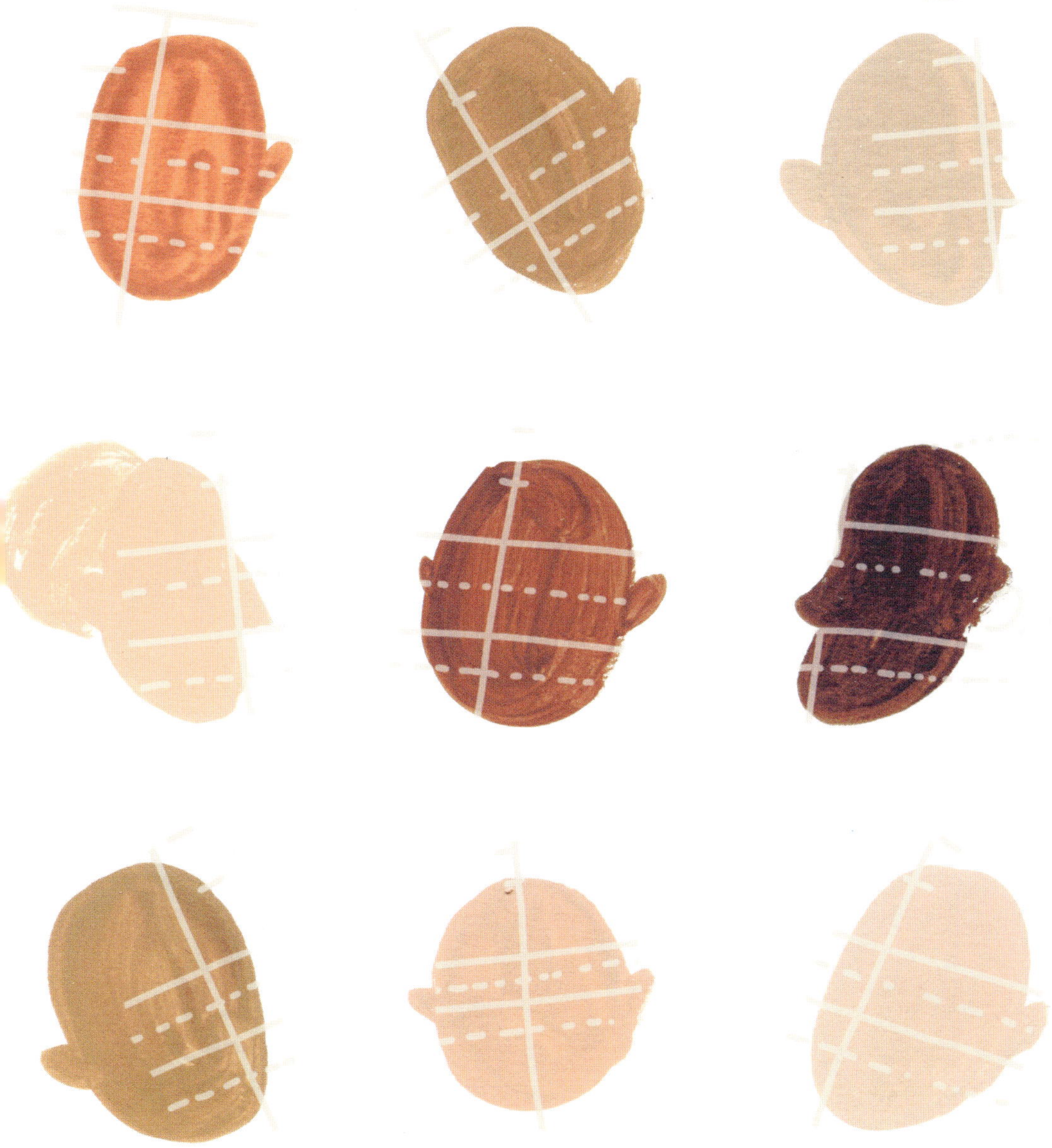

WHAT MATERIALS ARE YOU USING? WHAT ARE YOUR FAVOURITE COLOURS? HOW DO YOU MAKE MARKS? LET'S PRACTISE HERE!

First, make swatches below of neutral shades for skin colours, using your favourite materials. Then add swatches of any other colours you want to use.

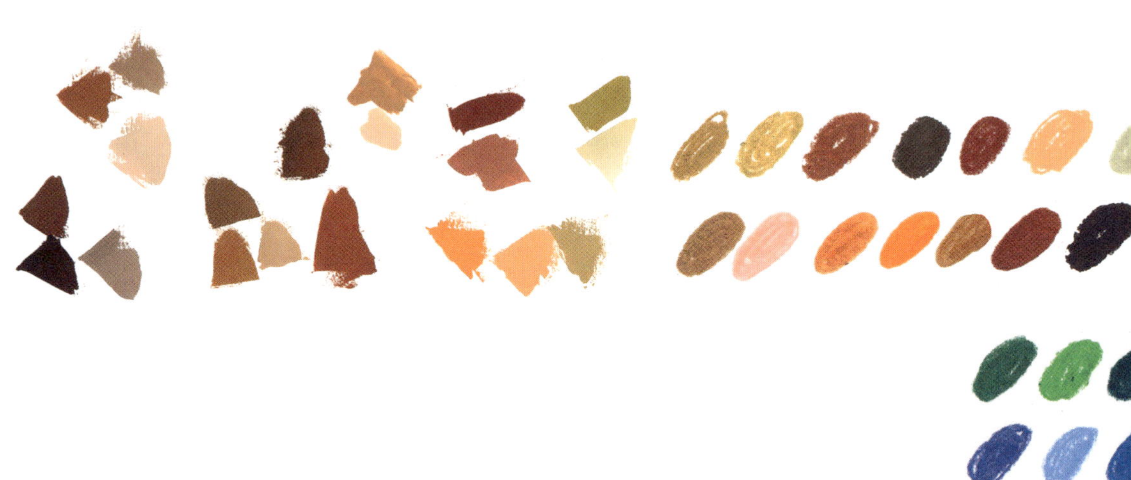

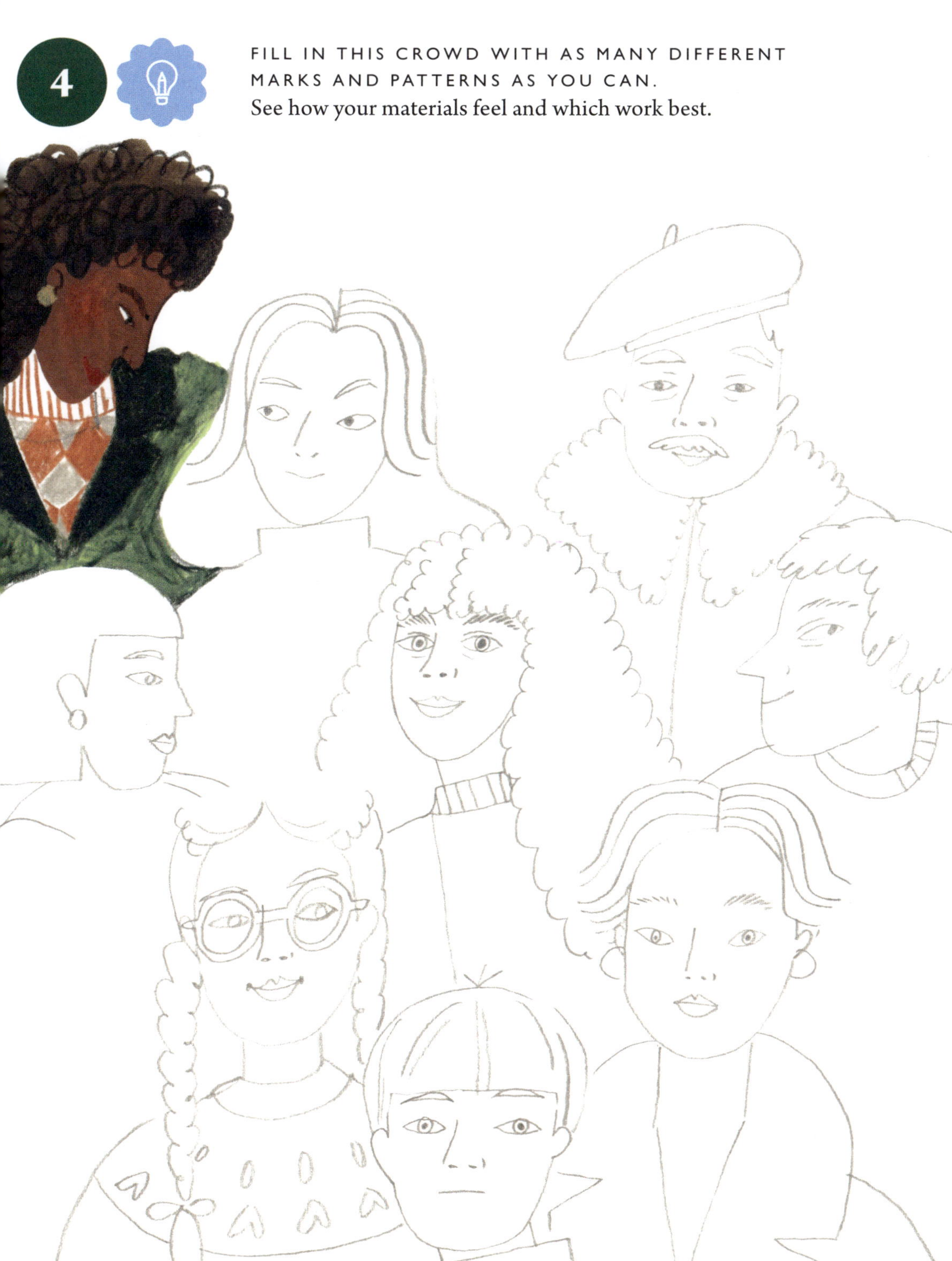

4
FILL IN THIS CROWD WITH AS MANY DIFFERENT
MARKS AND PATTERNS AS YOU CAN.
See how your materials feel and which work best.

CREATE A LIBRARY OF DIFFERENT FACIAL FEATURES THAT
YOU CAN USE FOR YOUR WORK THROUGHOUT THE BOOK.
How many different ways can you draw an eye, a nose or a mouth?
You can draw them realistically or choose to represent them as symbols.

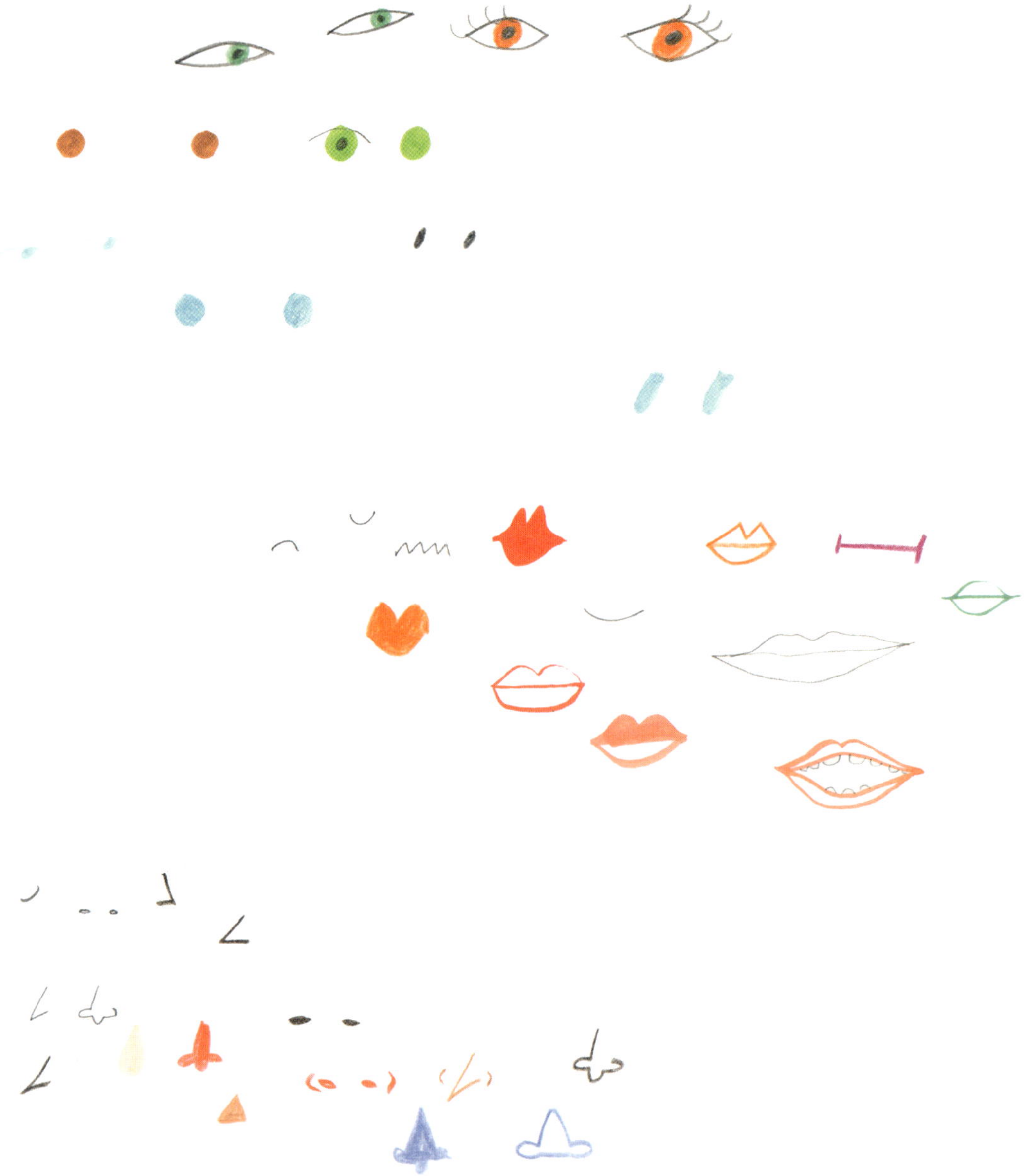

ADD FACIAL FEATURES AND HAIR TO THESE PEOPLE.
See which you like the most and which are most enjoyable to draw!

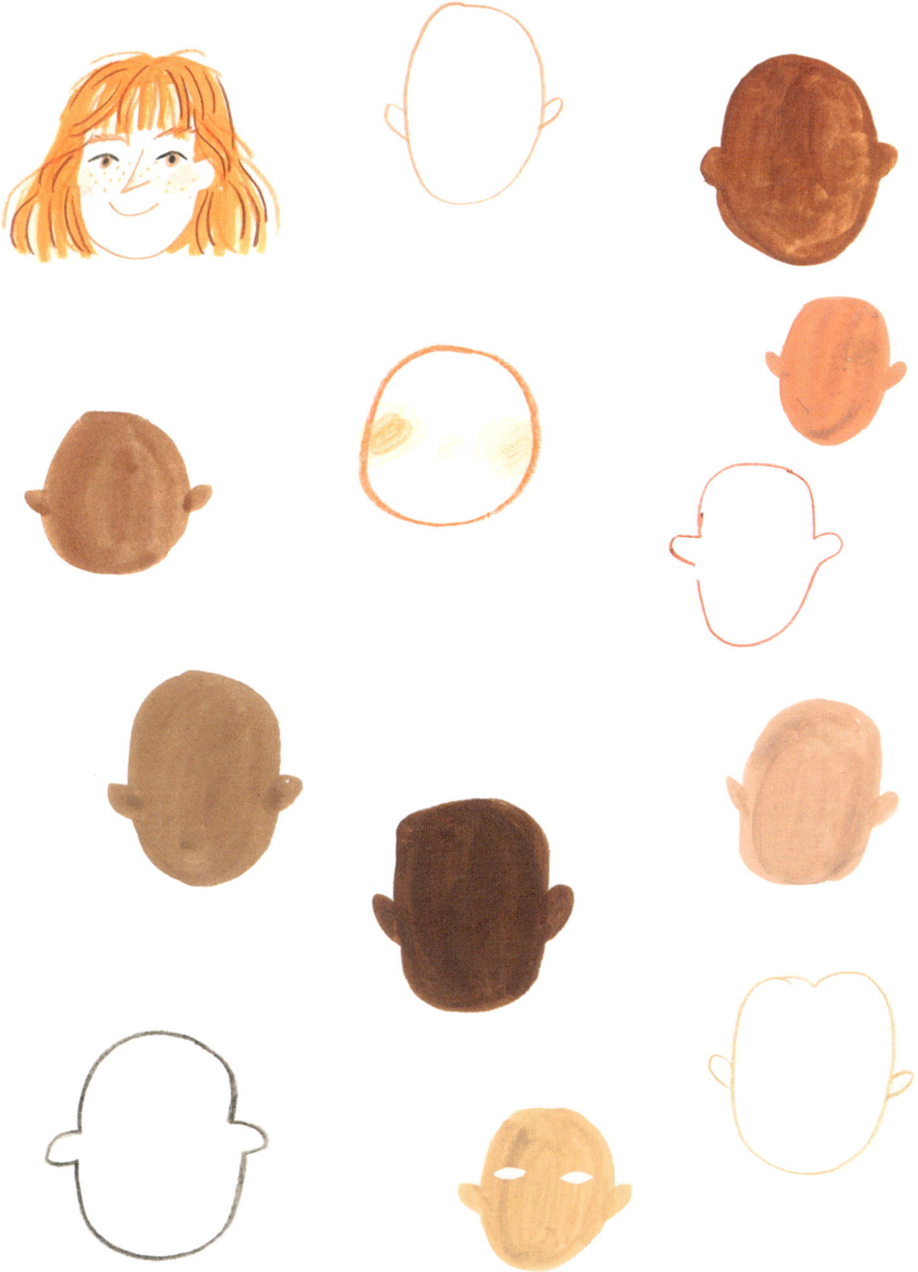

DRAW LOTS OF DIFFERENT SHOES.
Shoes are some of the best things to draw as part of a portrait.
They can add personality and tell a story!

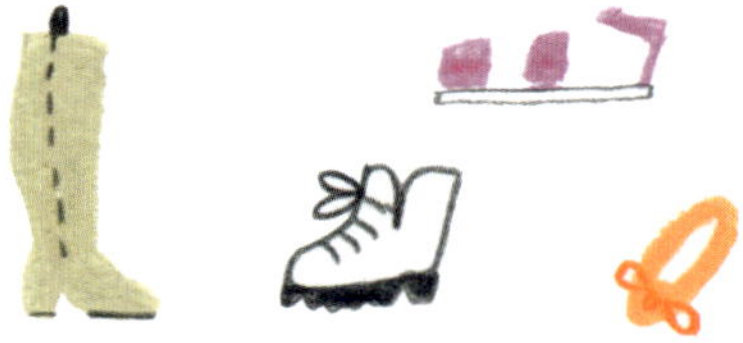

DRAW ACCESSORIES.
You could try glasses, bags or jewellery, but don't stop there.

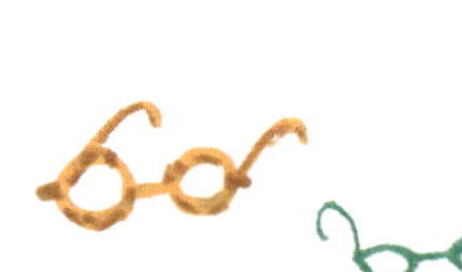
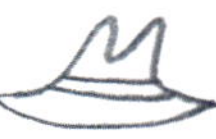
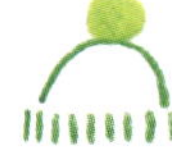
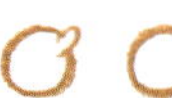
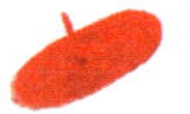
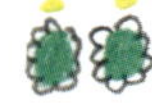

 **9** DRAW TOPS.
Sweaters, shirts, tank tops and blouses – what else can you dream up?

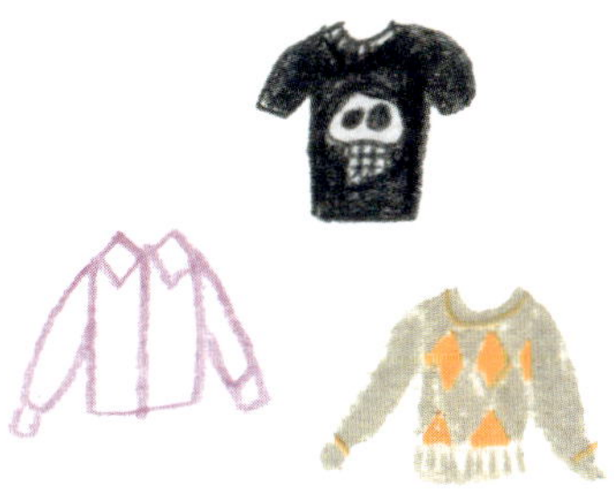

 **10** DRAW BOTTOMS.
How do you style your trousers, shorts or skirts?

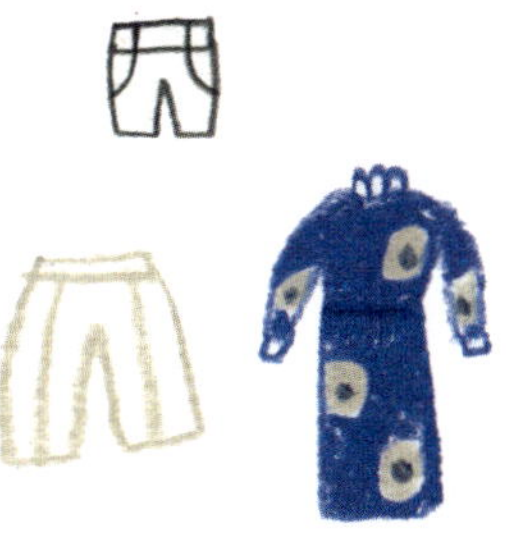

ADD OUTFITS AND ACCESSORIES TO THESE PEOPLE.
Think of who they are and what they would wear then play
around with different colours and patterns.

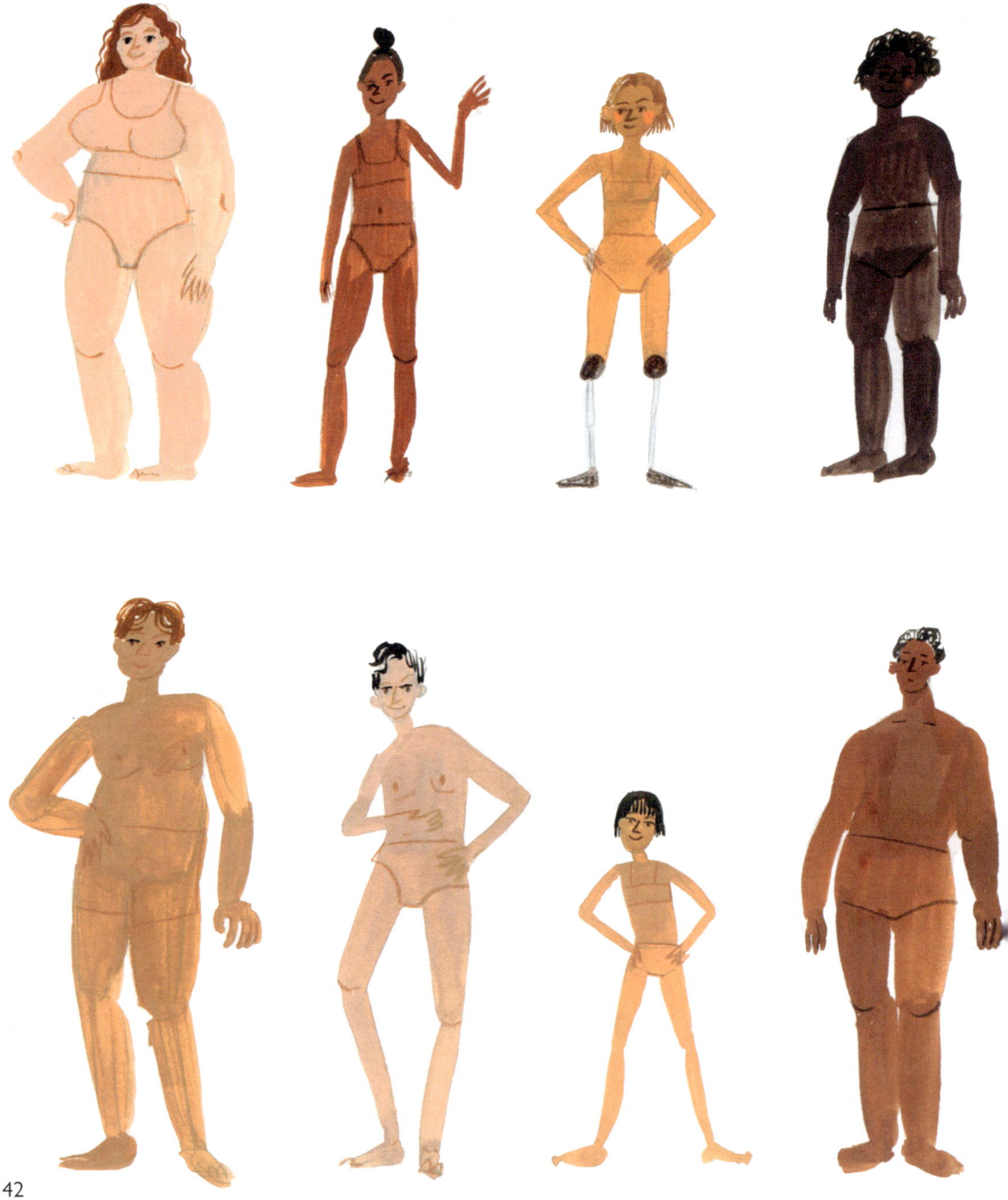

FILL IN THIS DRESS WITH A PATTERN.
Think mark making, colour and fun!

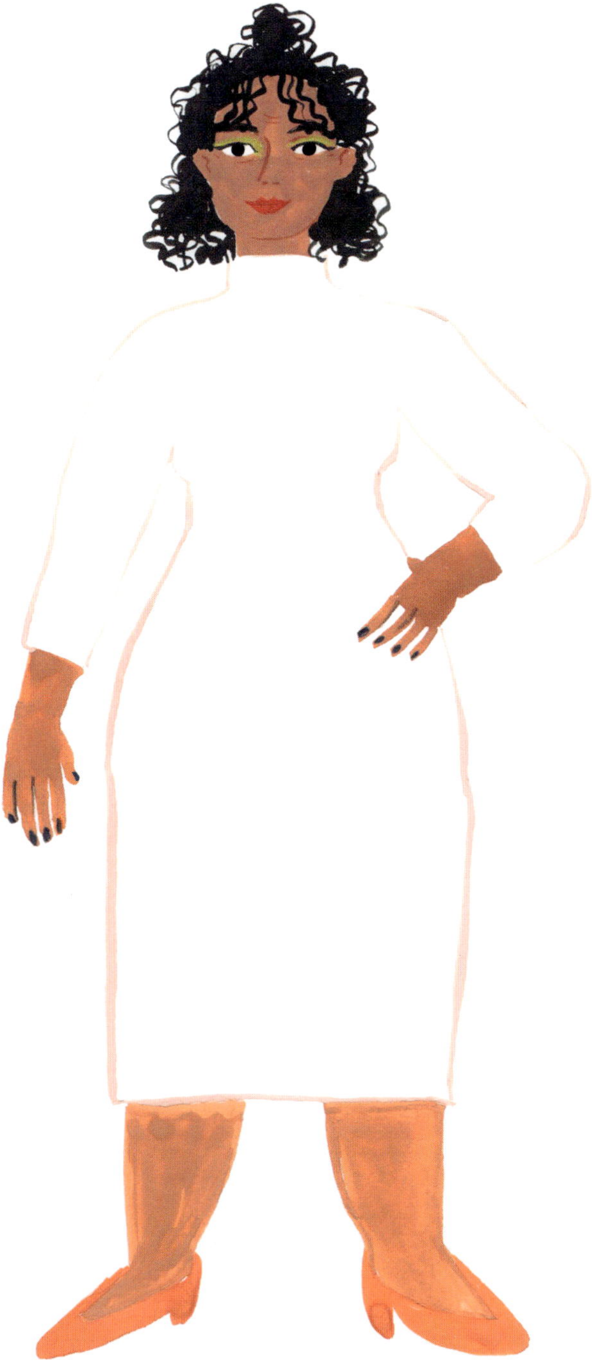

TRAIN YOUR EYE TO SEE FACES IN UNLIKELY PLACES.
Add details to these blobs, a little face, full figure or just tiny details.
Fill the pages with quirky characters and let your imagination run wild!

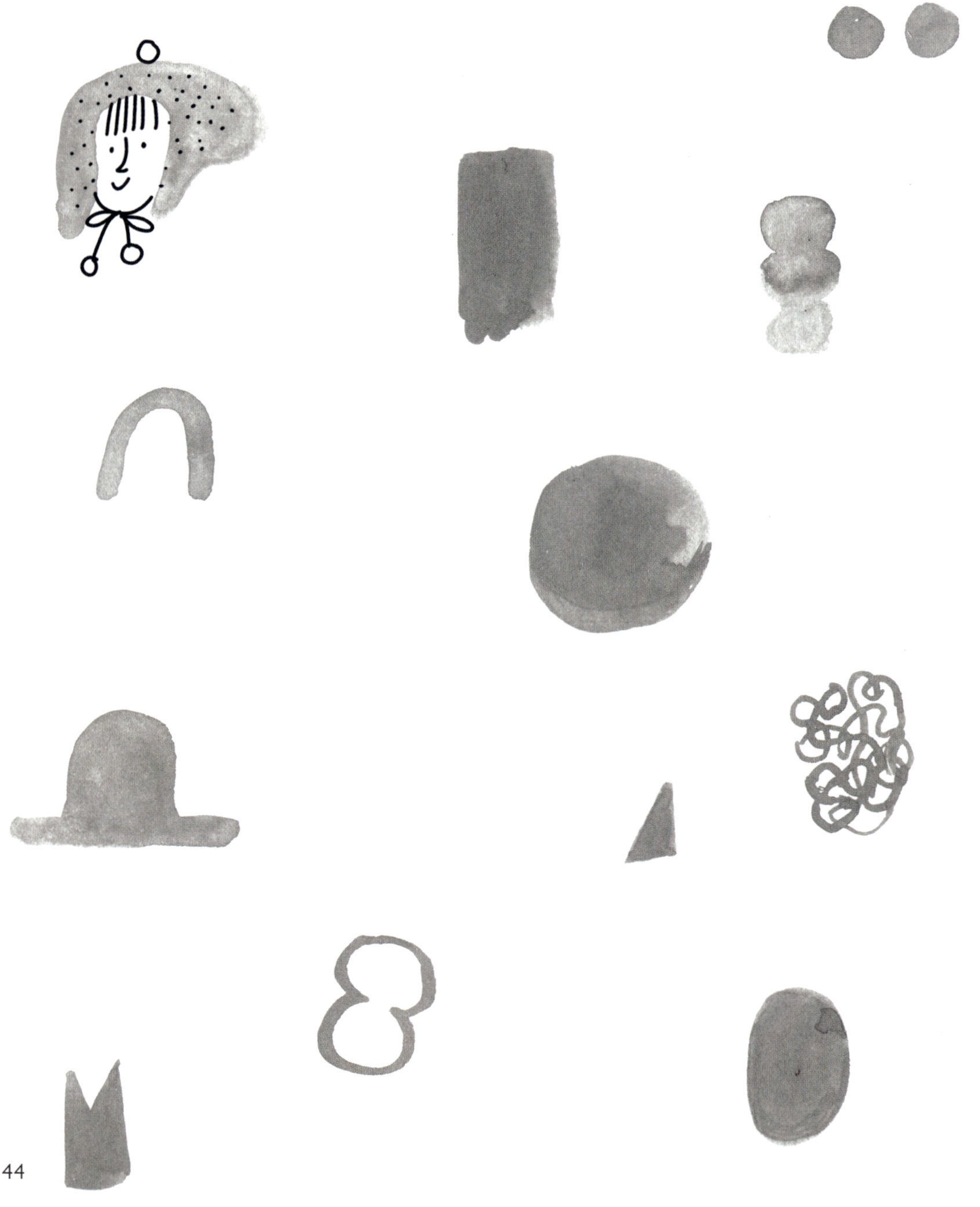

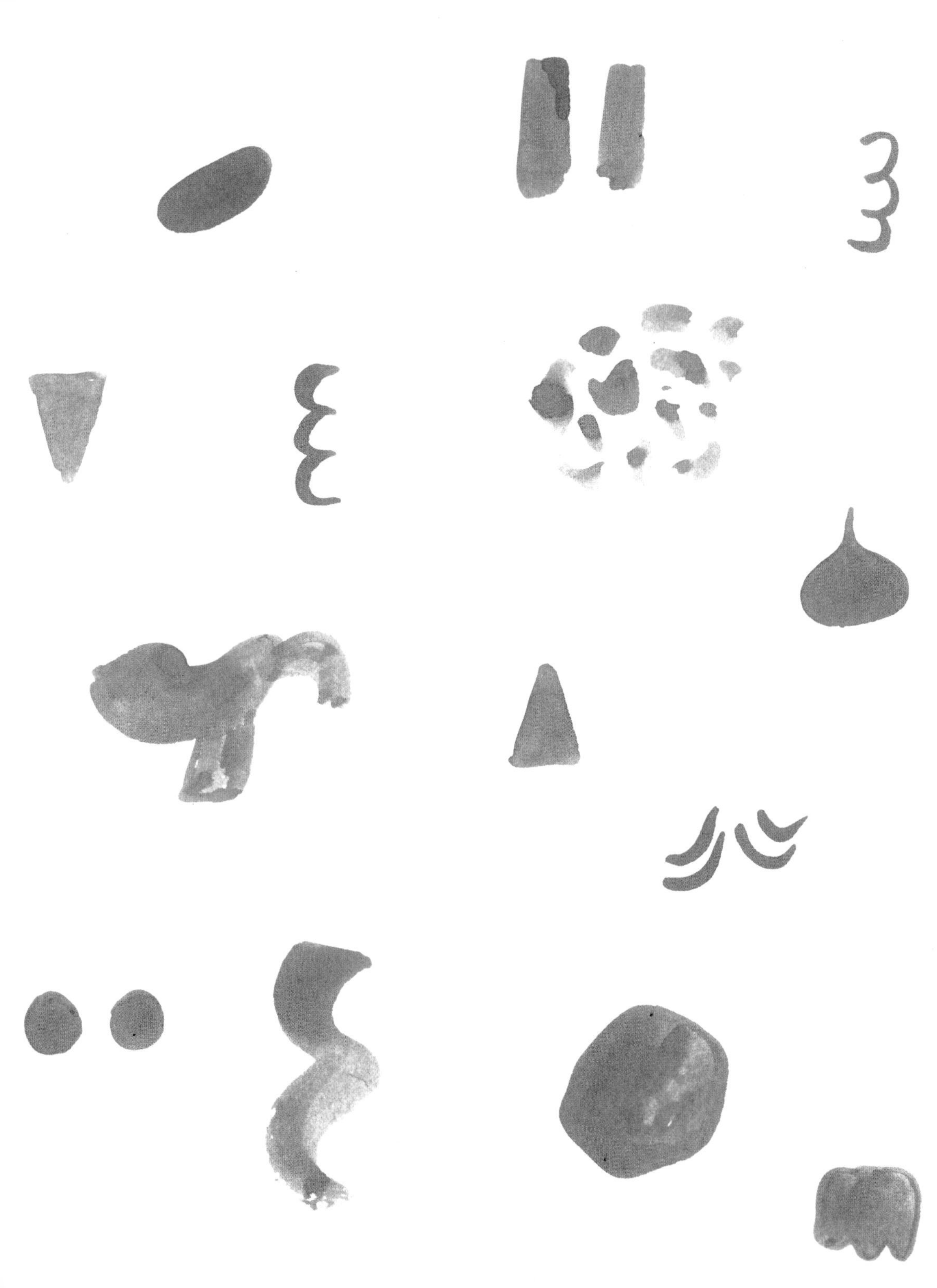

EXPLORE FACIAL SHAPES.
Each of us has a unique and special face. If we get the shape of the face right, the portrait is a better likeness. Try drawing as many facial shapes as you can see and imagine!

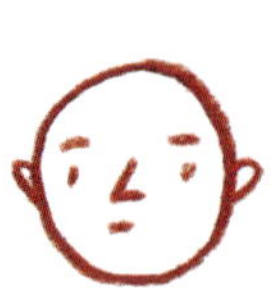 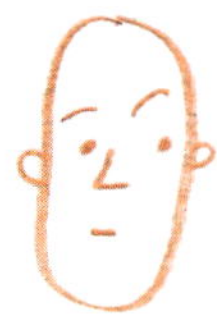 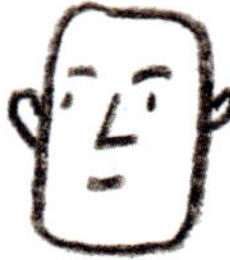 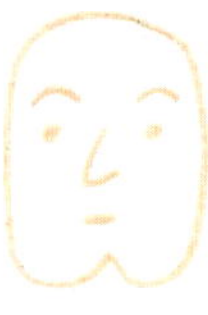 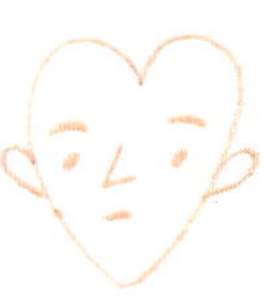 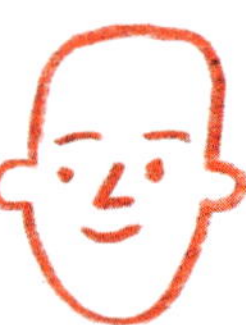

CHANGING FACIAL PROPORTIONS
There are rules for these, of course, but each one of us is so individual that these rules often go out of the window. Play around with changing proportions and see how many different faces you can draw. Notice how the personality changes with each detail. I've made a start ... now try for yourself!

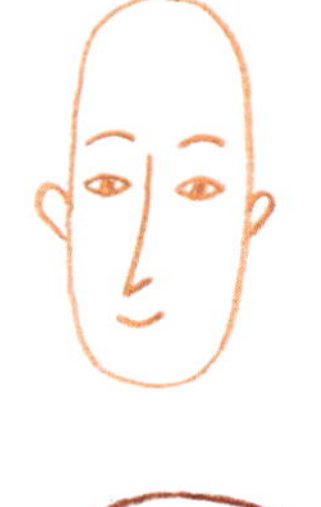 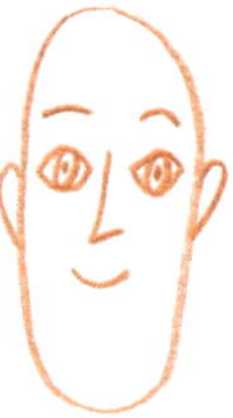 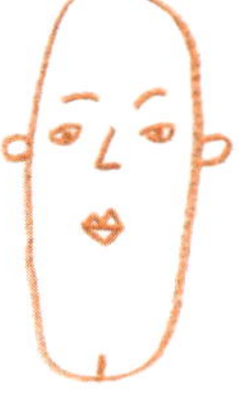 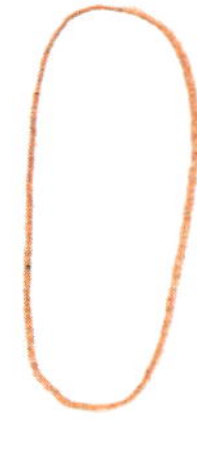 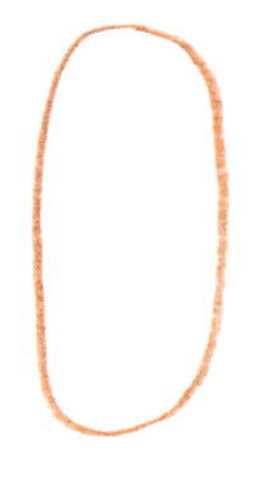 

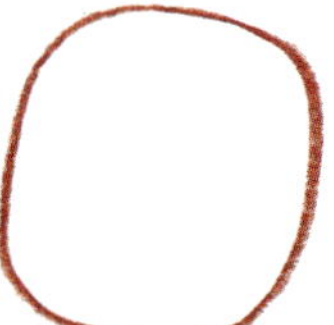 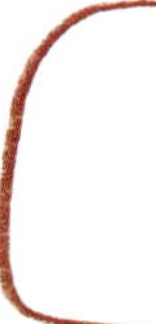 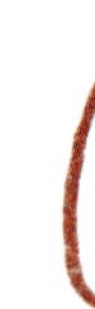 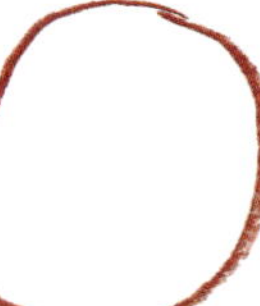 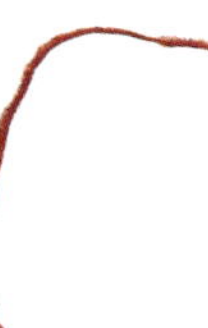 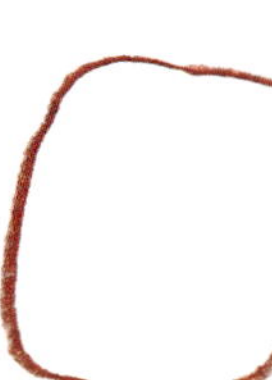

A WIG MAKES A GREAT DISGUISE, AND A MOUSTACHE OR BEARD CAN ALTER THE APPEARANCE ENORMOUSLY. Changing these features completely changes the face. Try drawing as many different options for moustaches, beards or hair as you can and see how it changes the character!

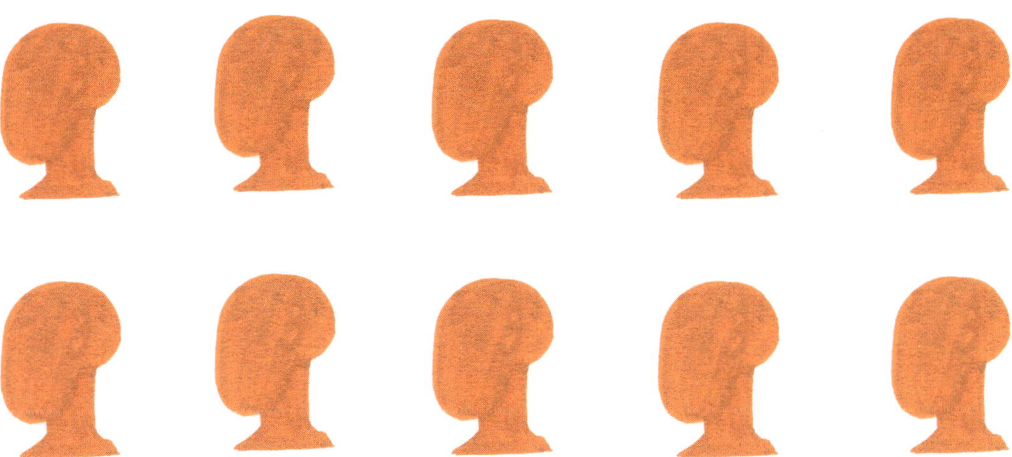

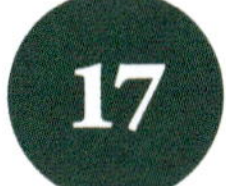 

EYEBROWS ADD CHARACTER AND CAN COMMUNICATE SO MUCH. Try drawing different eyebrows to convey a range of emotions and see how they change the facial expression, too.

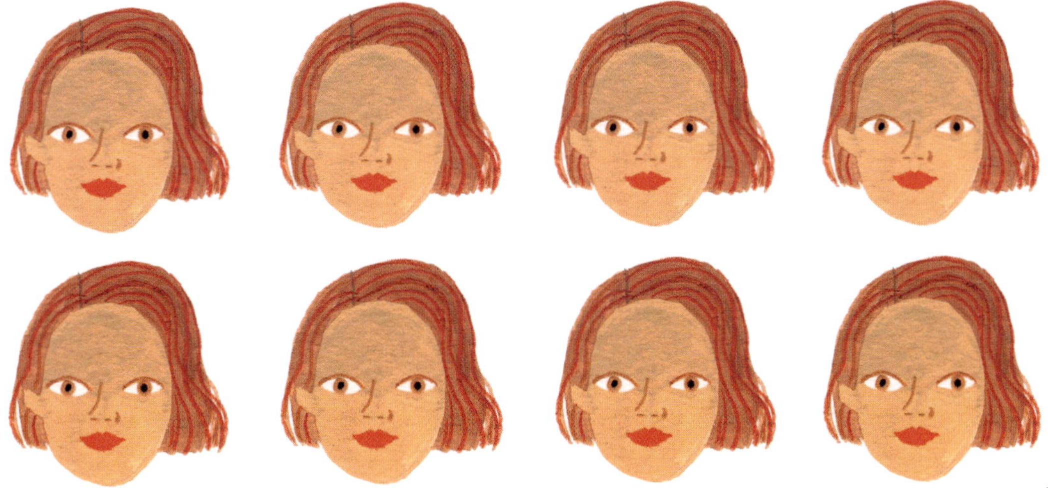

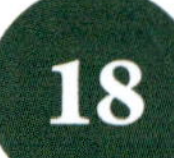

DRAW SOME PEOPLE USING
THESE COLOUR PALETTES,
THEN COME UP WITH YOUR
OWN COLOUR COMBINATIONS.
Either use these colours as inspiration
for outfits or create more abstract
portraits with expressive use of colour.

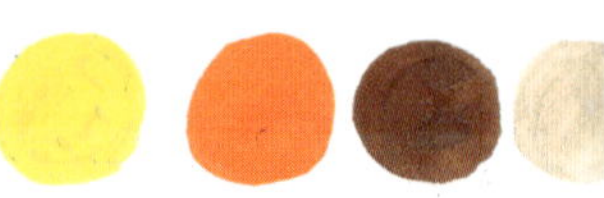

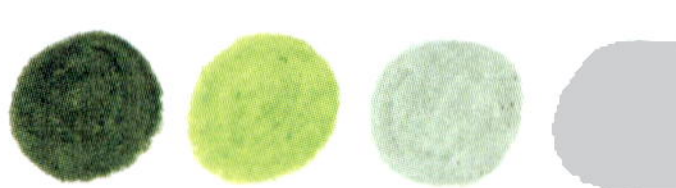

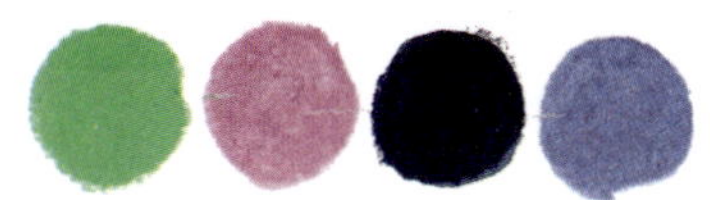

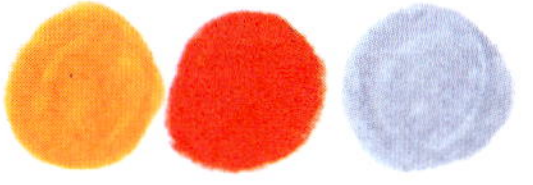

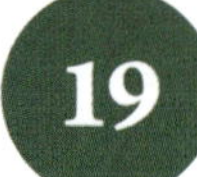 

MARK MAKING
HAIR PRACTICE!
When drawing hair I like to add a thin layer of colour first, with something like watercolour, thin gouache, a marker or ink. Then I go over with pencil or a darker marker to add more definition and details.

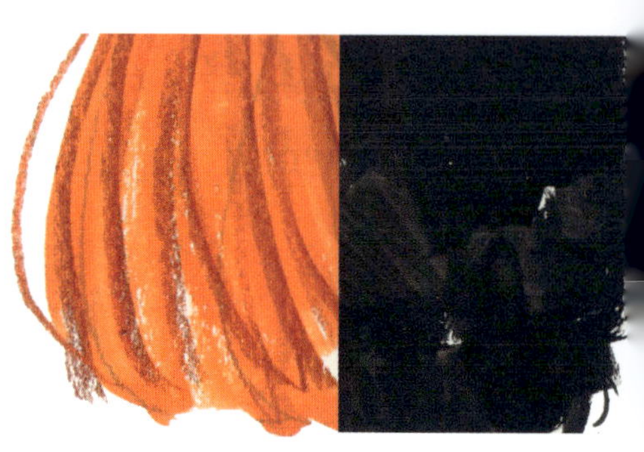

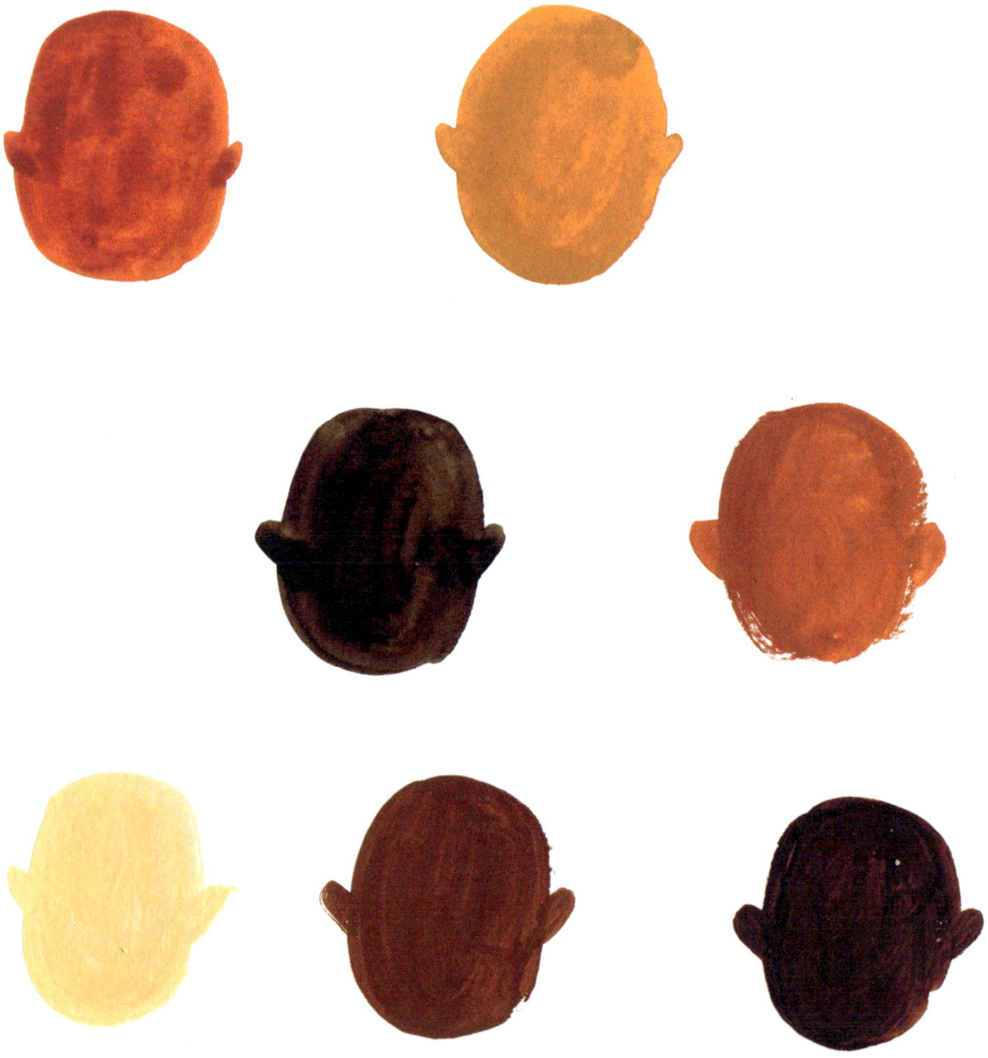

Here are lots of different faces, finish drawing them and add hair,
have fun with textures.

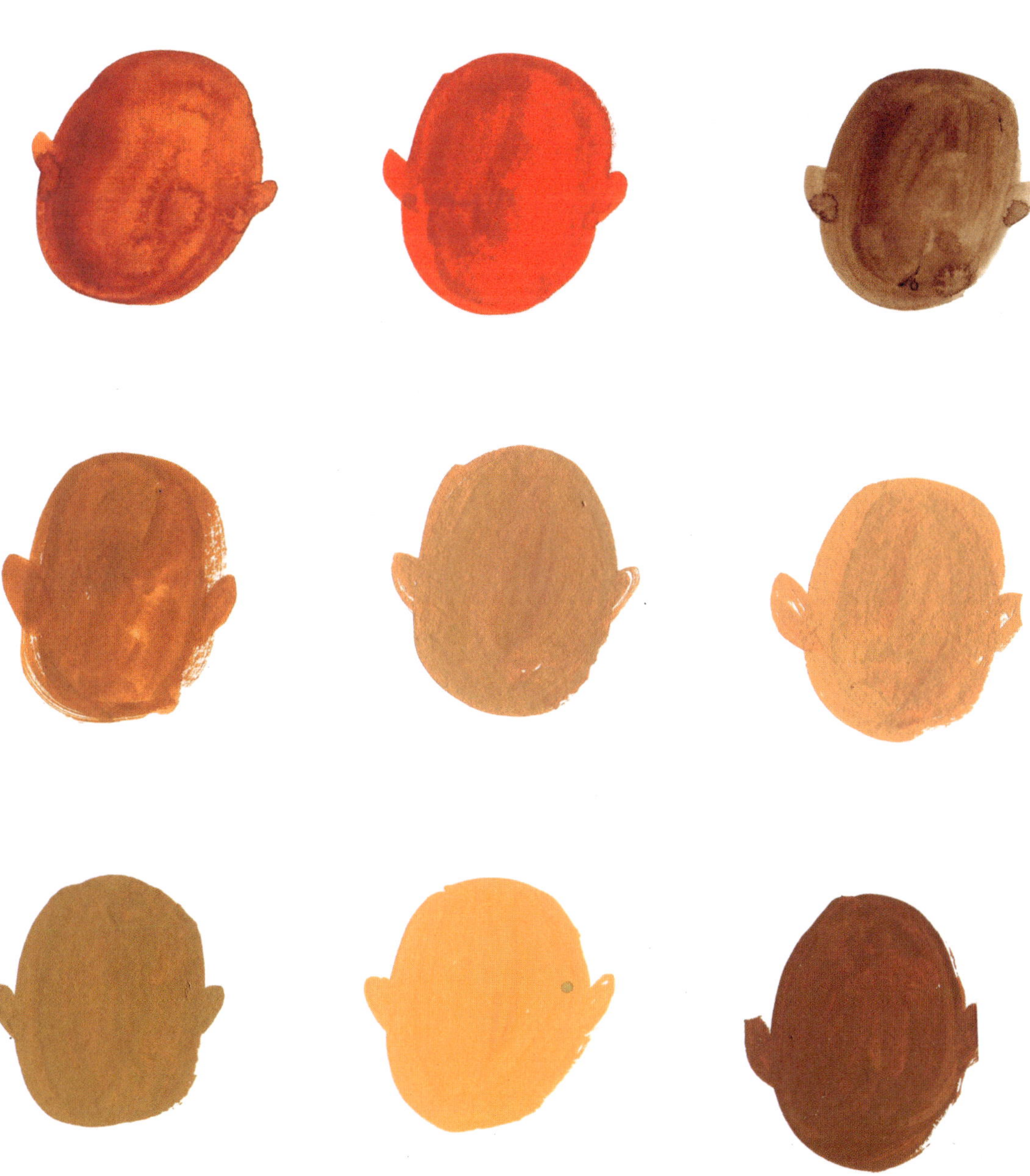

21
DRAW PEOPLE AT A BOTANICAL GARDEN. Use the stick figure method (pages 20–21) as a guideline. Who are they? What are they wearing?

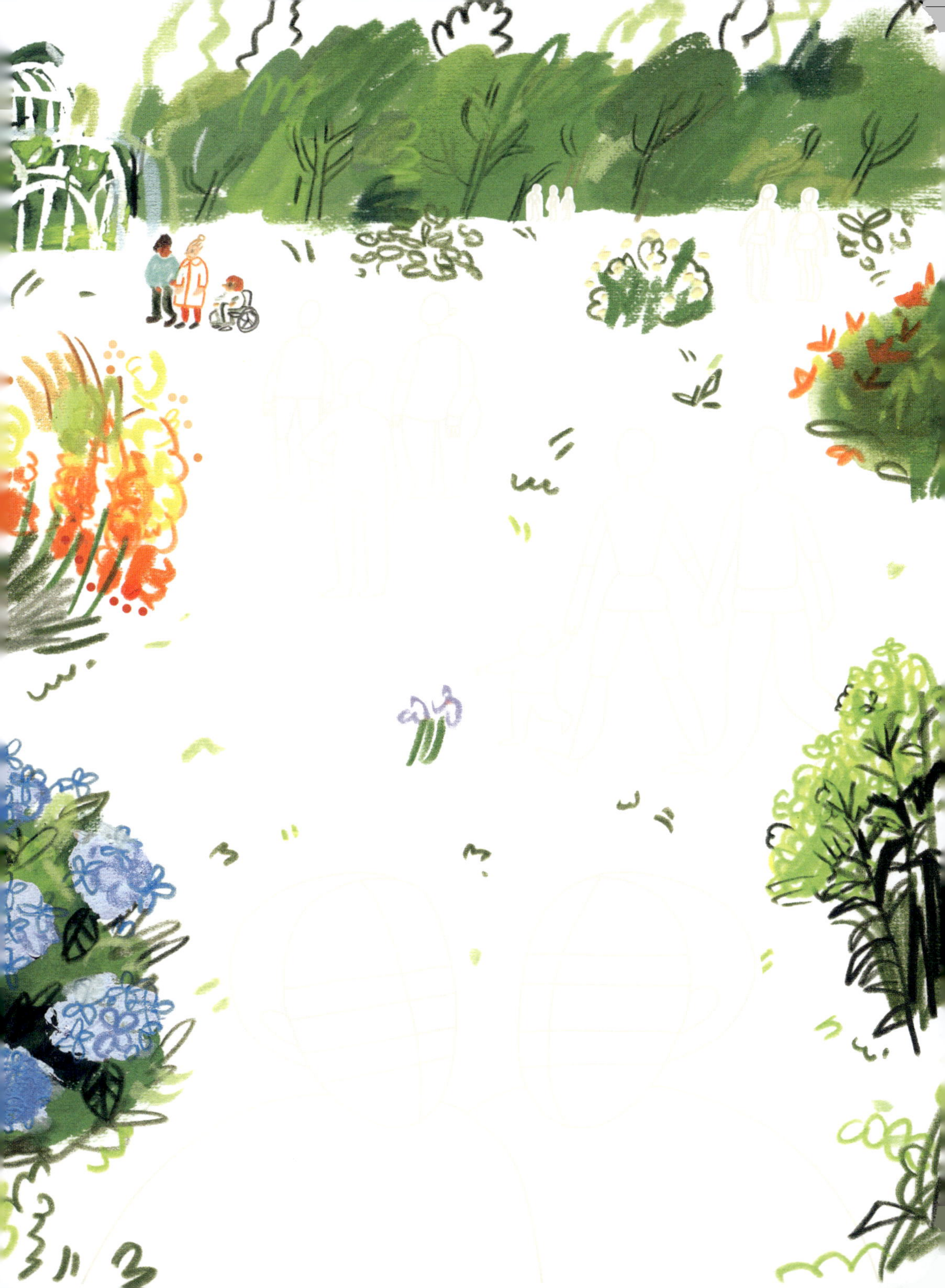

22

DRAW LOTS OF DIFFERENT PEOPLE IN ACTION.
Practise the wildest of poses using the stick figure approach
(see pages 20–21). Draw headstands, star jumps, cartwheels
and anything else you can think of.

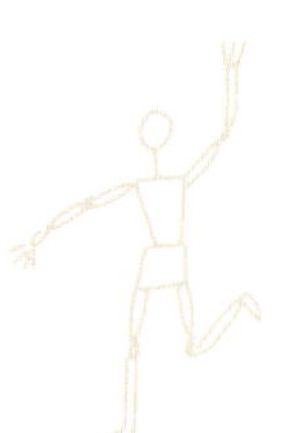
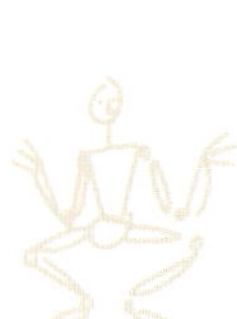
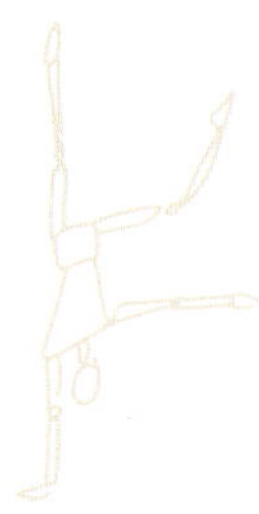

23

CHOOSE A FEW OF YOUR FAVOURITE
SKETCHES FROM ABOVE AND DRAW A TINY
CHARACTER BASED ON THE STICK FIGURES.
Add clothes and accessories, too!

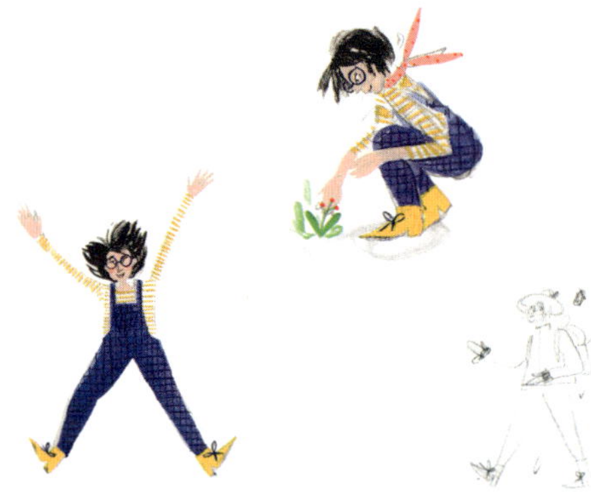

24 ADD CUTE OUTFITS AND SILLY DETAILS TO THESE PEOPLE. Imagine they are from the future – what would they look like, what kind of outfits would they need?

DRAWING EMOTIONS IS SO MUCH FUN. Try drawing a happy, angry, sad, excited, curious or worried person. You can make faces in a mirror as a reference to perfect the various expressions.

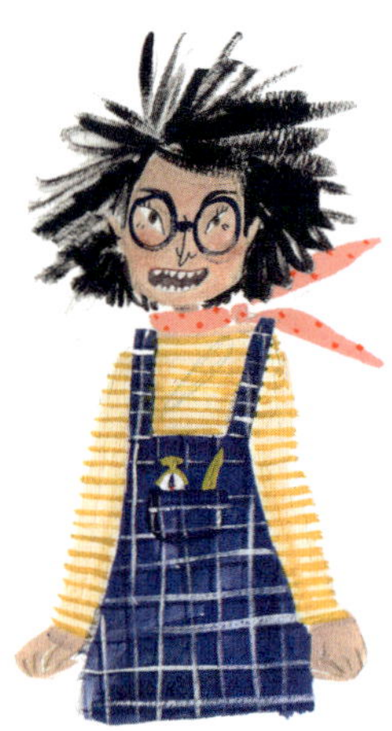

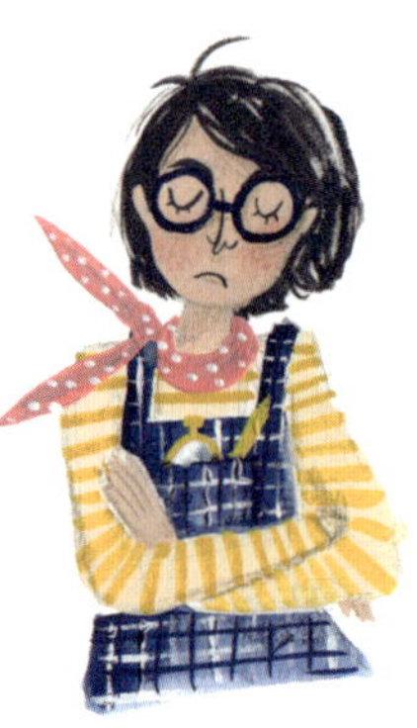

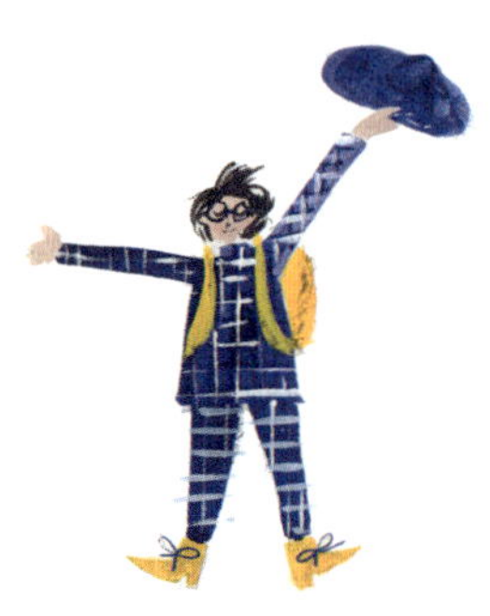

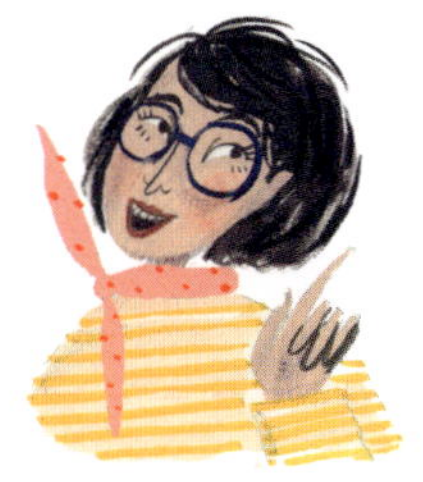

STICK FIGURES ARE A GREAT STARTING POINT
FOR ANY DIFFICULT POSE.

Draw people doing yoga, tracing the stick figures to
begin with. Then add two more people on the empty
mats in any pose, freehand!

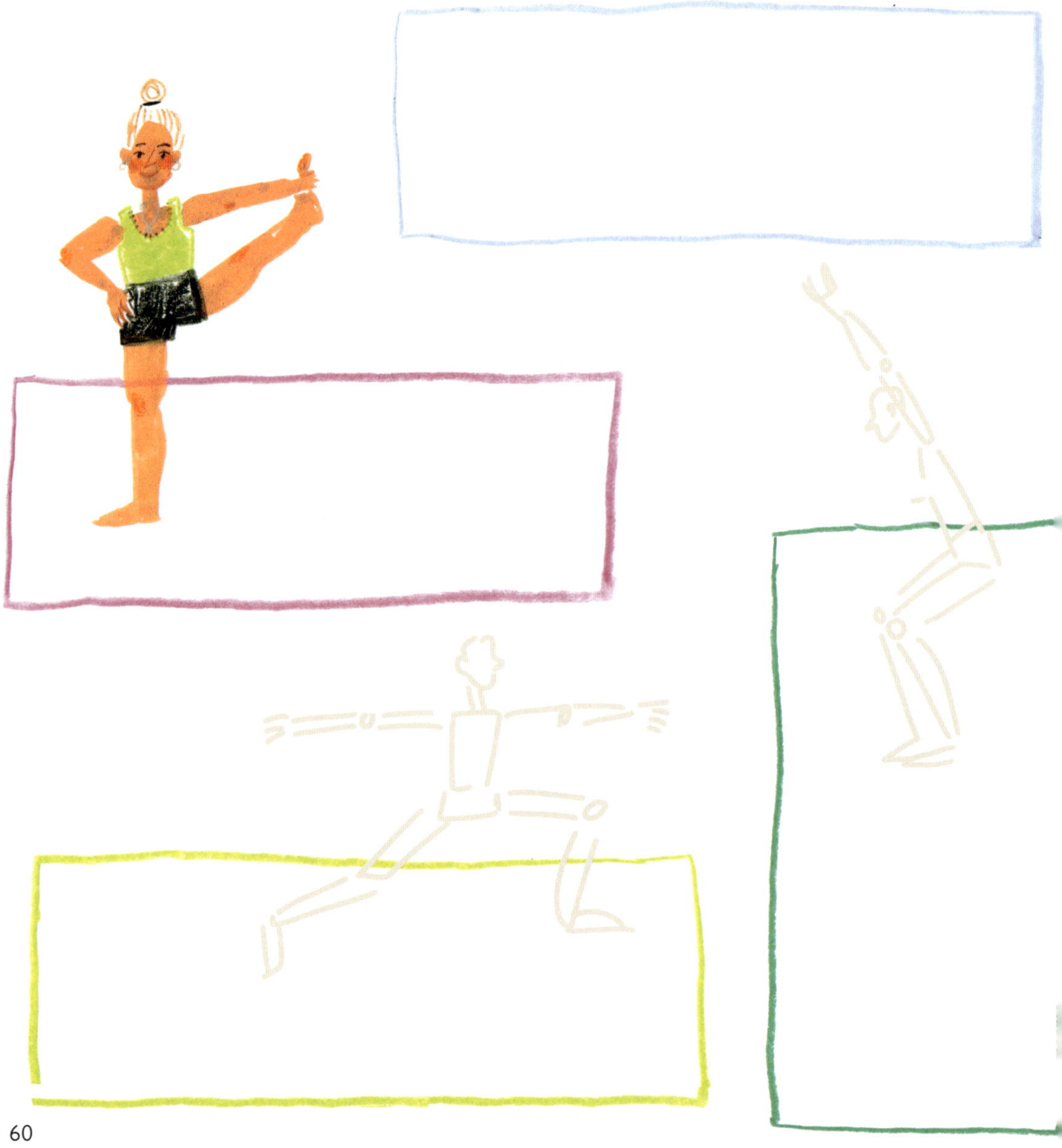

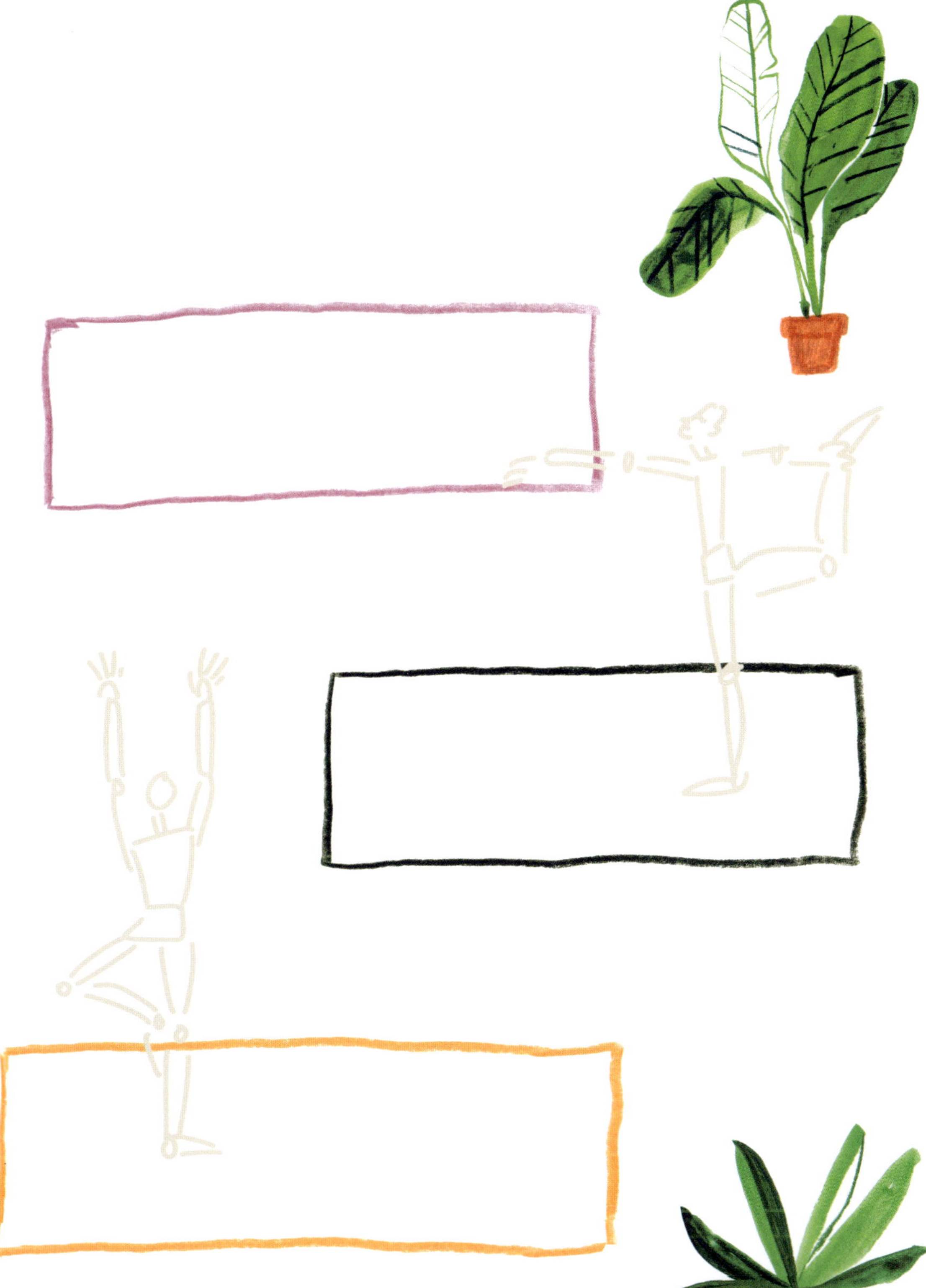

27 DRAW A FACE USING A CONTINUOUS LINE.
Don't take your pencil off the page, and don't worry about
coming back on yourself, making extra lines or creating scribbles.
This is such a wonderful exercise for warming up and loosening up!

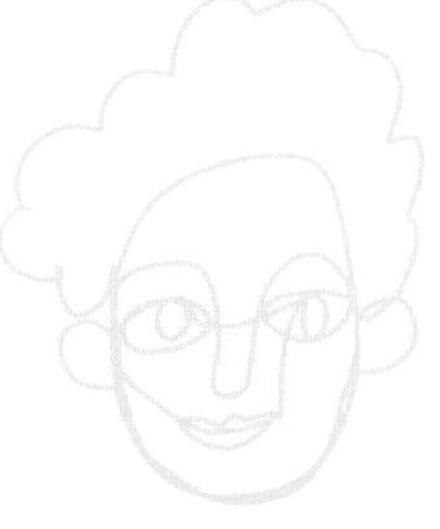

28 NOW DRAW A FULL FIGURE WITHOUT TAKING
YOUR PENCIL OFF THE PAGE.

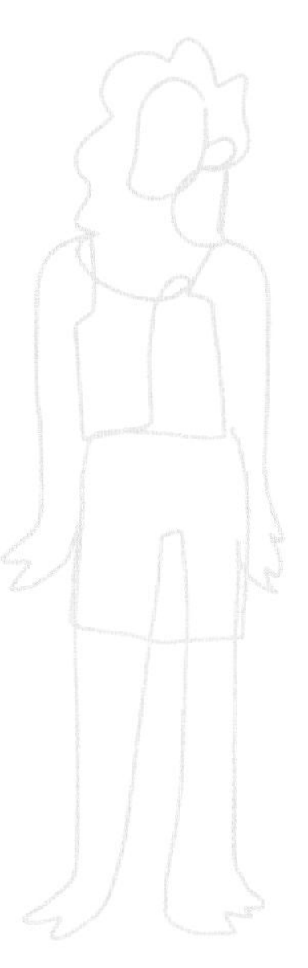

DRAWING HANDS STEP-BY-STEP.

Hands are probably the most difficult parts of a person to draw. But our hands are so expressive in life – they can add energy, tell a story or communicate emotions – so it's worth spending a little time getting them right.

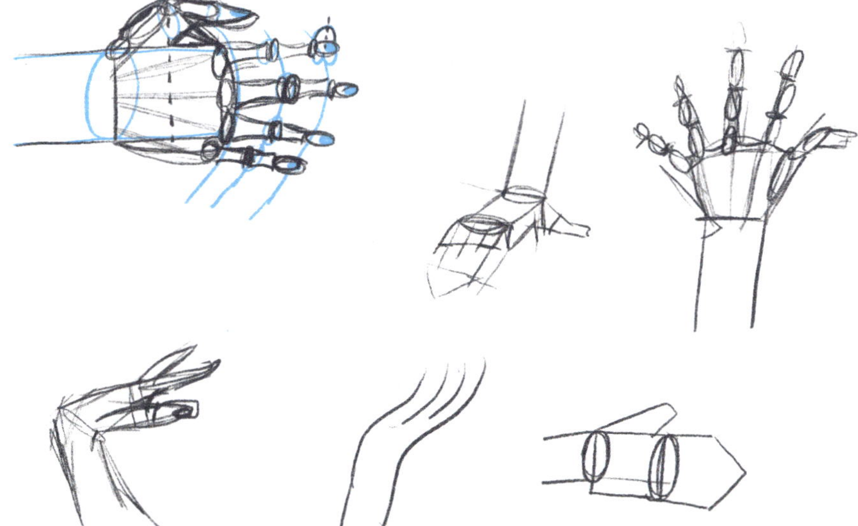

Using a graphite pencil, sketch a rough outline of a head and shouders. Start drawing one of the hands as a mitten, with the palm turned towards the face, touching the chin, fingers closed. Add a little triangle at the side for the thumb.

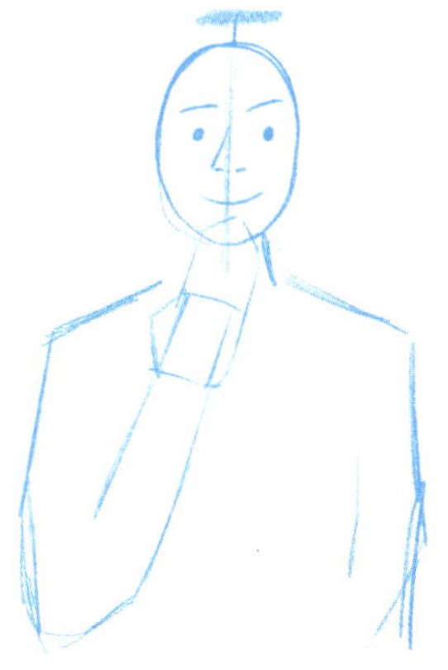

Add more details to the drawing – hair, freckles, ears, etc. – and then return your focus to the hand. Draw the finger and thumb phalanges (three sections for each finger and two for the thumb).

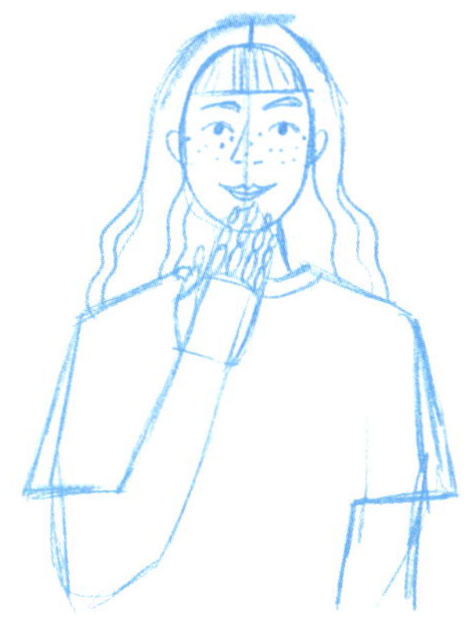

Go over the outline of your sketch, rubbing out all of the marks you made.

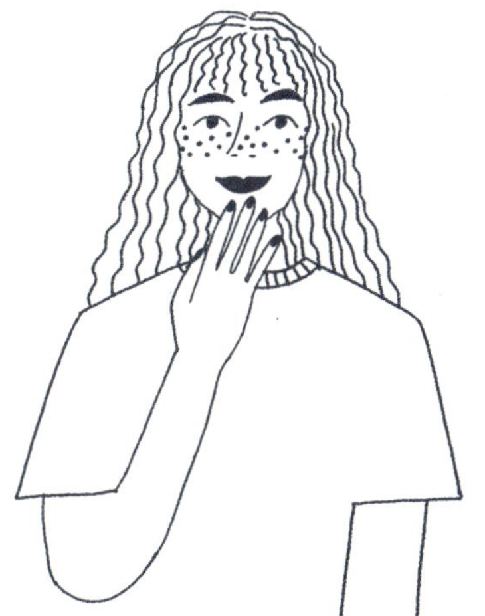

TIP: *When sketching your hands, think of geometric shapes. Imagine all the joints in the wrists and fingers as spheres, and the palm shape as a rectangle or triangle. Once you have the shapes finessed, you can then add the details.*

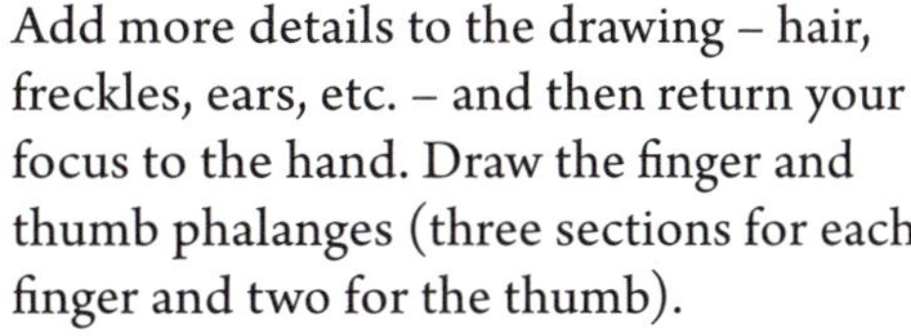

HAND SELF-PORTRAITS.
Using your own hands as reference, draw them
holding a pen, having a cup of coffee, playing
the piano or anything else that takes your fancy.

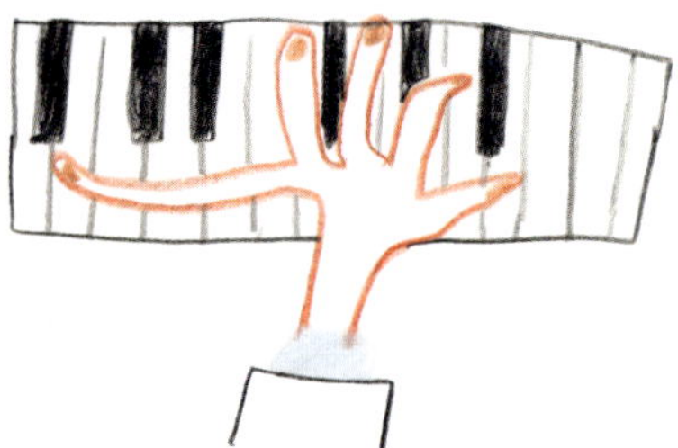

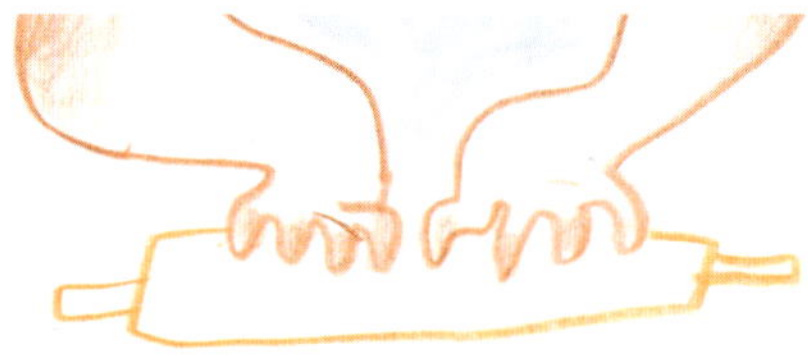

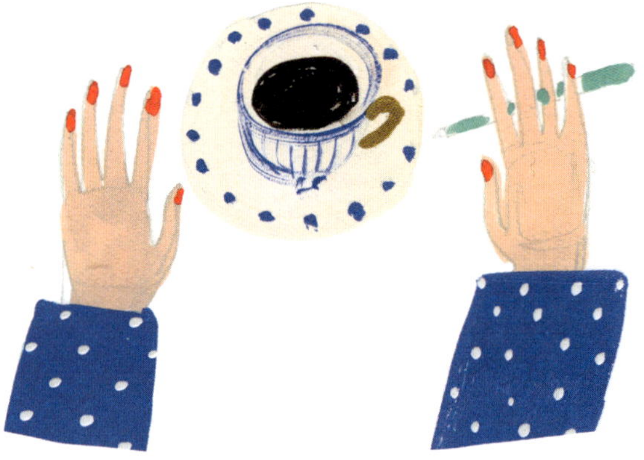

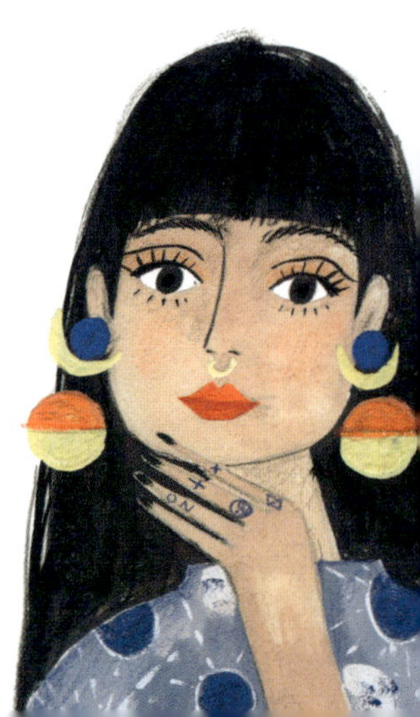

DRAW AS MANY UNUSUAL HAIRSTYLES AS YOU CAN.
Complete your portraits using only one other colour.
Sometimes setting limitations is an invitation to play.

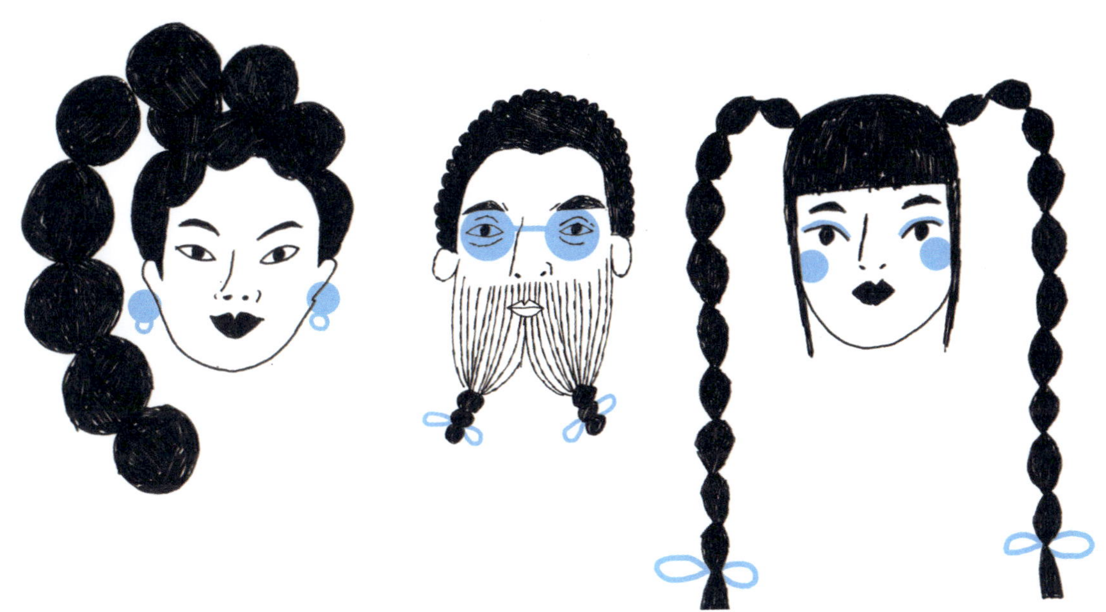

DRAW A SERIES OF PORTRAITS IN DIFFERENT COMPOSITIONS.
They can be full height, close-up or upper body only. Follow the guidelines below for inspiration.

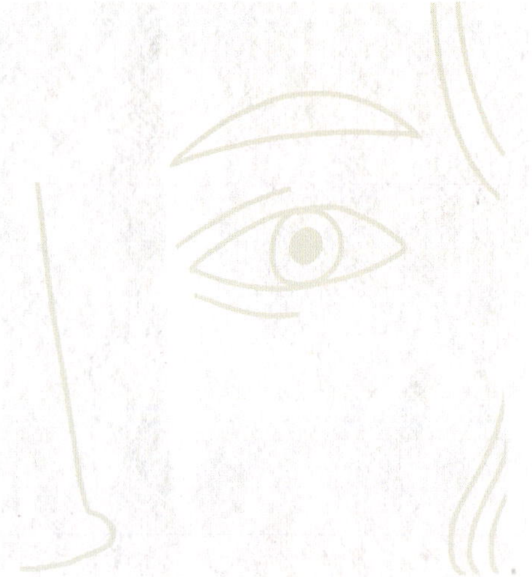

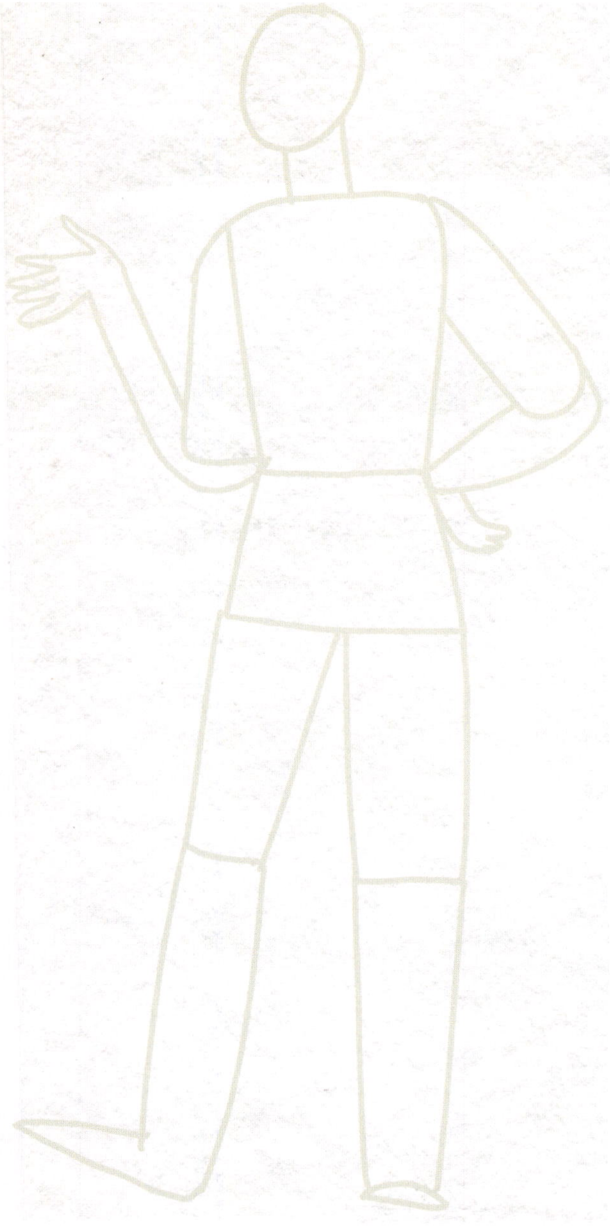

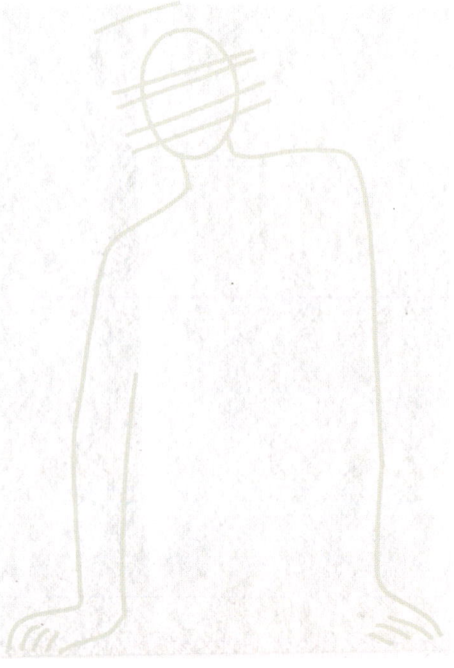

DRAW A FULL-BODY SELF-PORTRAIT.

34 ADD DETAILS TO THESE SCULPTURES.

Give them faces, hands, outfits or wigs. Have a blast and be silly!

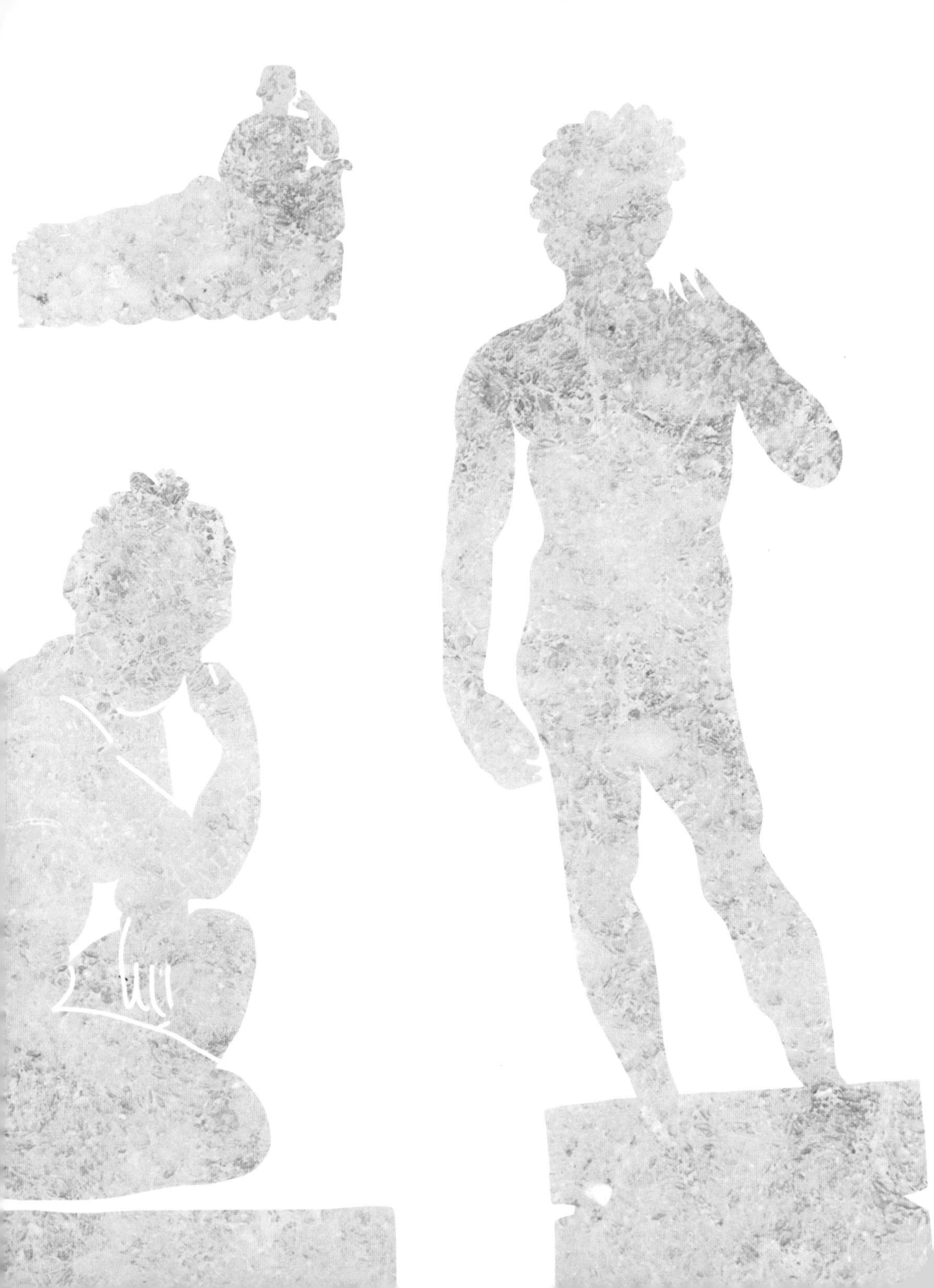

DRAW DOG OWNERS TO MATCH THESE PETS.

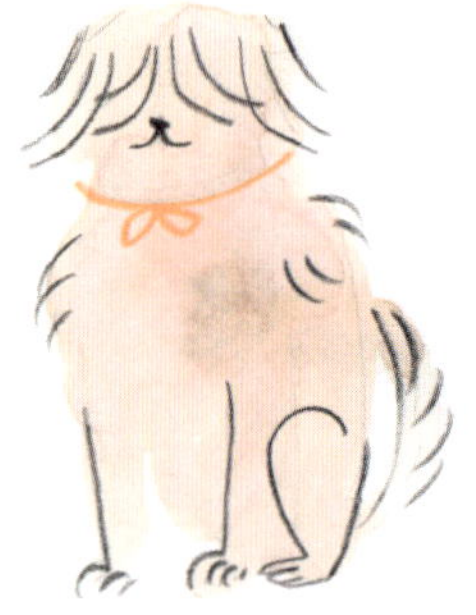

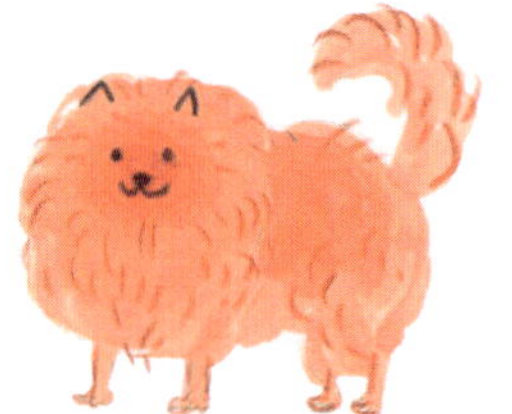

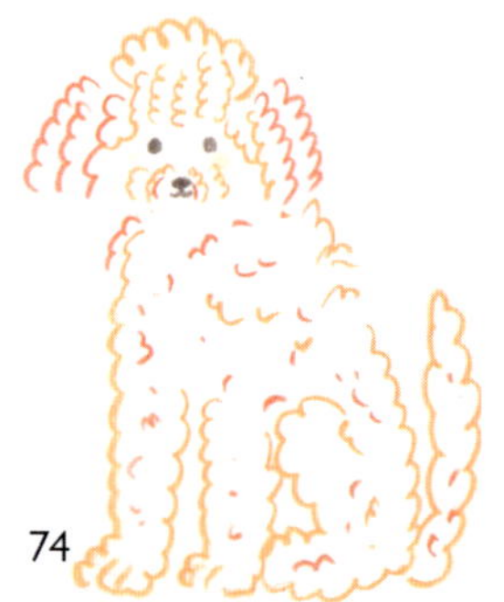

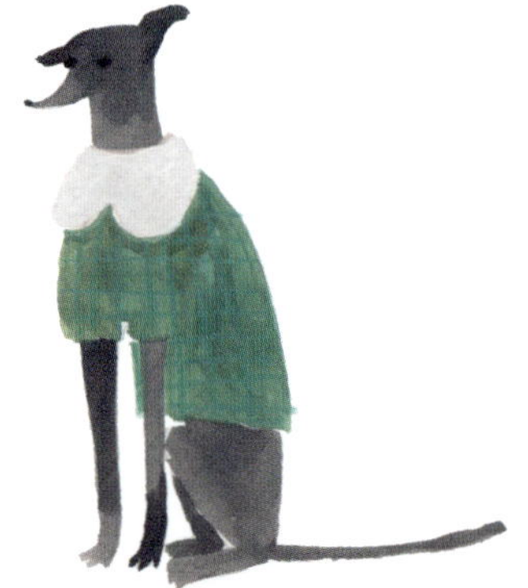

DRAW PEOPLE IN THE CITY.
Use the stick figure outlines or add your own characters to the scene.

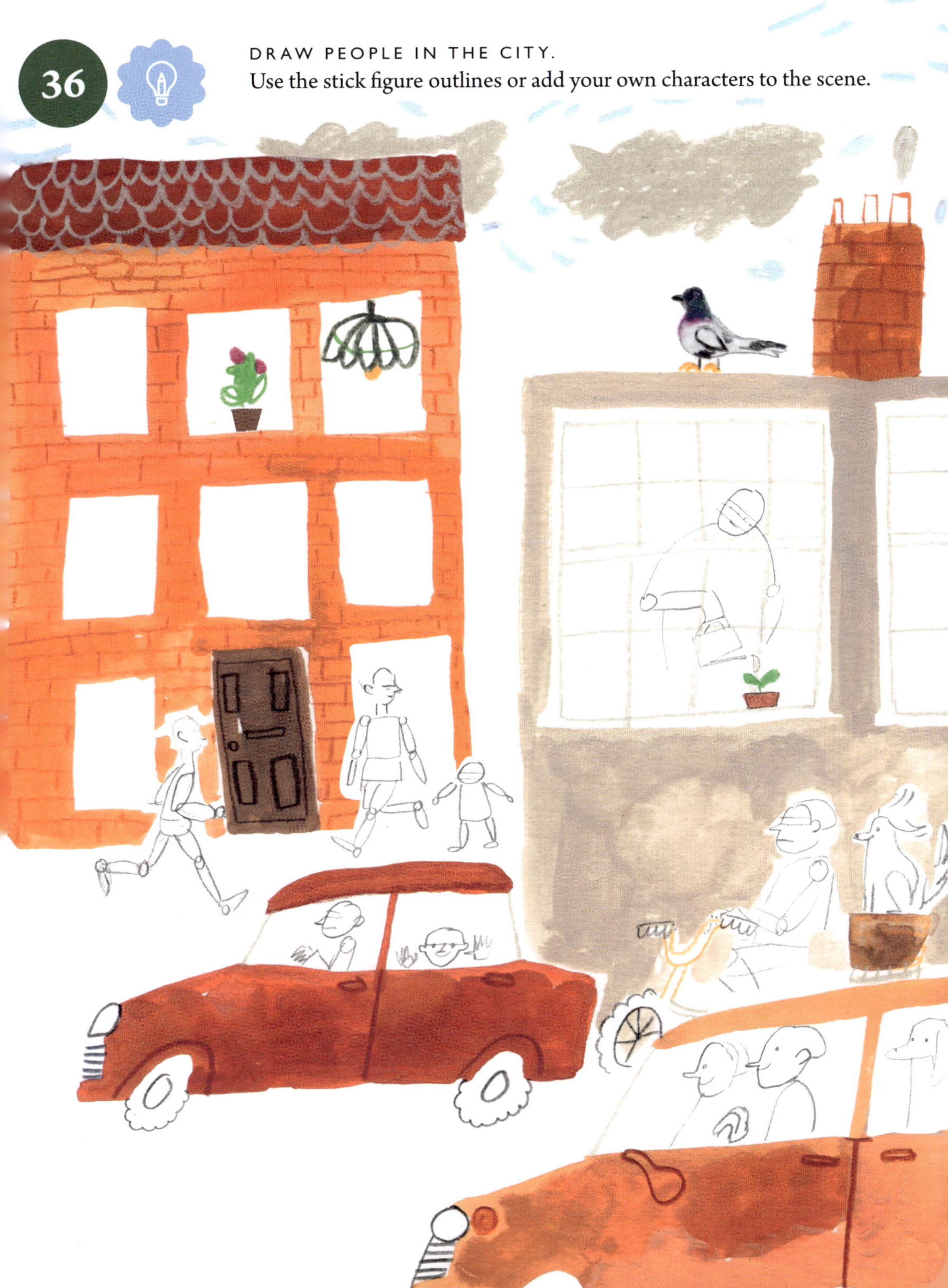

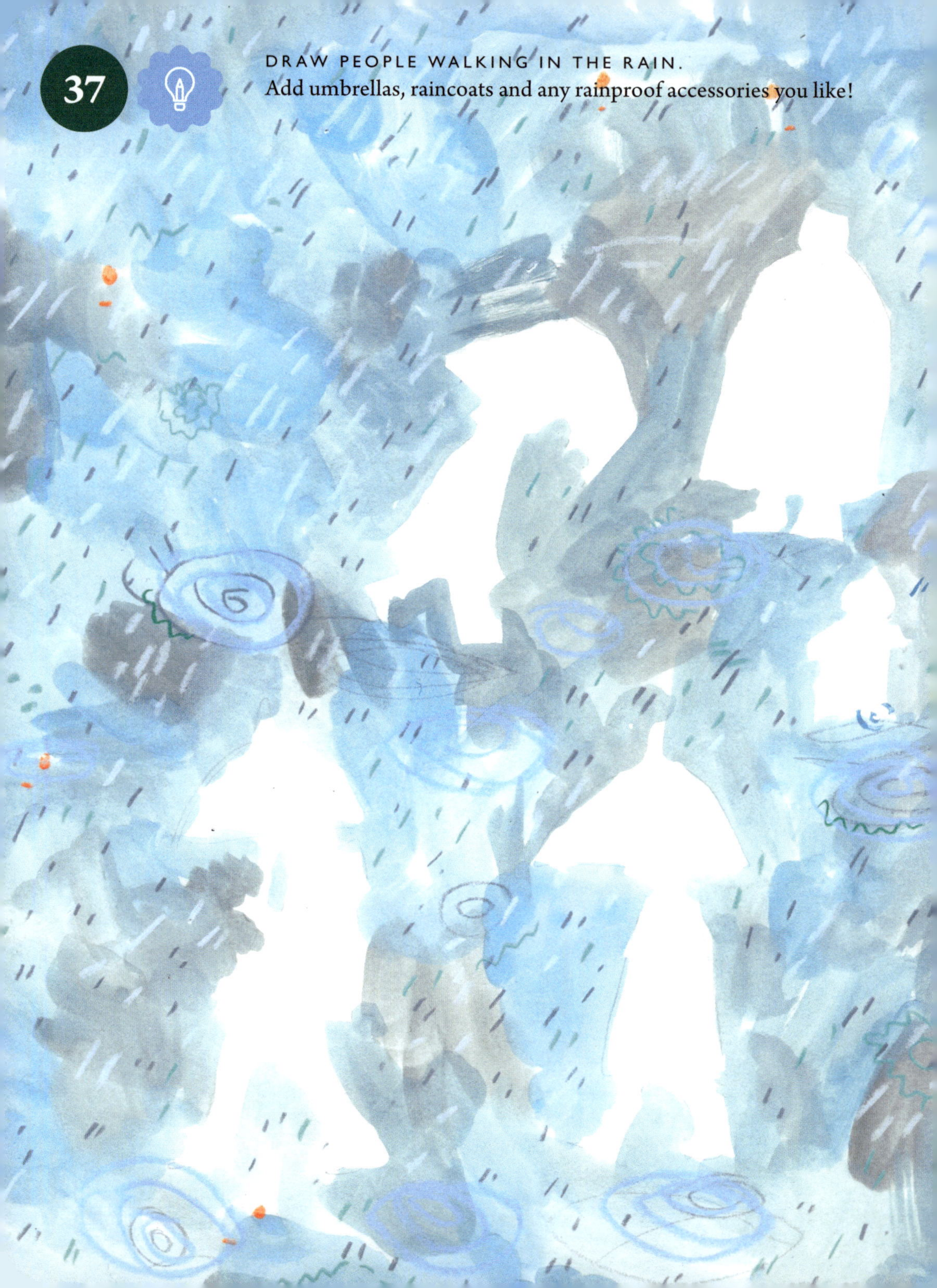

37

DRAW PEOPLE WALKING IN THE RAIN.
Add umbrellas, raincoats and any rainproof accessories you like!

38

ADD PEOPLE TO THESE COATS.

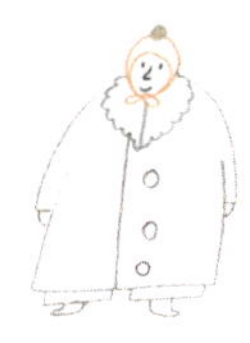

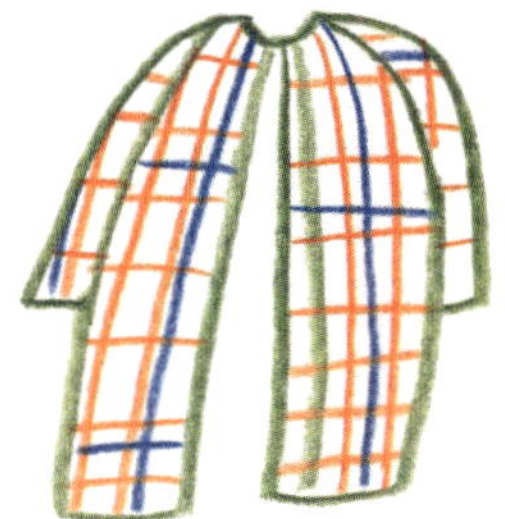

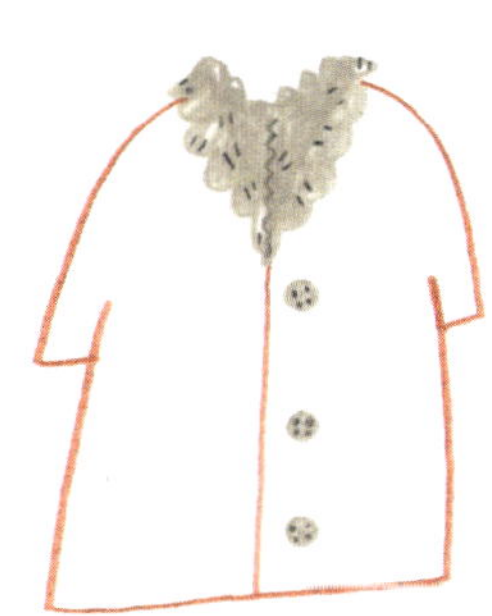

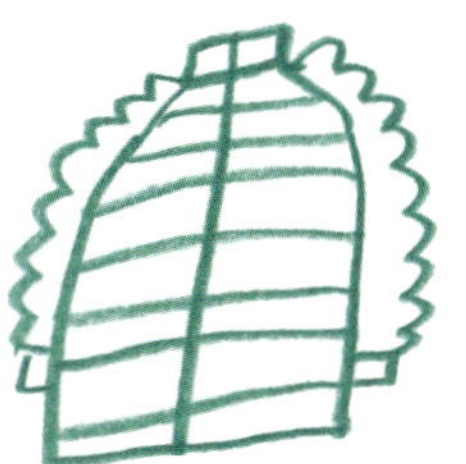

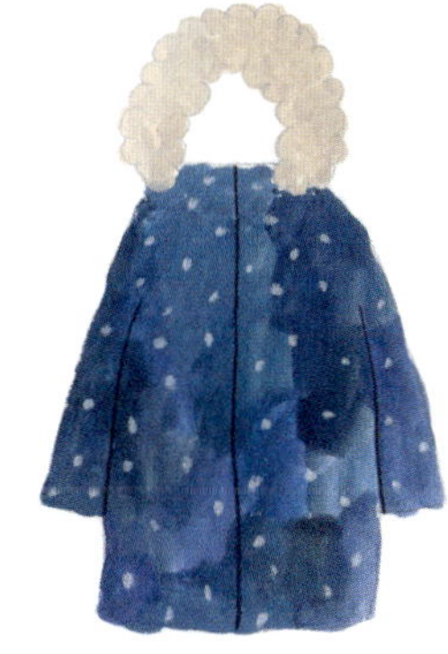

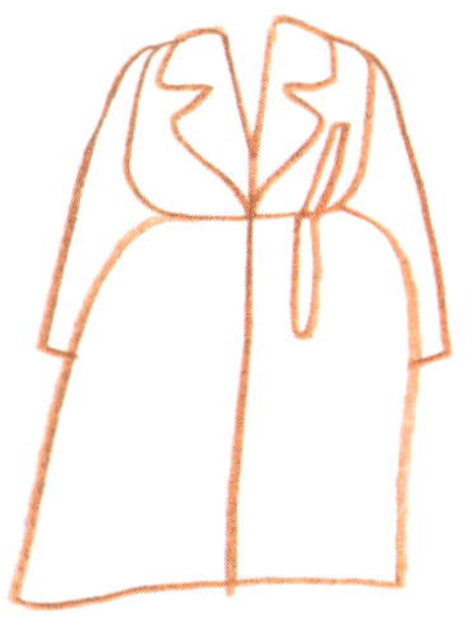

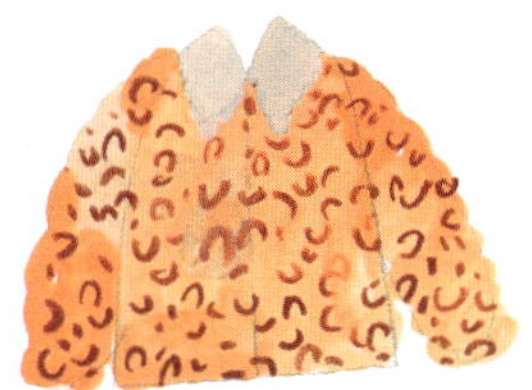

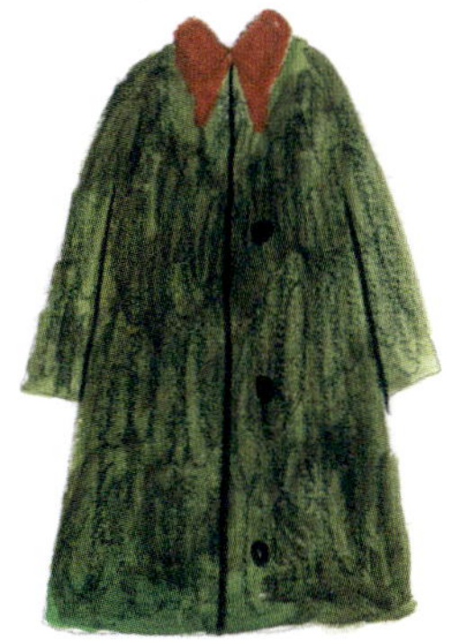

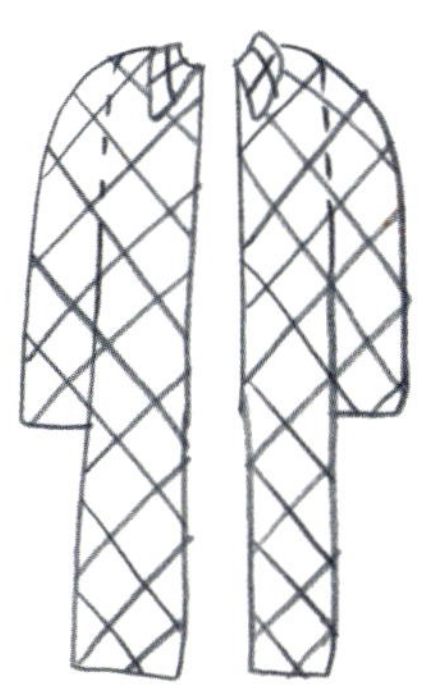

39

DRAW LITTLE SKIERS GOING DOWN THE HILL.

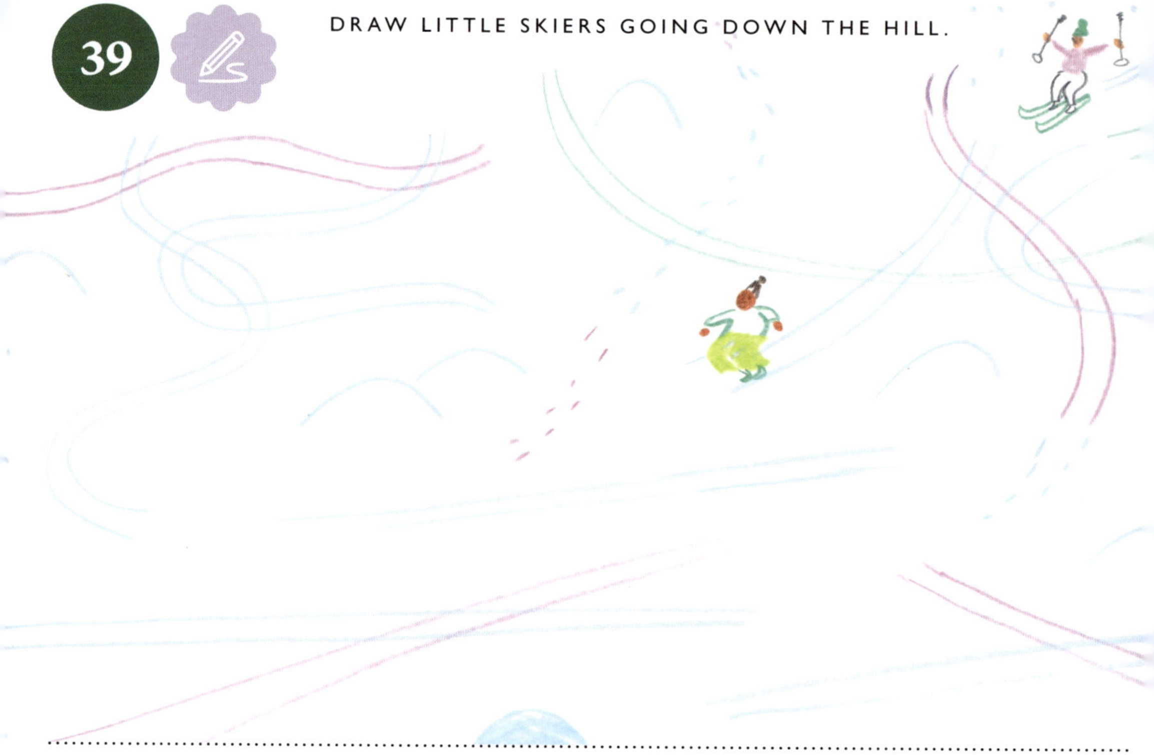

40

SKETCH DIFFERENT ICE SKATING POSES, ADDING SYMBOLS TO COMMUNICATE MOVEMENT. Think about energy and shape and less about proportions here.

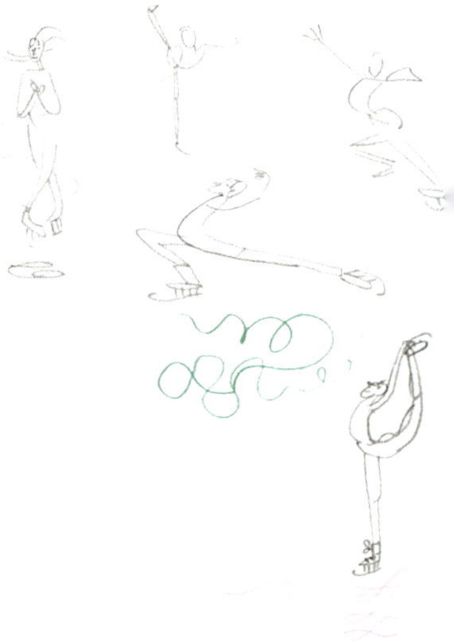

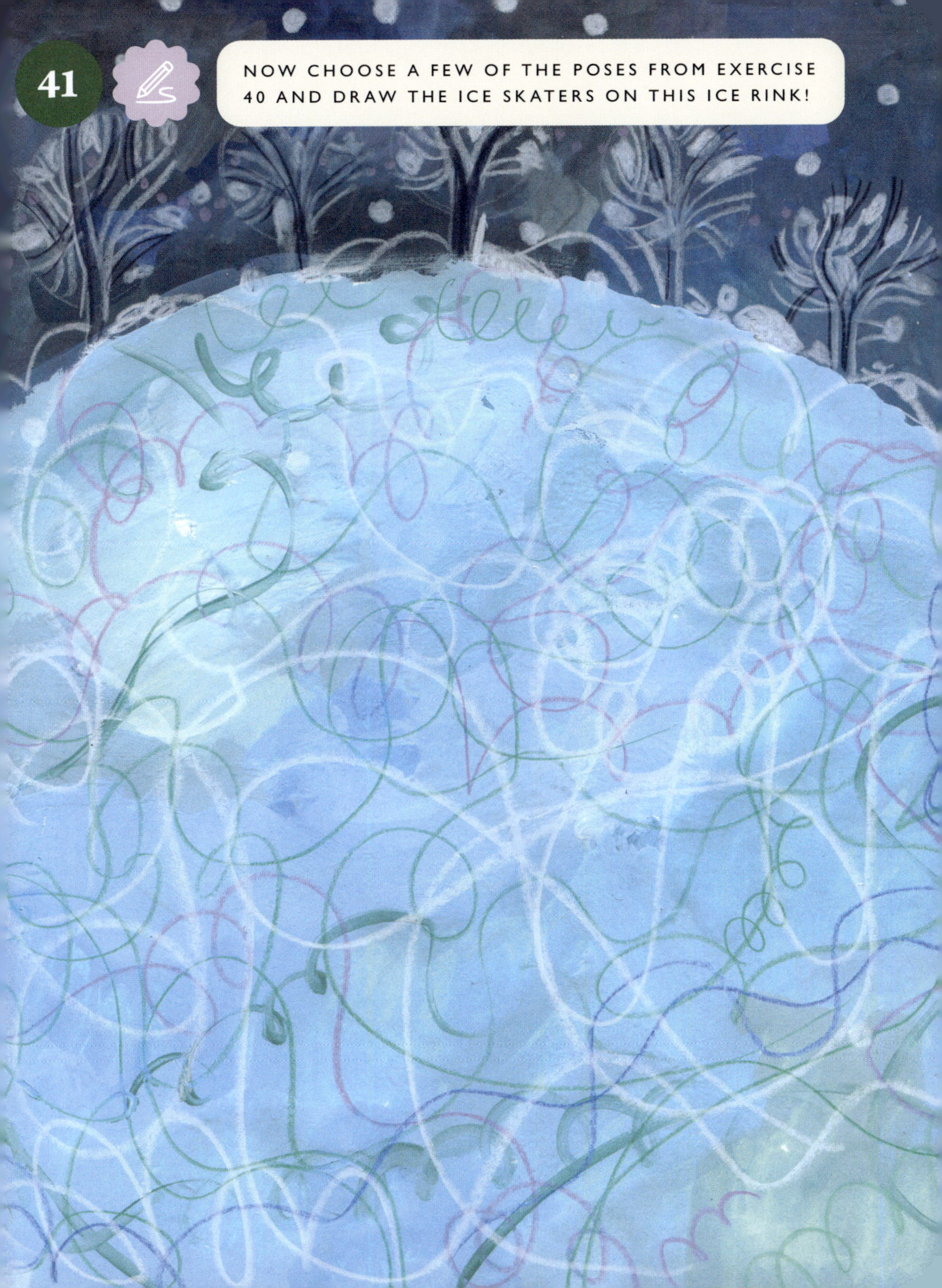
41
NOW CHOOSE A FEW OF THE POSES FROM EXERCISE 40 AND DRAW THE ICE SKATERS ON THIS ICE RINK!

DRAW PEOPLE CLIMBING.
Use the stick figure method first (see pages 20–21)
if you are not sure about poses!

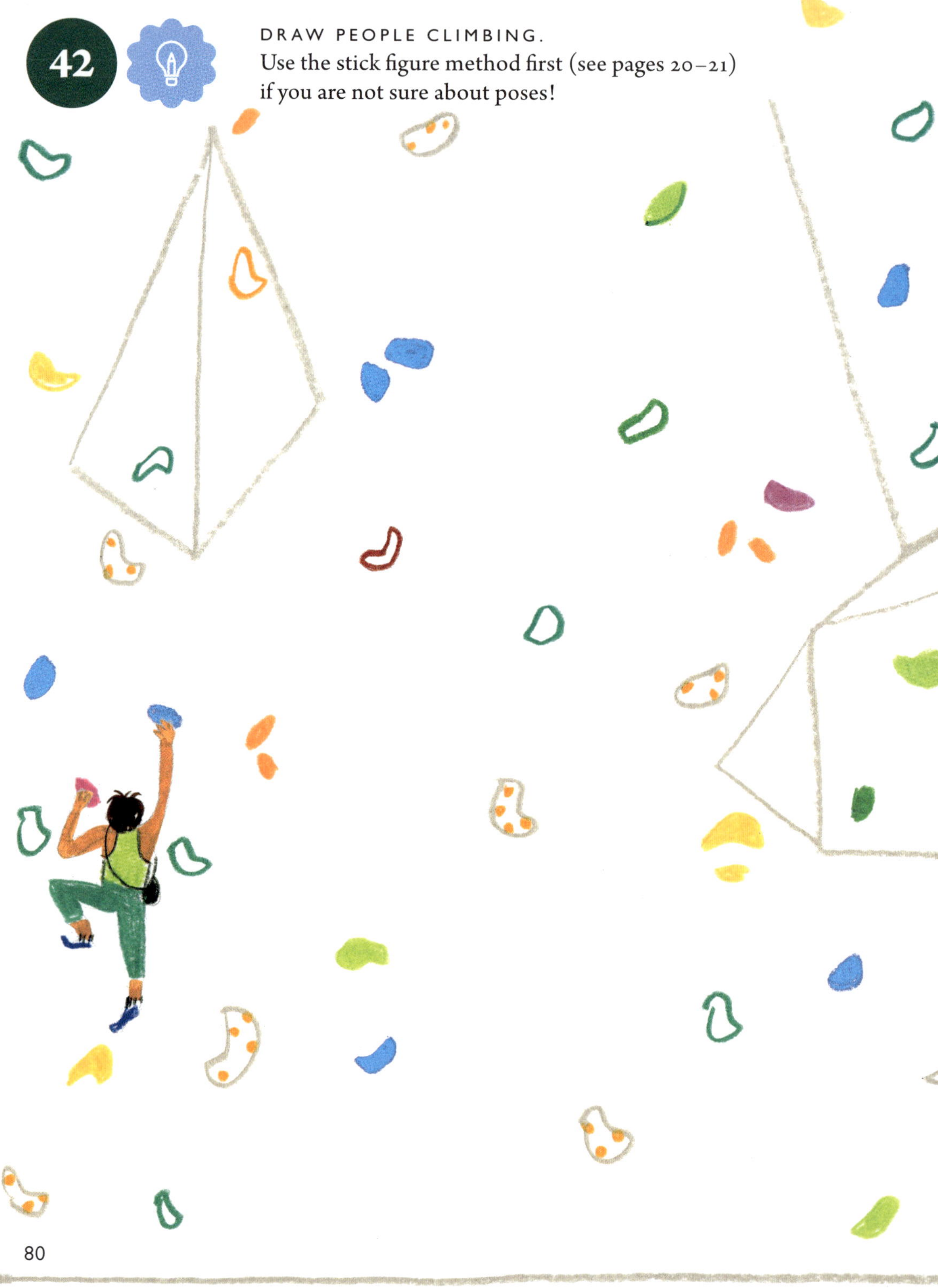

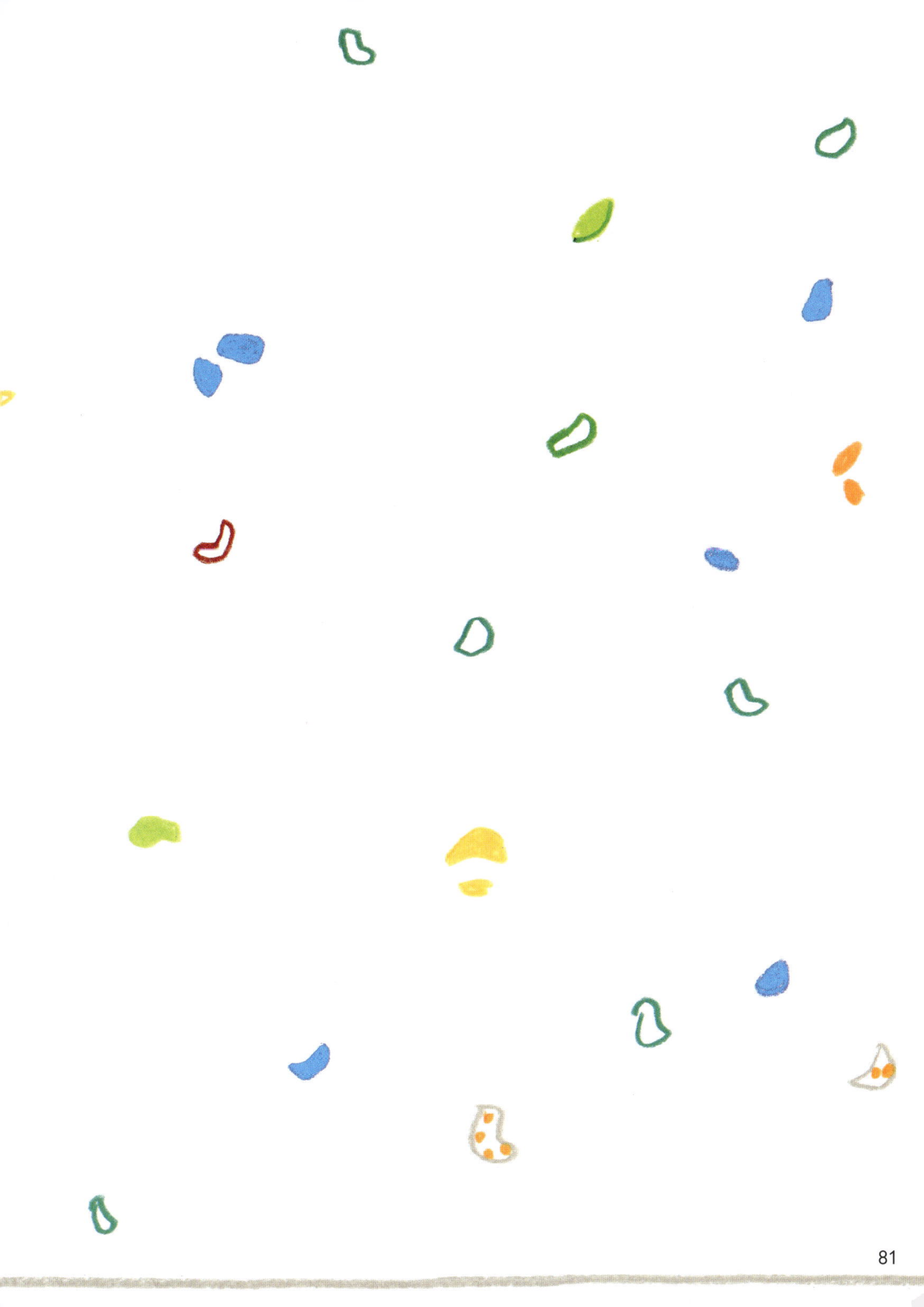

DRAW LOTS OF TINY PEOPLE IN THIS SQUARE.
Are they tourists? Taking pictures? Having coffee? Feeding pigeons?

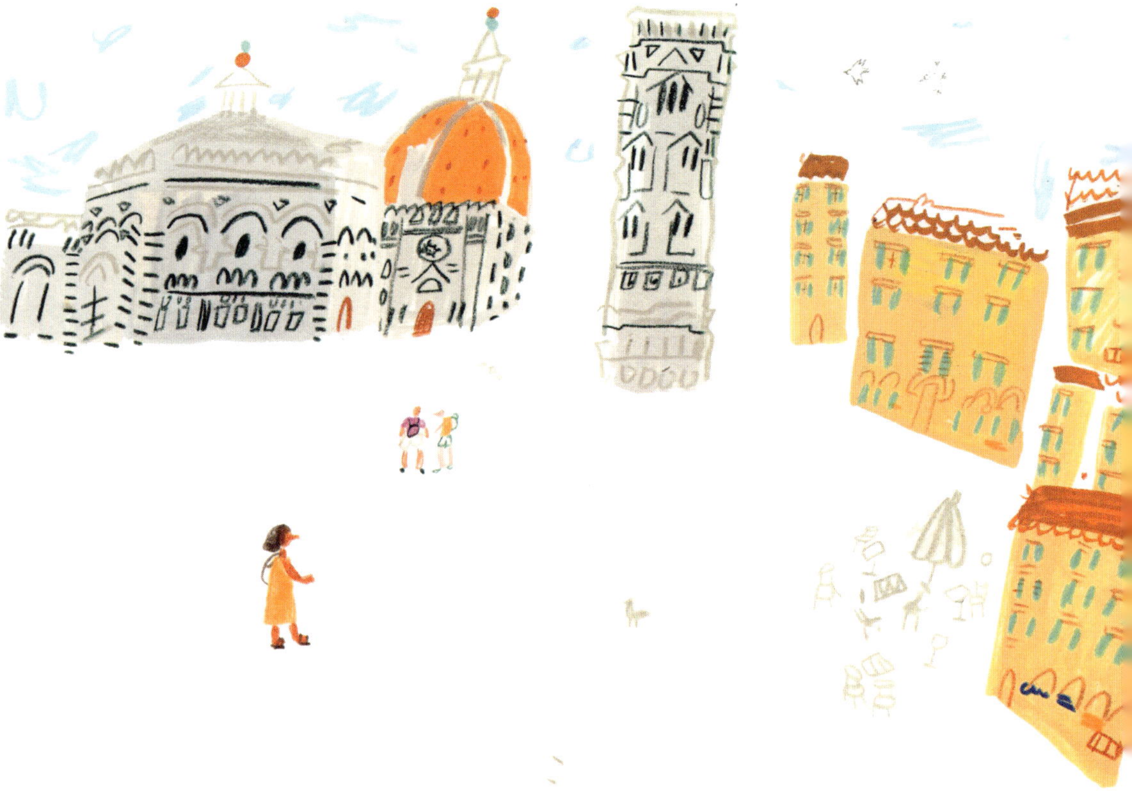

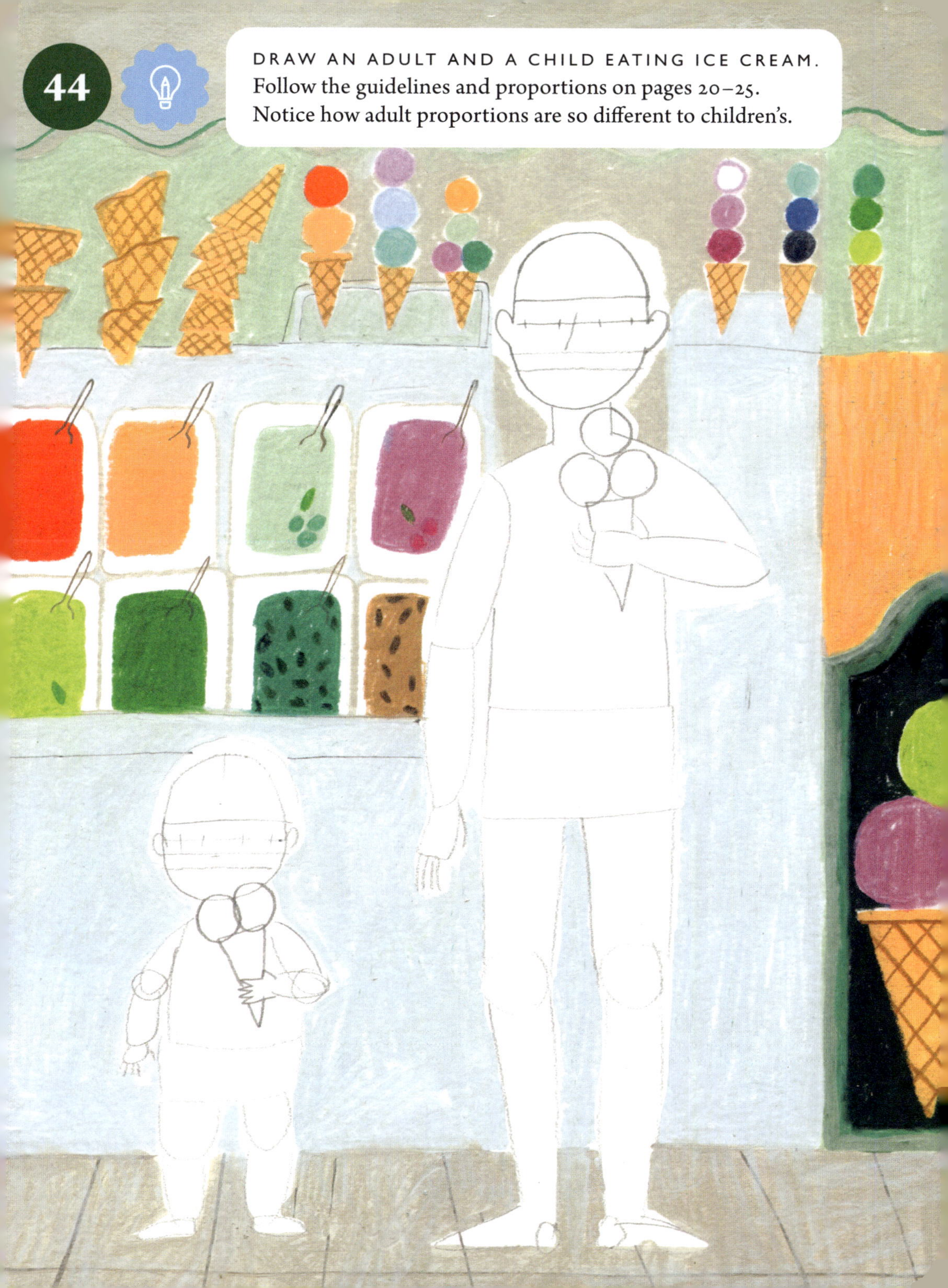

DRAW AN ADULT AND A CHILD EATING ICE CREAM.
Follow the guidelines and proportions on pages 20–25.
Notice how adult proportions are so different to children's.
44

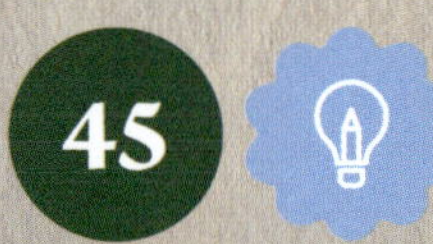

DRAW PEOPLE SITTING AND HAVING COFFEE IN THIS CAFÉ.
Who are they? Are they girlfriends/boyfriends? Sisters? Brothers?

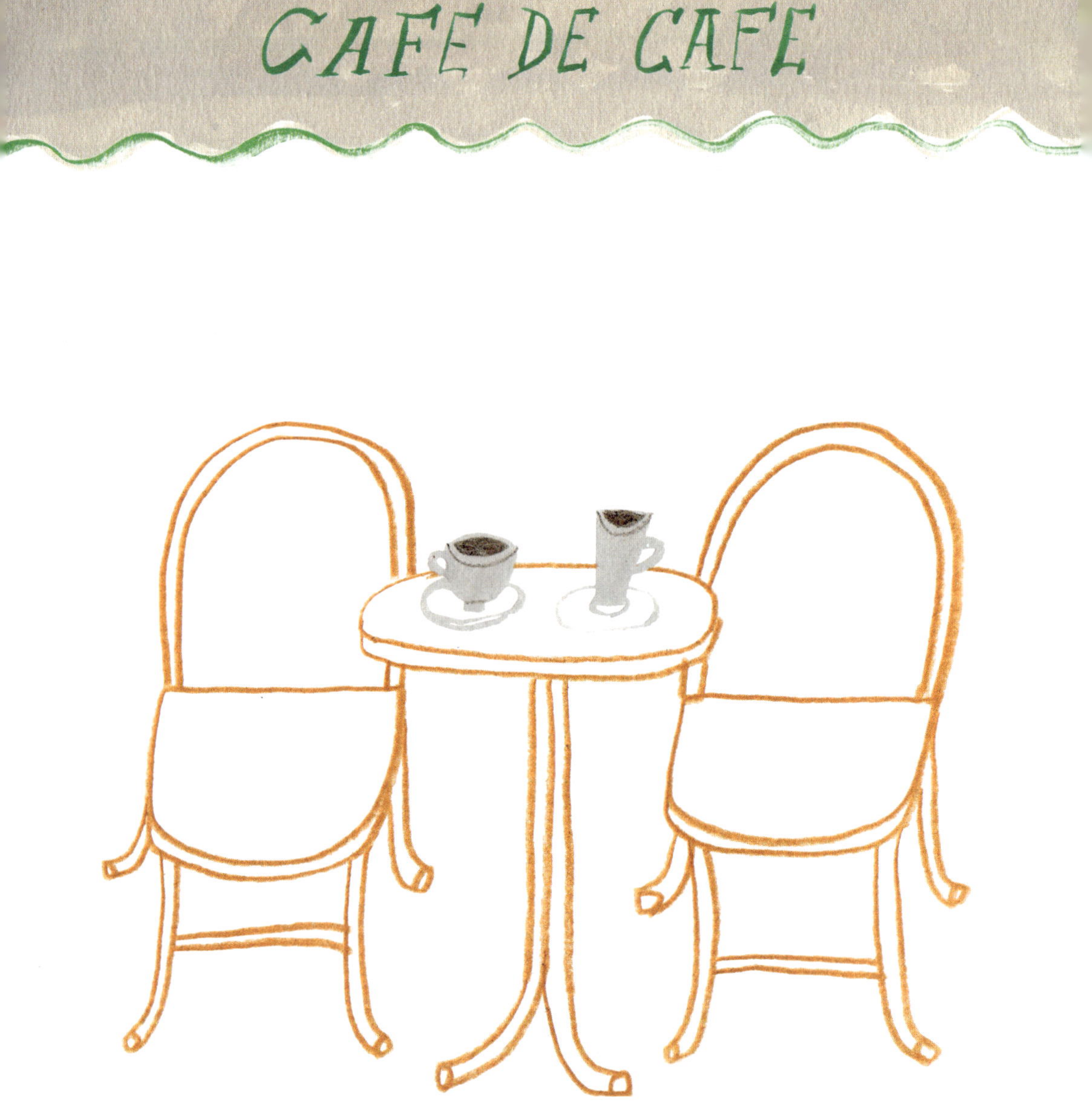

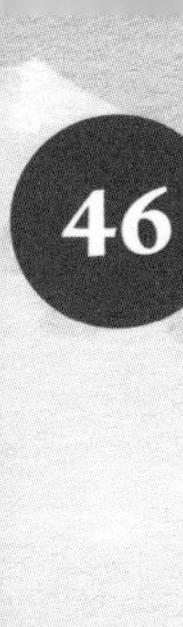 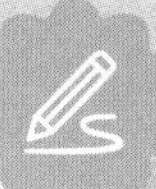

DRAW PEOPLE CLIMBING THIS ICY PEAK.
You can give them climbing equipment or perhaps a flag.
You decide how small or large people should be!

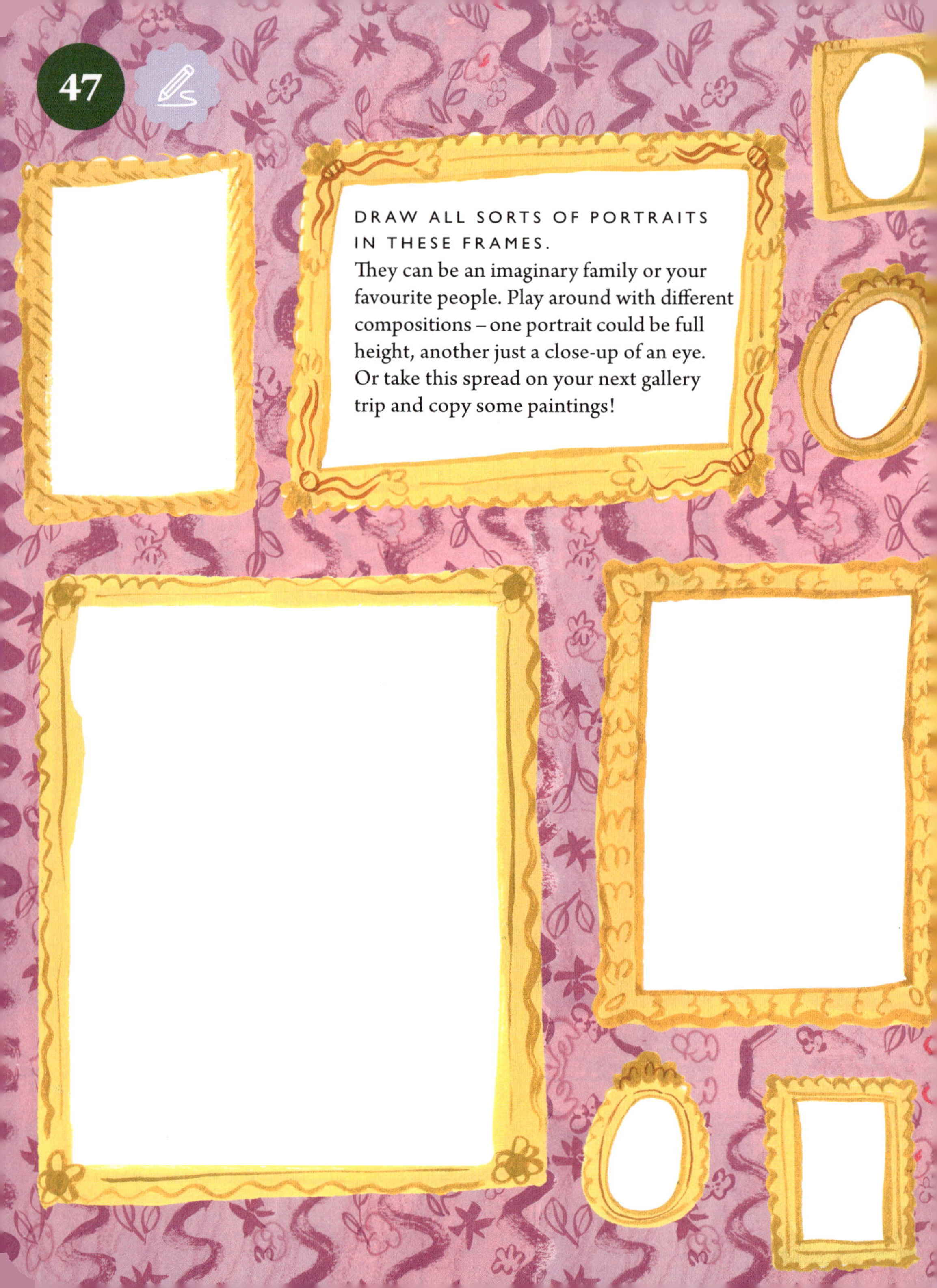

DRAW ALL SORTS OF PORTRAITS IN THESE FRAMES.

They can be an imaginary family or your favourite people. Play around with different compositions – one portrait could be full height, another just a close-up of an eye. Or take this spread on your next gallery trip and copy some paintings!

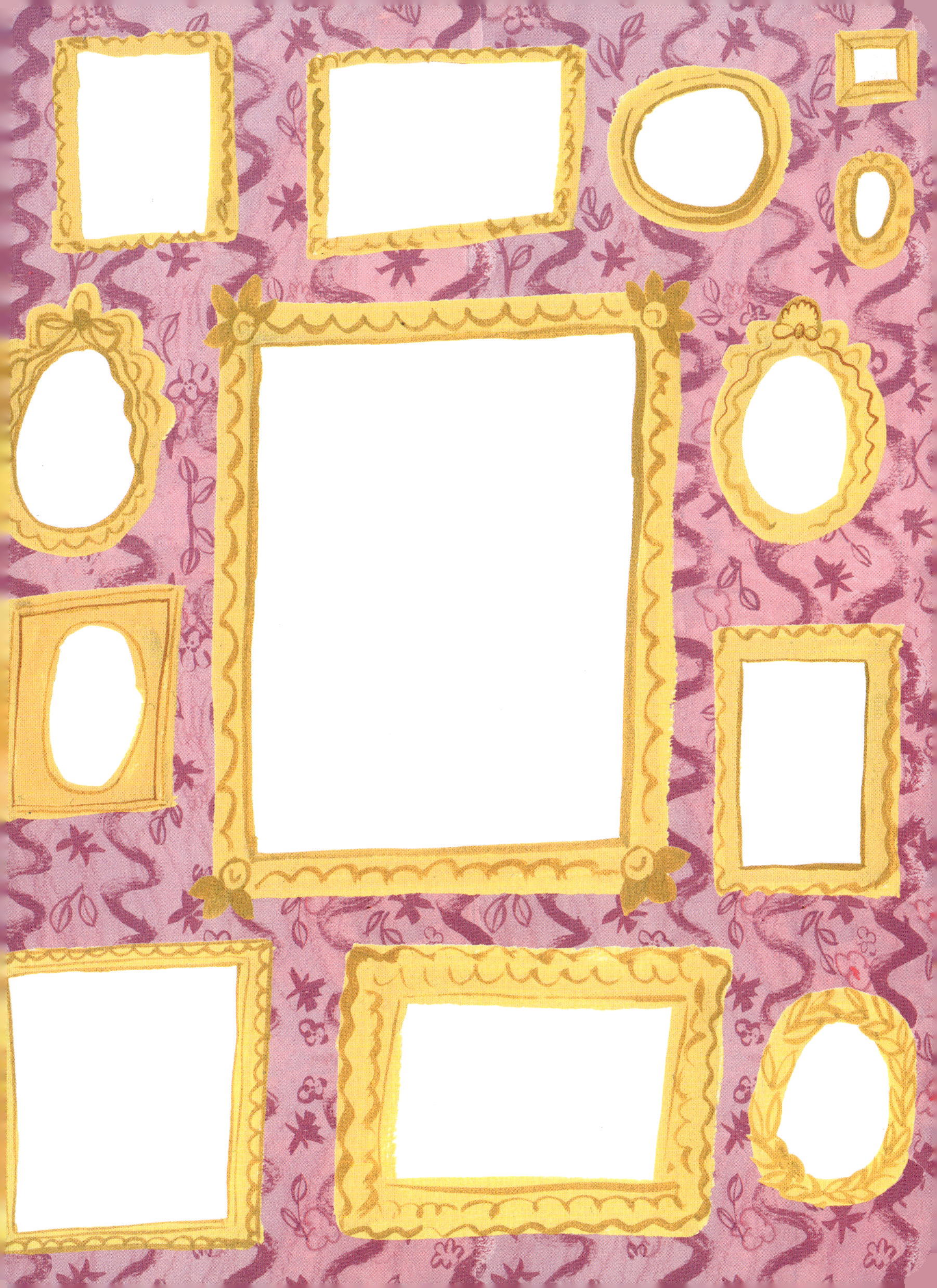

DRAW A CROWD.

Using figures of different sizes is an easy way to communicate depth and distance. If we draw people large closer to us and smaller figures towards the top of the page it creates depth, and can help us gauge the size of the scene. Try drawing a crowd to fill in the gaps and play with different scales.

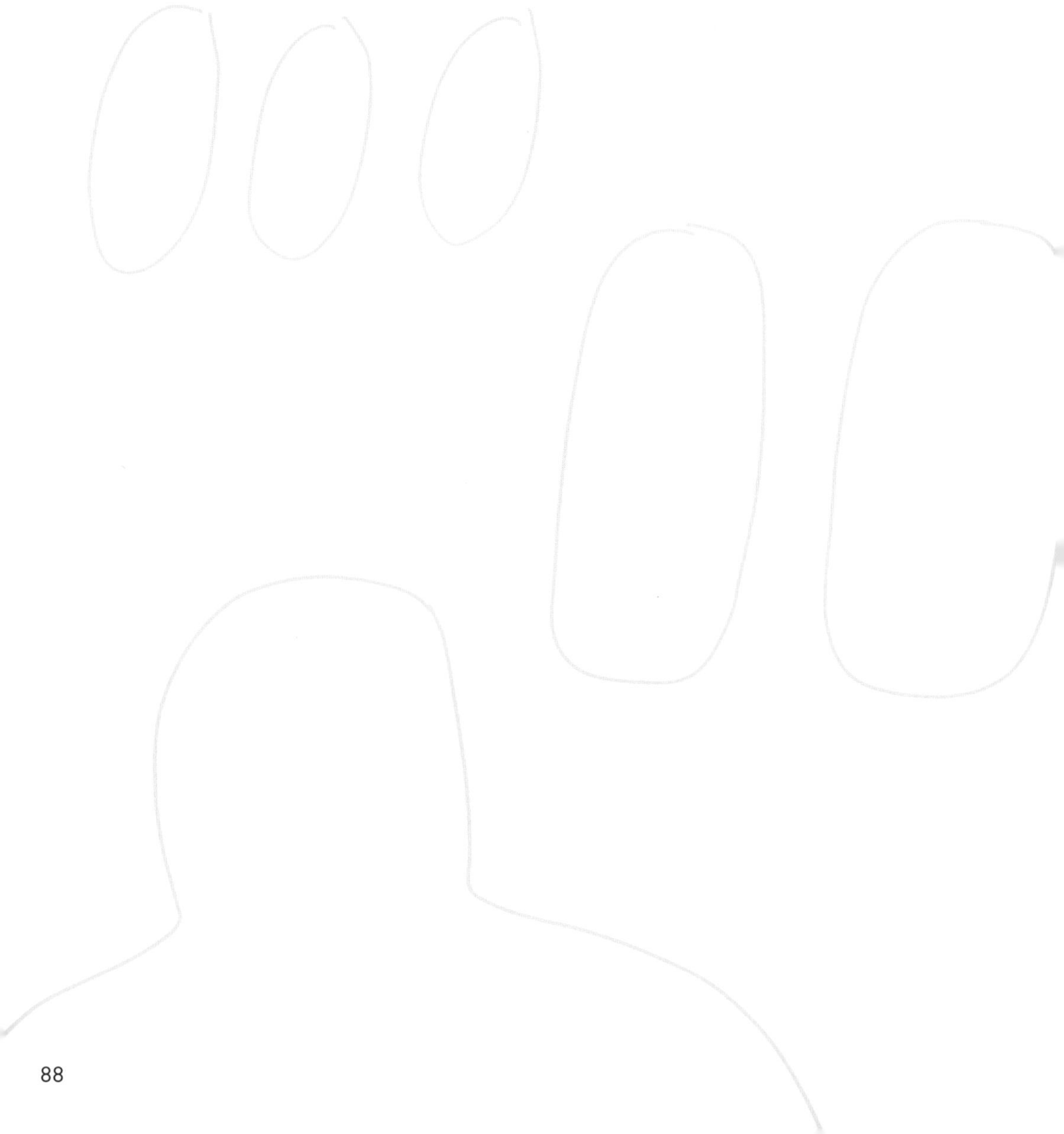

DRAW THE SAME PERSON
IN FOUR DIFFERENT WAYS.

USING
LINES.

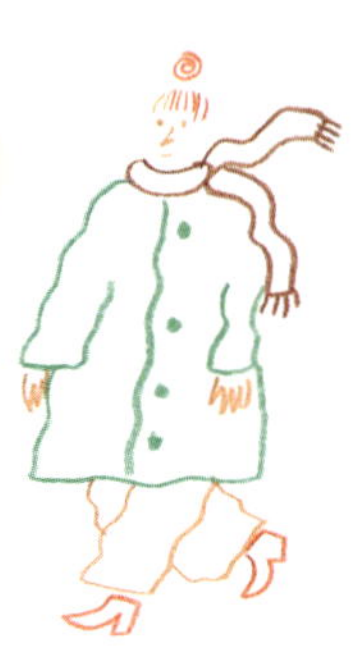

USING
COLOUR.

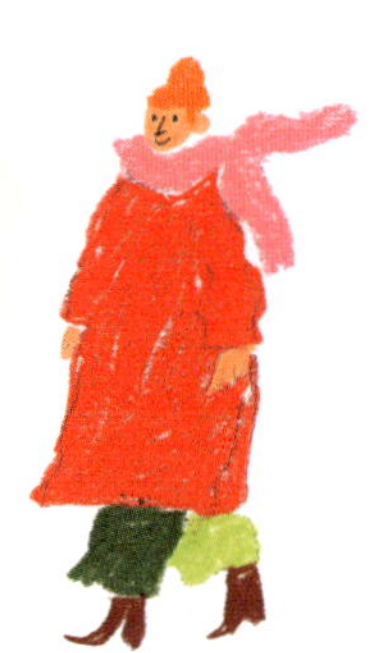

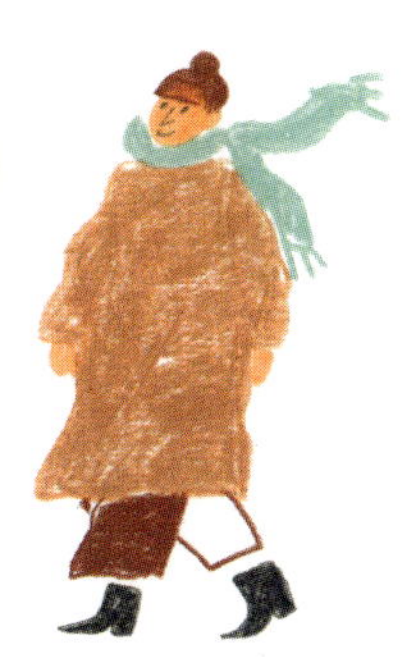

USING
SHAPES.

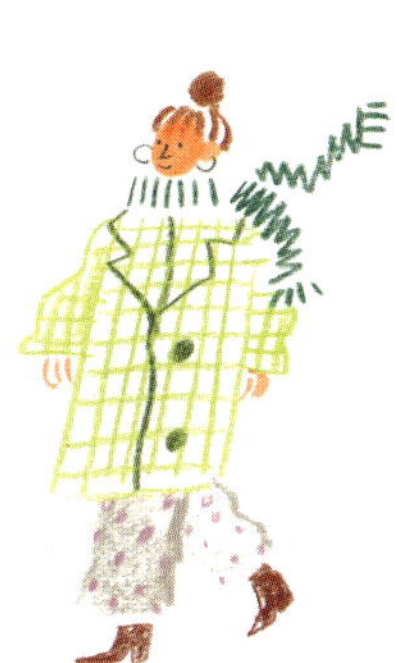

USING
MARK
MAKING.

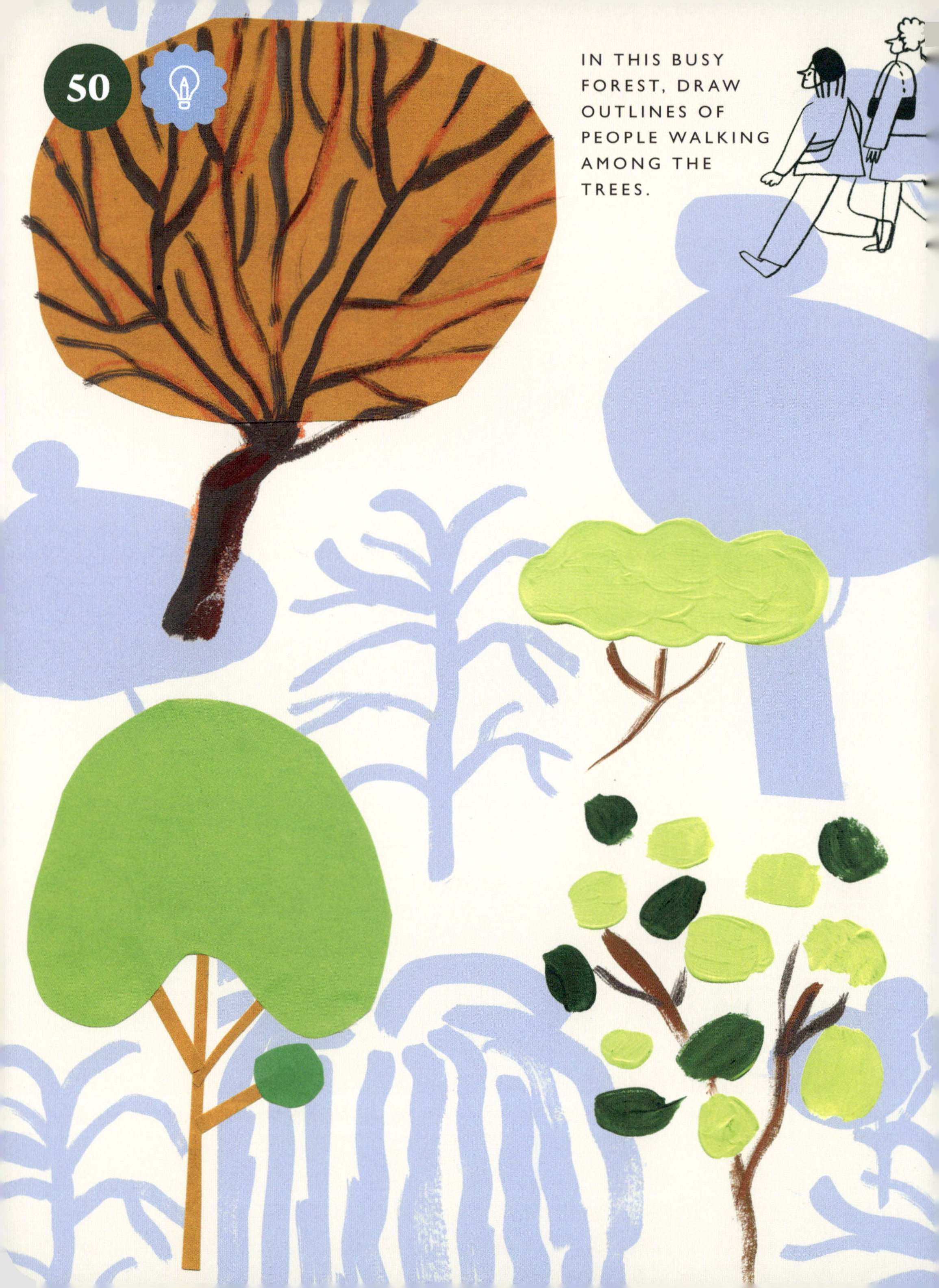
50
IN THIS BUSY
FOREST, DRAW
OUTLINES OF
PEOPLE WALKING
AMONG THE
TREES.

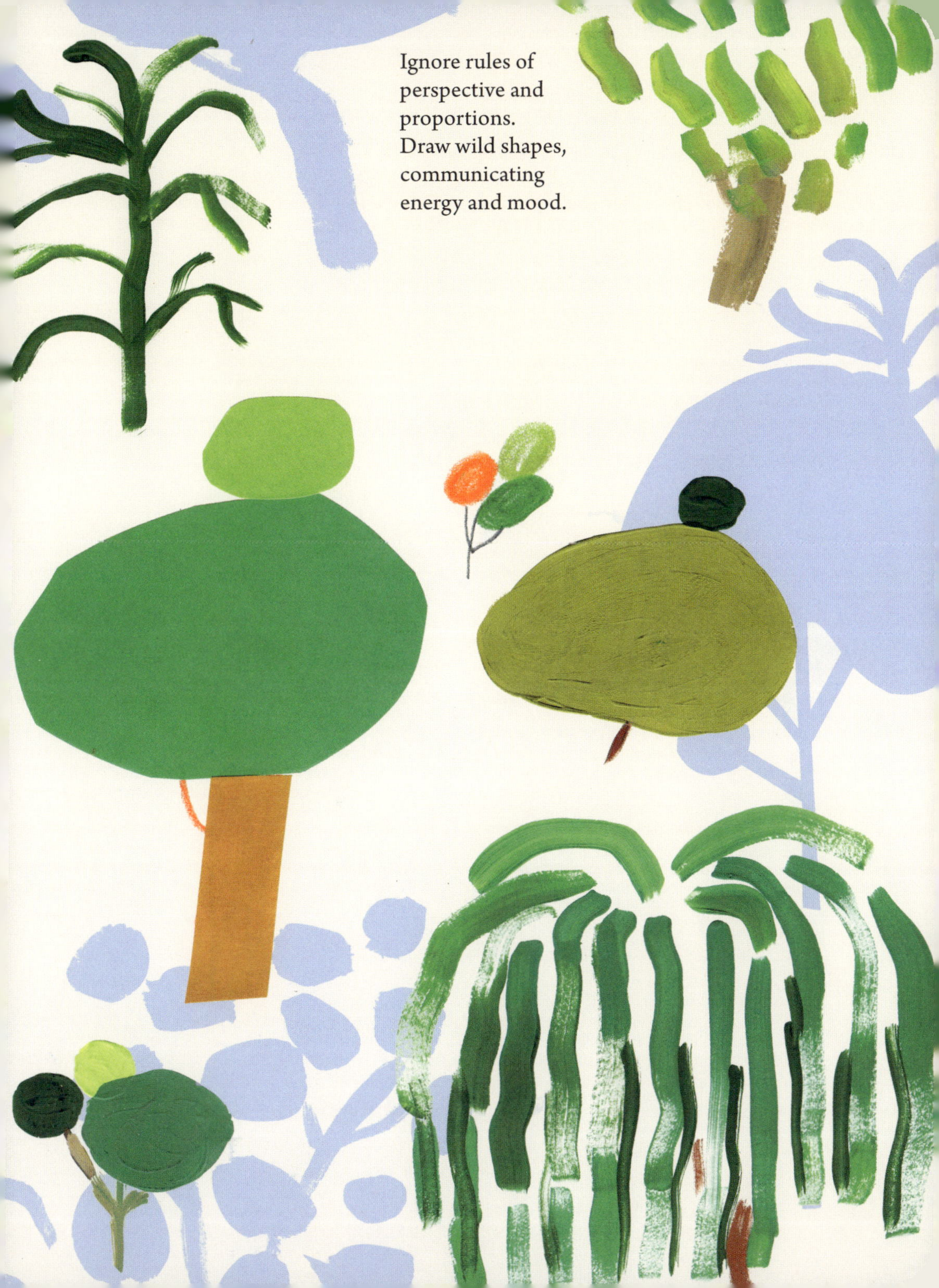

Ignore rules of
perspective and
proportions.
Draw wild shapes,
communicating
energy and mood.

SHADOWS CAN ADD DEPTH AND ATMOSPHERE TO A DRAWING AND PLACE YOUR CHARACTER IN A SCENE. Try drawing shadows, imagining there is the source of light behind, in front and above these figures. What kind of shadows would the different light placements create? Short? Long? Angled?

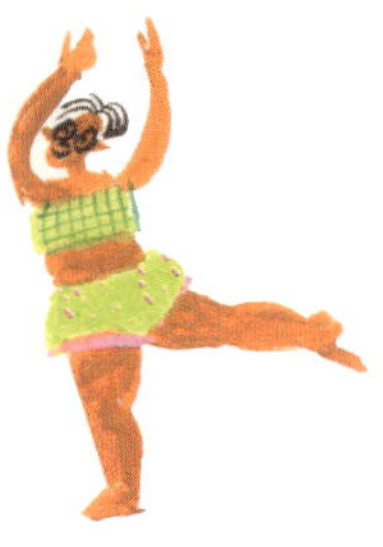

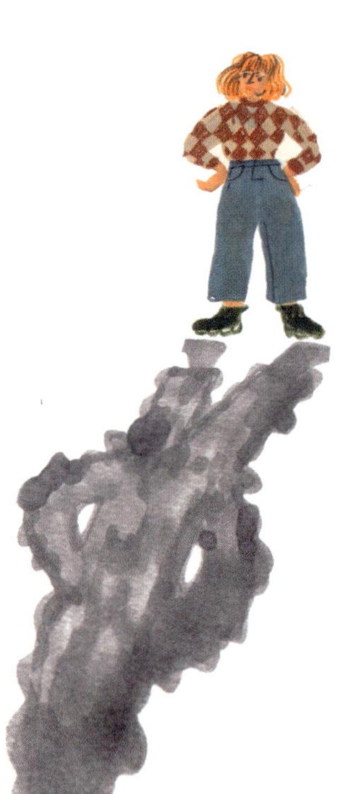

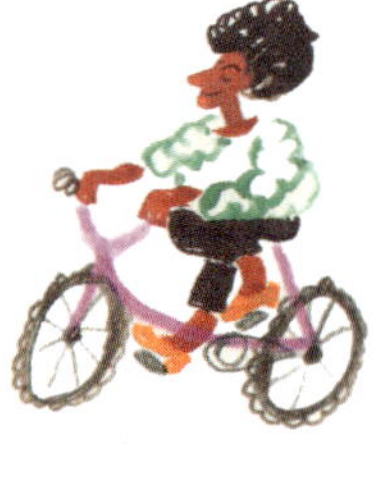

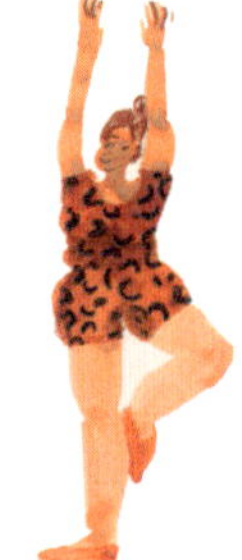

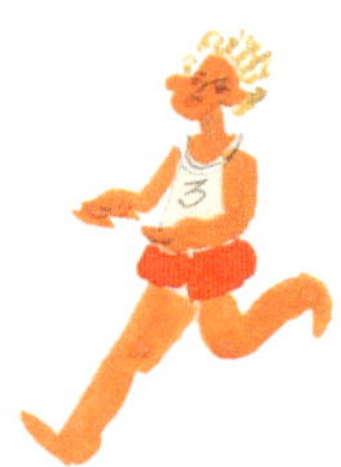

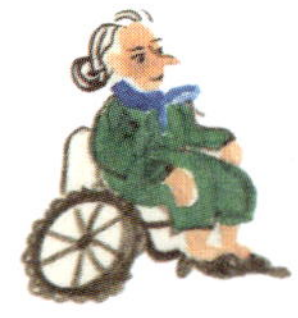

52

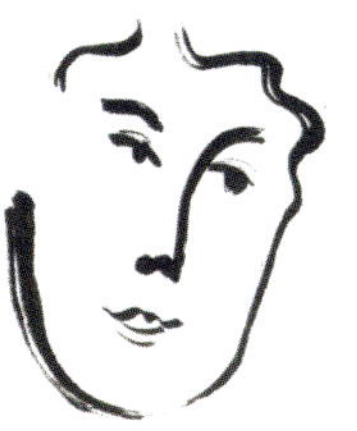

Try drawing a portrait in their style!

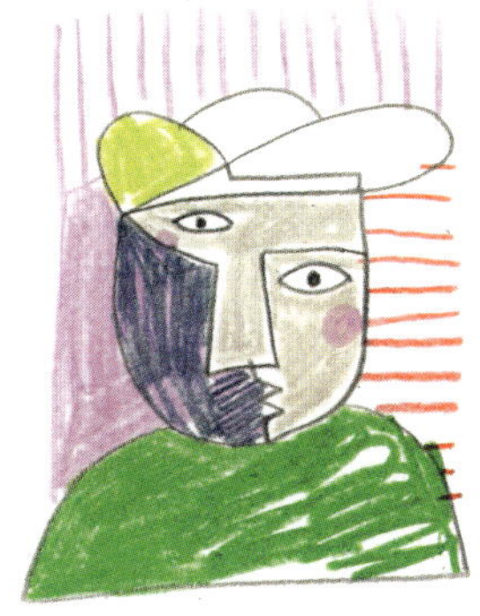

ADD DETAILS TO THE SWIMMING FIGURES AND DRAW MORE PEOPLE HAVING THE BEST TIME AT THE BEACH. Play around with different sizes, adding people in both the background and foreground. Some could be sunbathing, some running, some swimming!

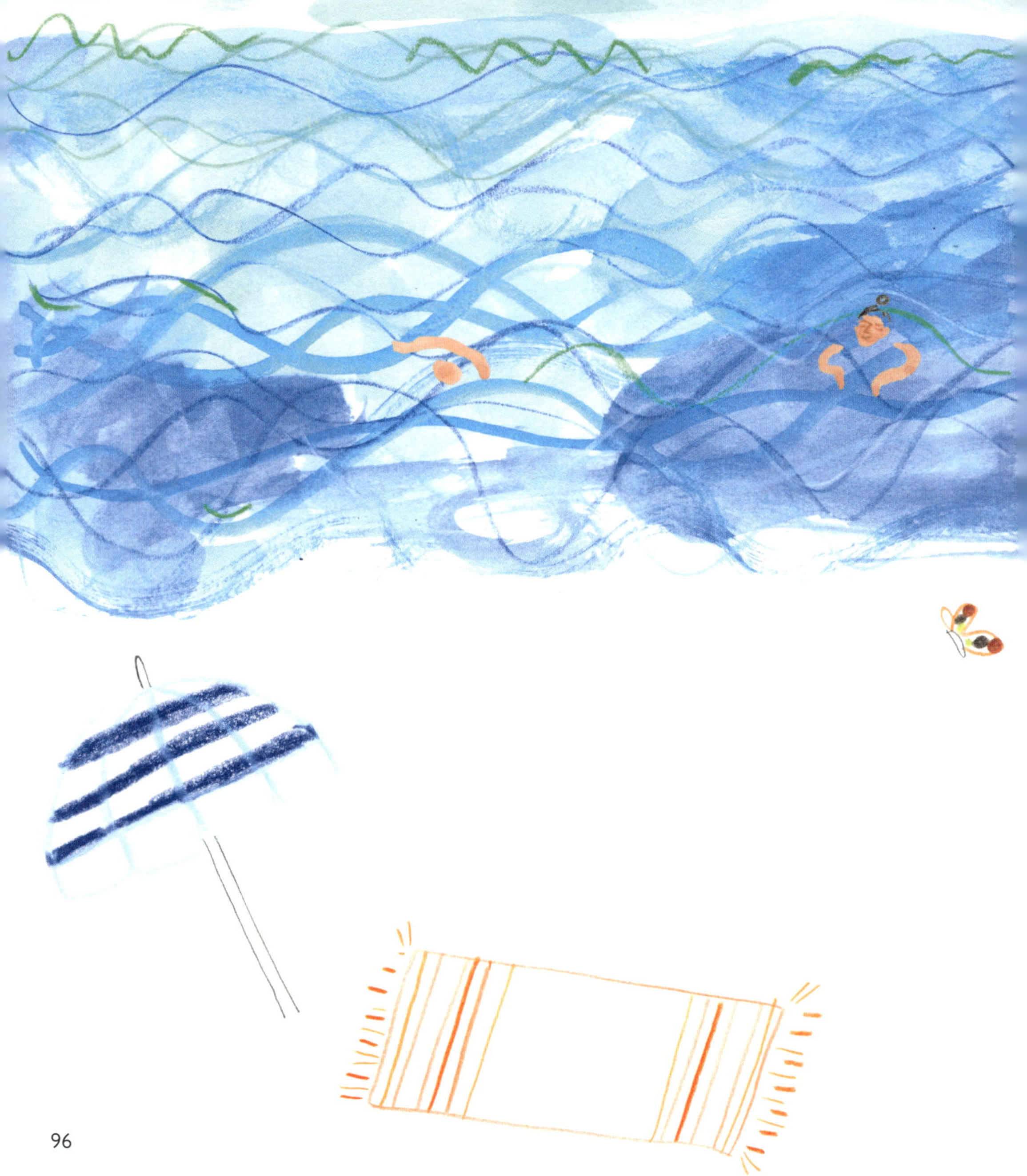

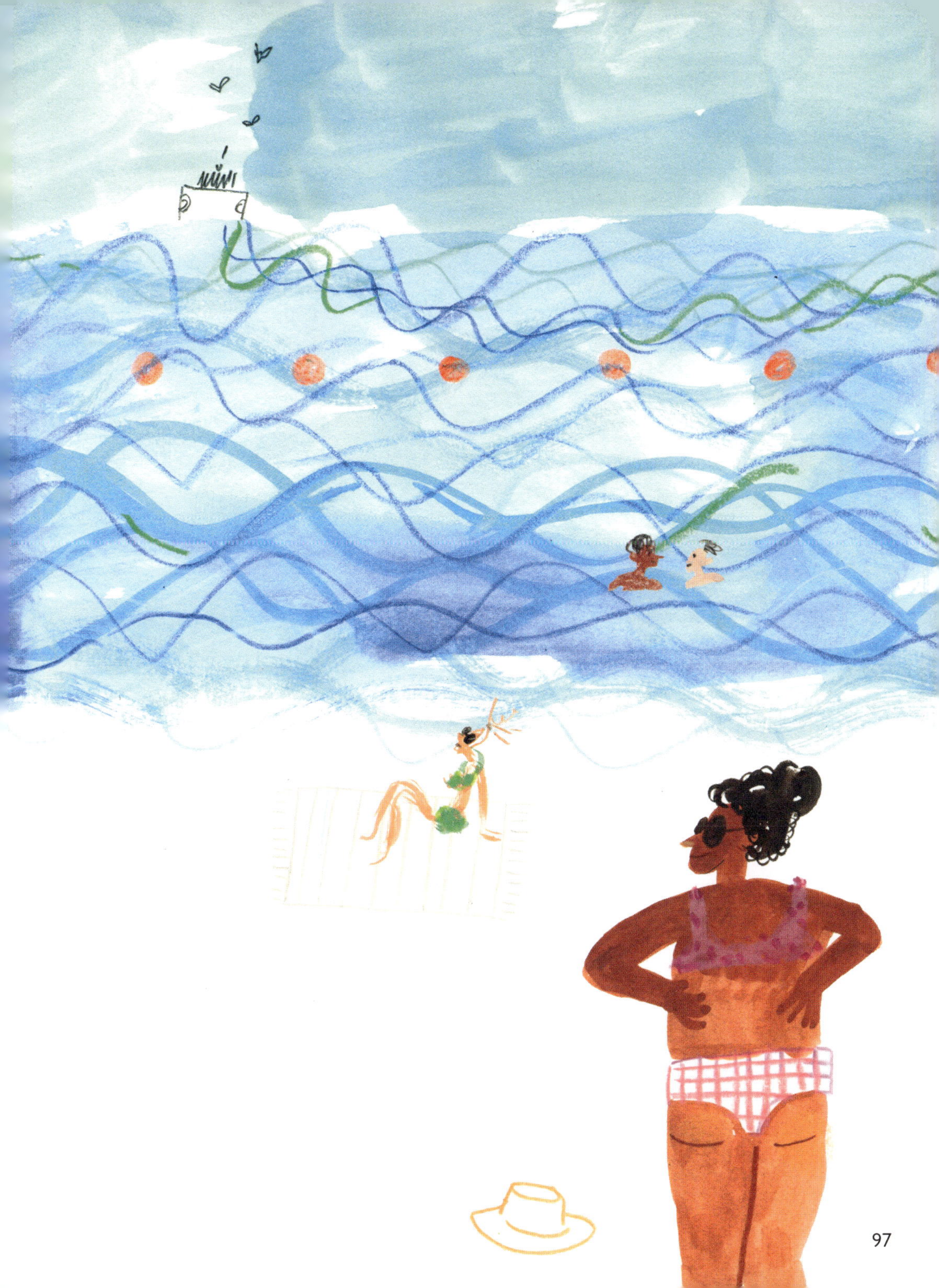

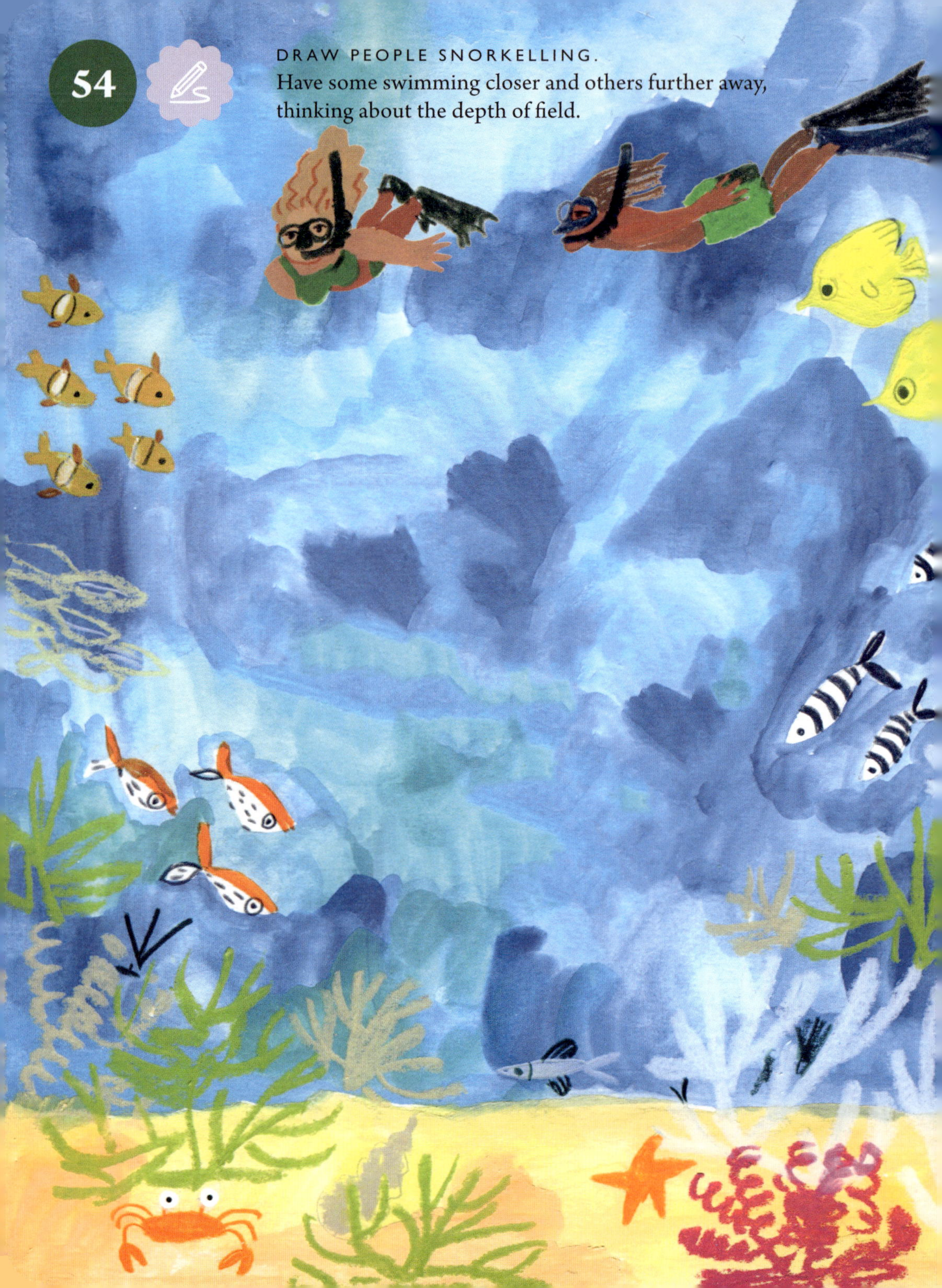

54
DRAW PEOPLE SNORKELLING.
Have some swimming closer and others further away,
thinking about the depth of field.

DRAW PEOPLE SITTING AND LAYING DOWN
IN DIFFERENT AND UNUSUAL ANGLES.
Perhaps their arm is in the foreground, held out
in front of them, phone in hand, to take a selfie.

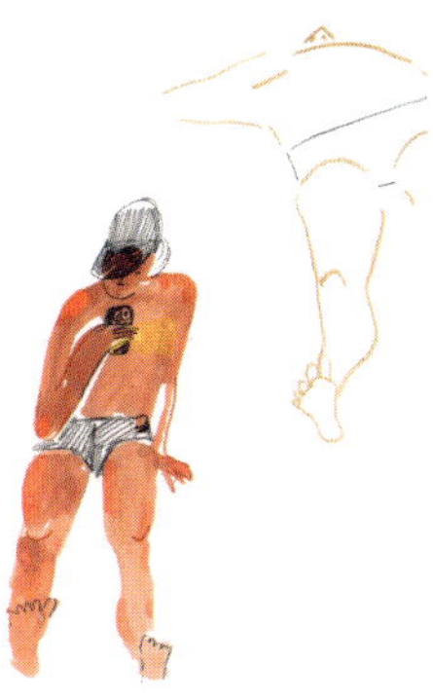

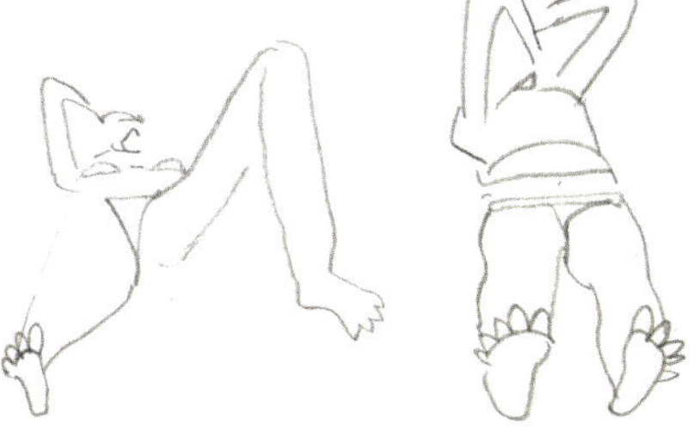

DRAWING FABRICS & TEXTILES STEP-BY-STEP.

In this project I want to take you through several options for drawing garments. First a solid heavy fabric, then a gentle, thinner-looking fabric and finally a see-through one. As always, I want you to use the materials you already have to hand. I will be using gouache and soft pastels. This exercise is all about mark making and layering!

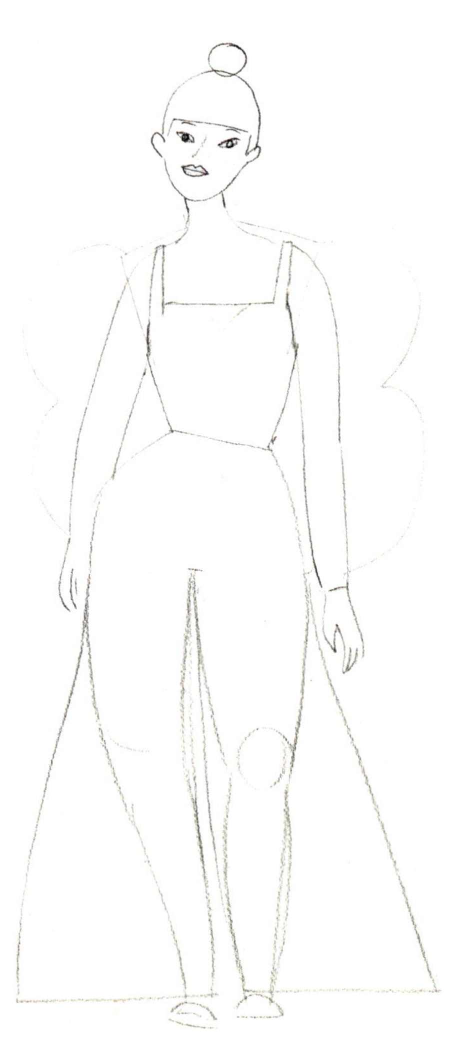

STEP 1

Let's sketch the body! I'm drawing a woman in a fancy outfit, with lots of floating elements and cool fabrics. Feel free to change her body shape.

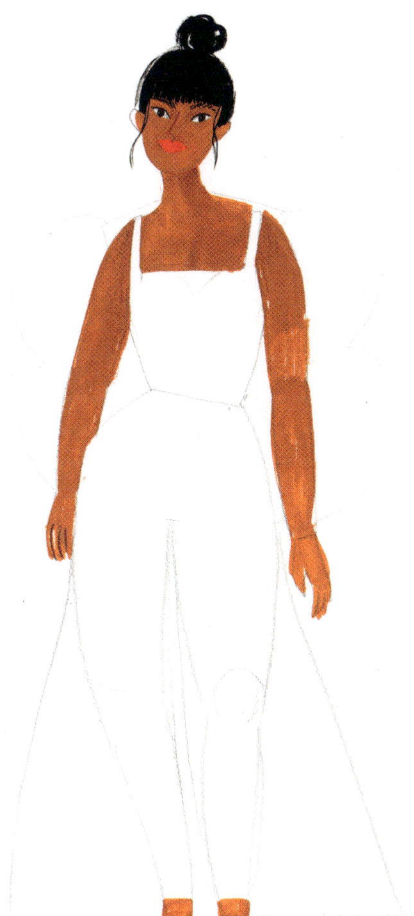

Paint the trousers and top. I am using watered-down gouache in aqua blue for the trousers and mint green for the top. I want the layers to be a little bit see-through, in contrast to the skin and hair. Markers, soft pencils or watercolours will work for this layer too.

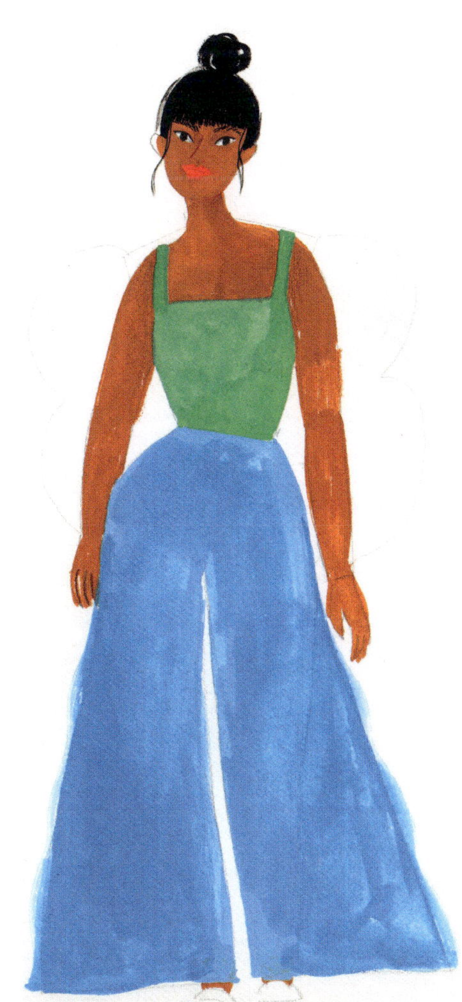

STEP 2

Paint the skin tone and face, adding in the facial details. I am using gouache for this step, but you can use whatever you have – markers, watercolours, acrylic or pencils.

Let's add details! I am using gouache and colouring pencils. You can also use markers in a darker colour, or mix watercolours with some white acrylic paint and use crayons or pencils on top. If you don't have materials that are opaque enough to cover the initial layer of colour, opt for a darker colour. I am decorating her outfit with little shining stars. On the top I have used a lighter blue and blue and on the bottom a green pencil, some lime and white. I added jewellery in this bright lime colour, too.

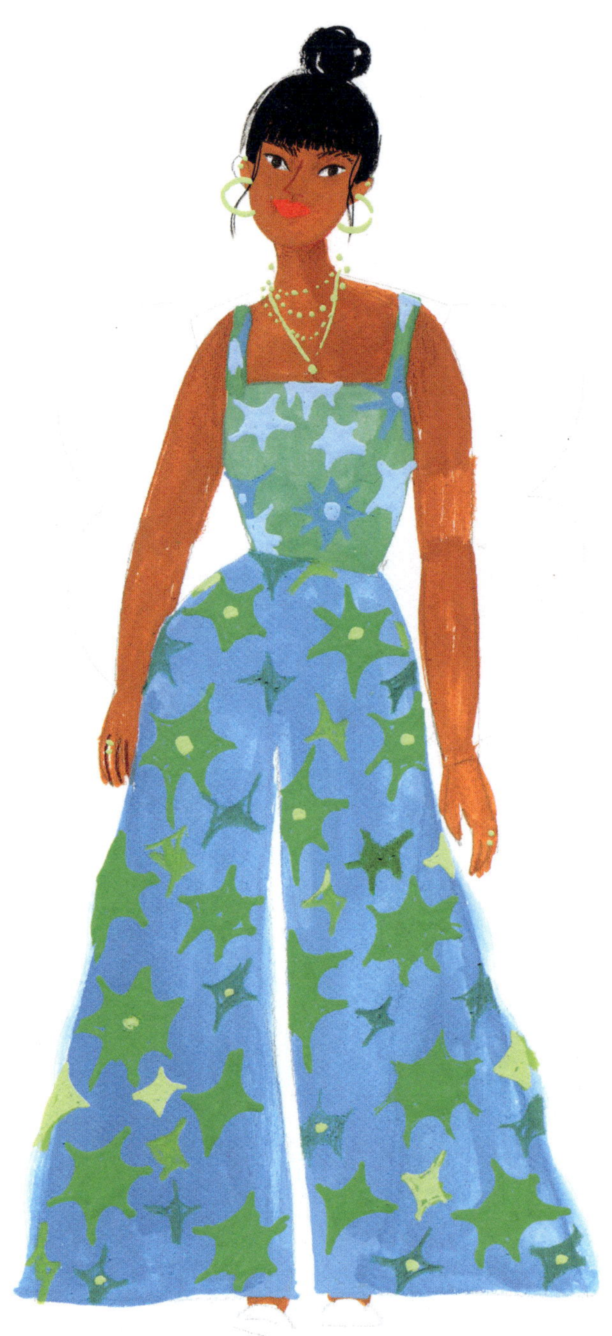

The last step … I want this airy see-through effect for the outer layer of her clothes, so I am using soft pastels and smudging them to achieve a translucent texture. Other options could be applying pencil in a very thin uniform layer or using watercolour wash (very watered-down), trying not to smudge other areas.

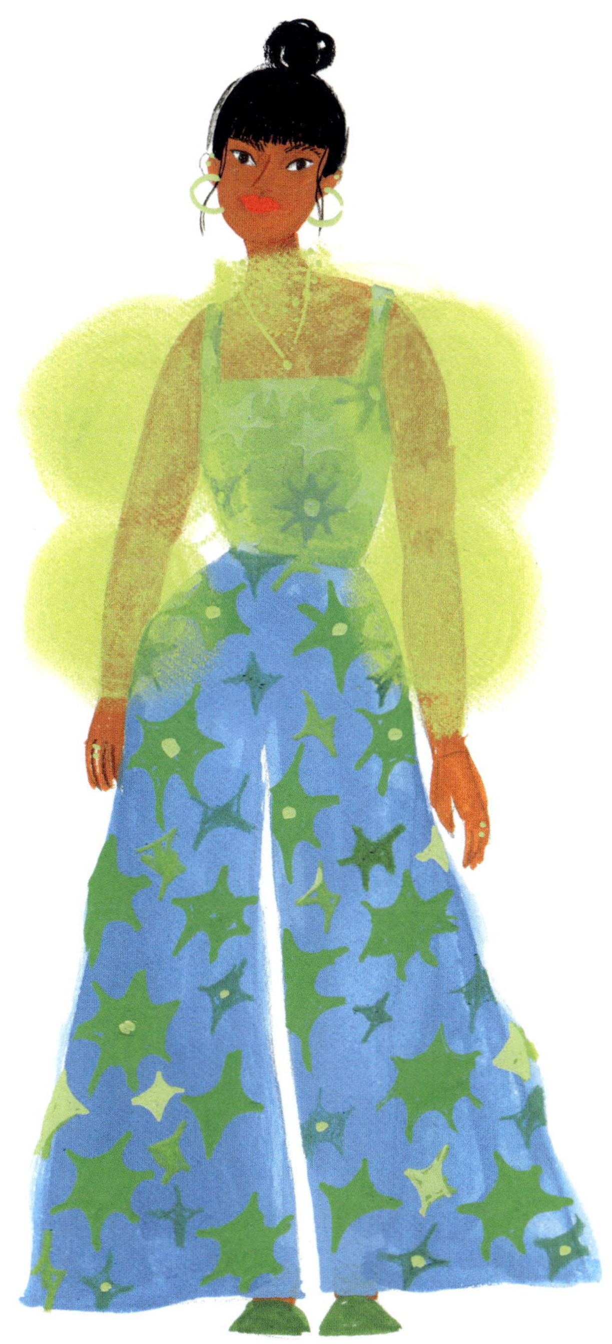

ADD BODIES AND CLOTHES TO THESE PEOPLE.
Play around with different mark making and don't limit
yourself with shapes!

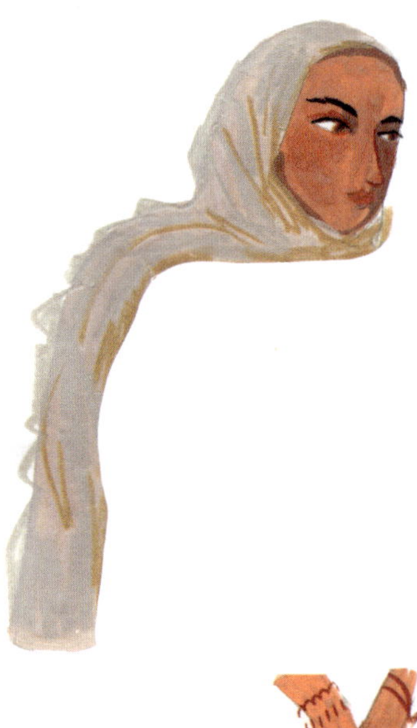

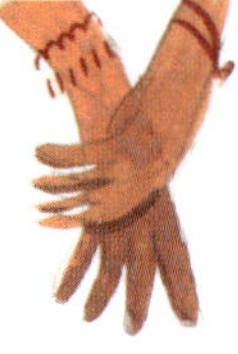

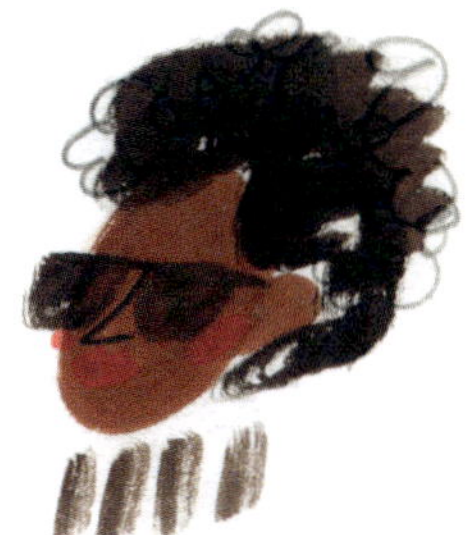

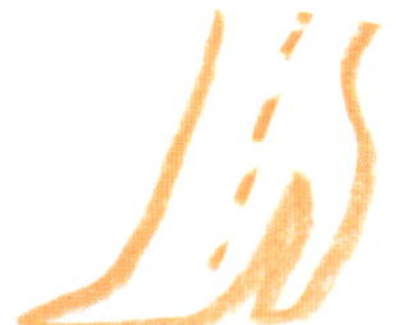

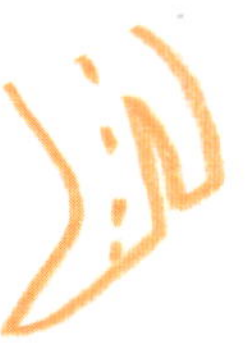

MAKE PEOPLE FROM THESE SHAPES.
Use these areas of colour as a starting point for outfits
and make your own marks, experimenting with textures!

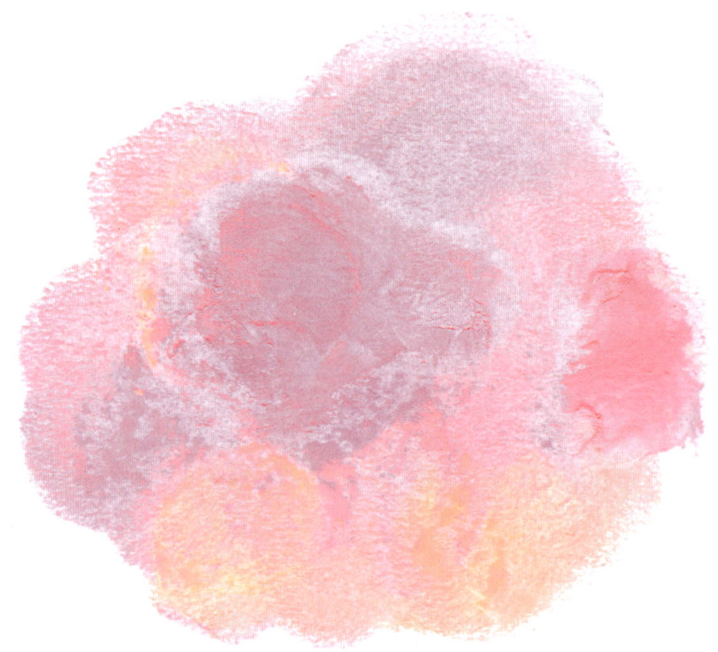

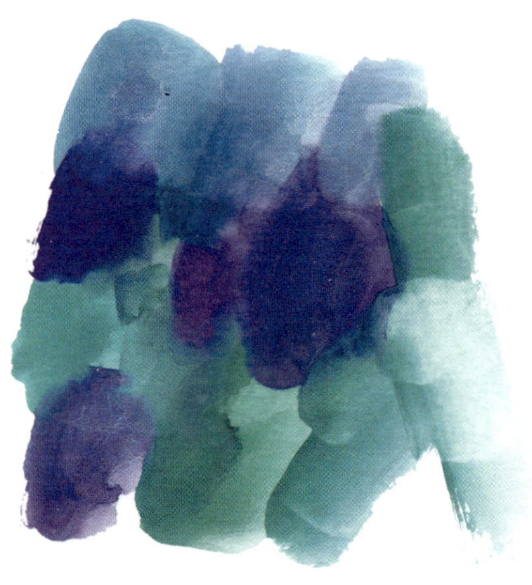

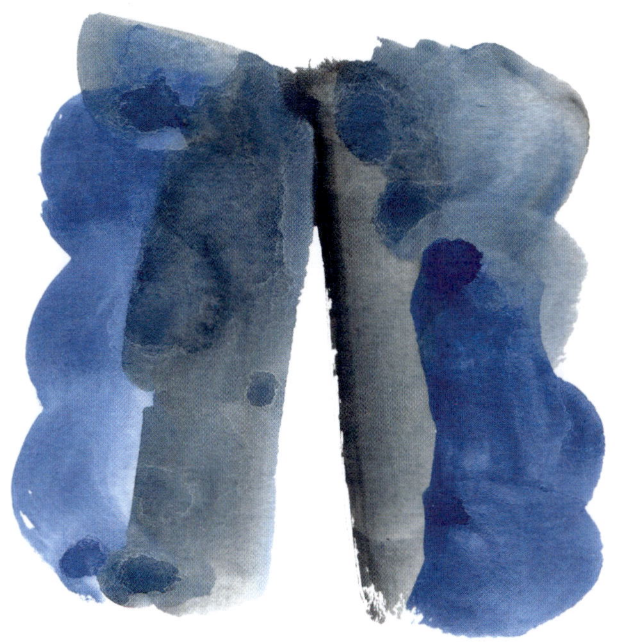

DRAW PEOPLE IN THESE SHAPES.
It can be inspiring to set some limitations on our drawings, so let's use these forms as a starting point!

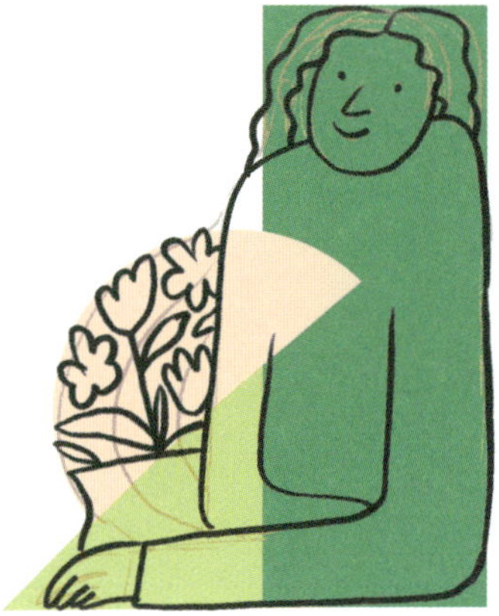

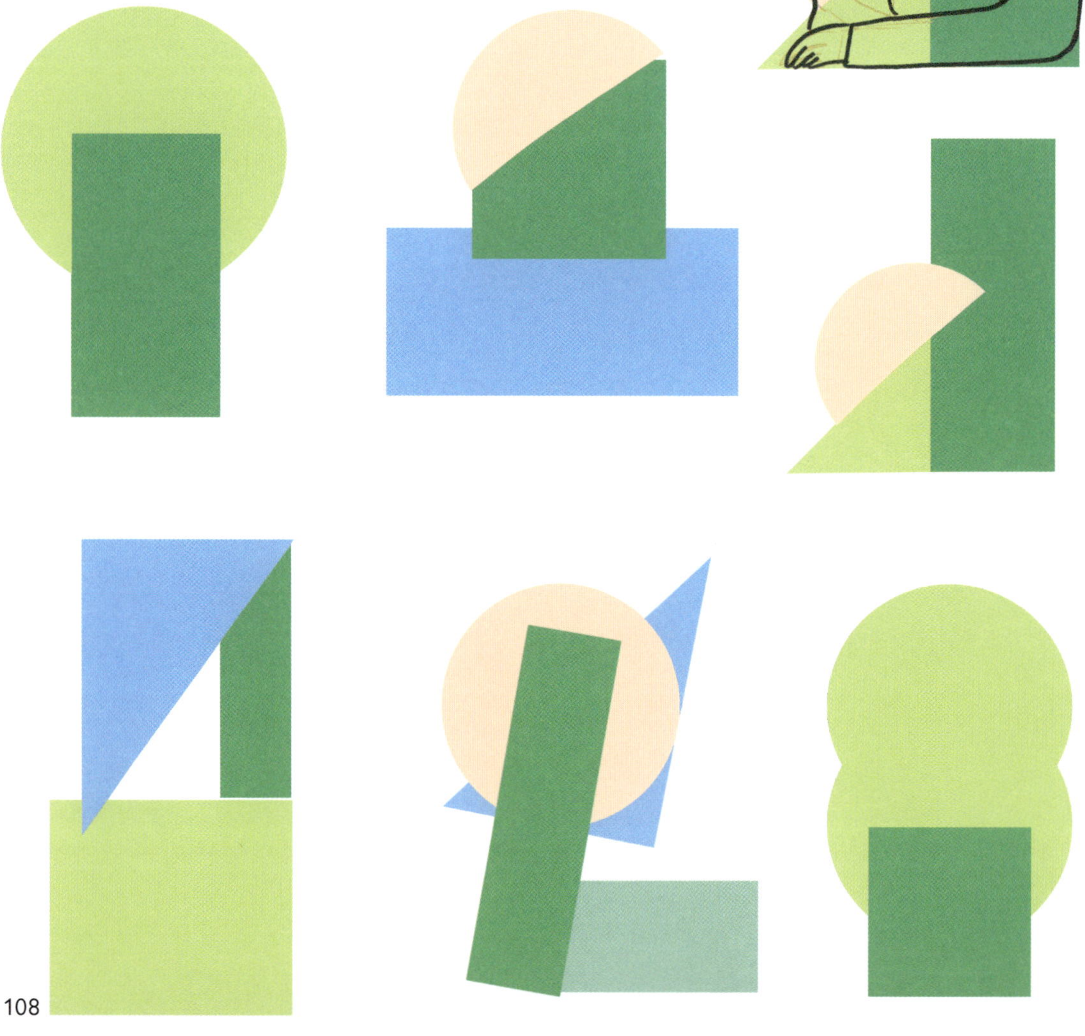

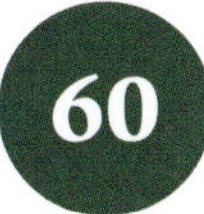 

60

DRAWING PEOPLE ALSO COVERS
DRAWING MYTHICAL BEINGS!
Draw a creature from legend or even invent
one! Here, I drew a mermaid, but the world –
real or imaginary – is your oyster!

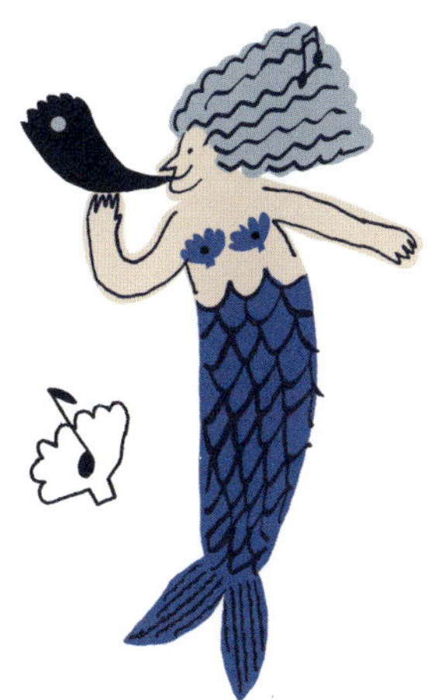

DRAW PEOPLE RUNNING.
Start by using the stick figure method and then
add more details as you go along.

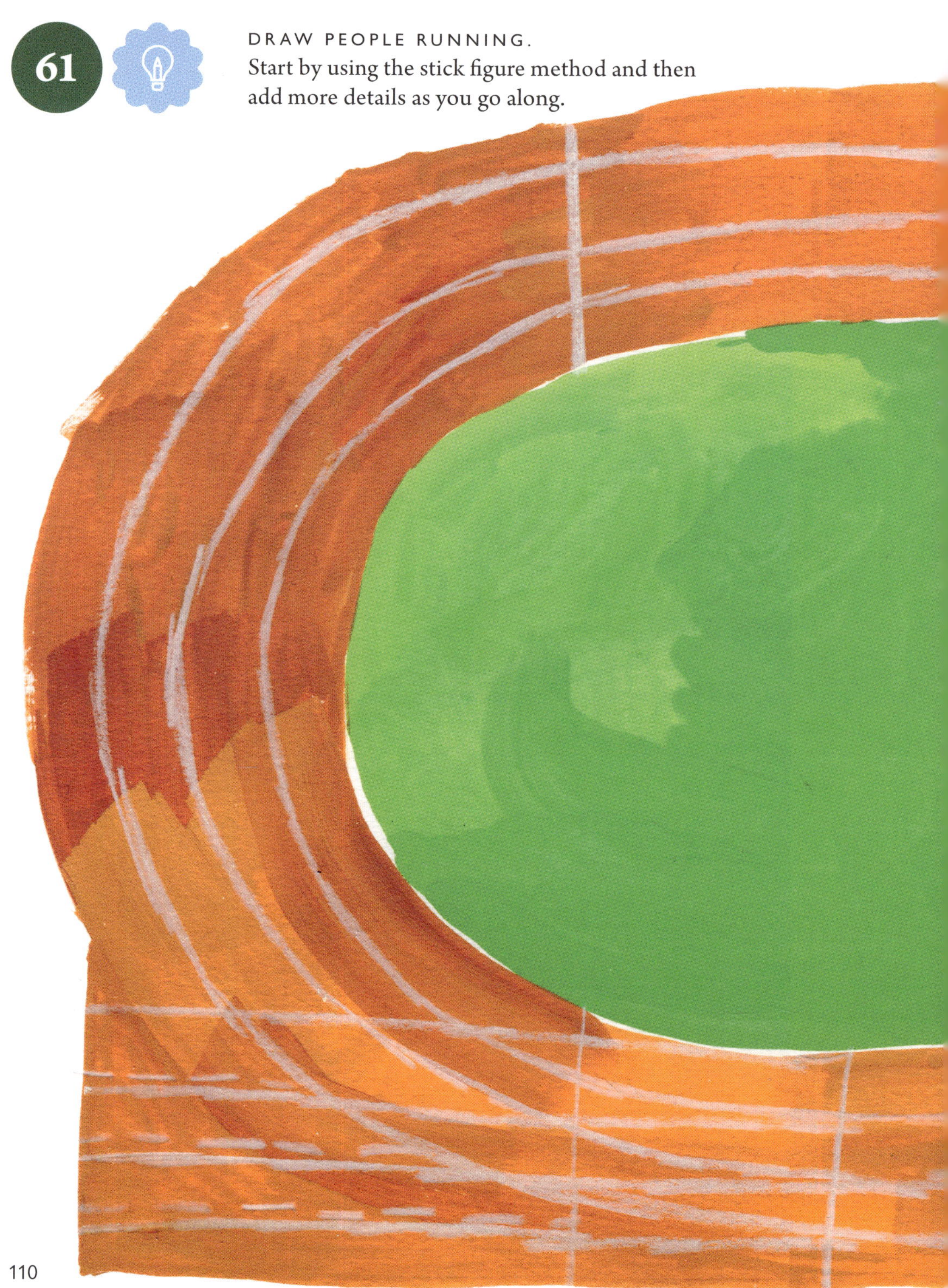

DRAW A POLE VAULTER.
Exaggerate movement (see page 27) or use graphic shapes.

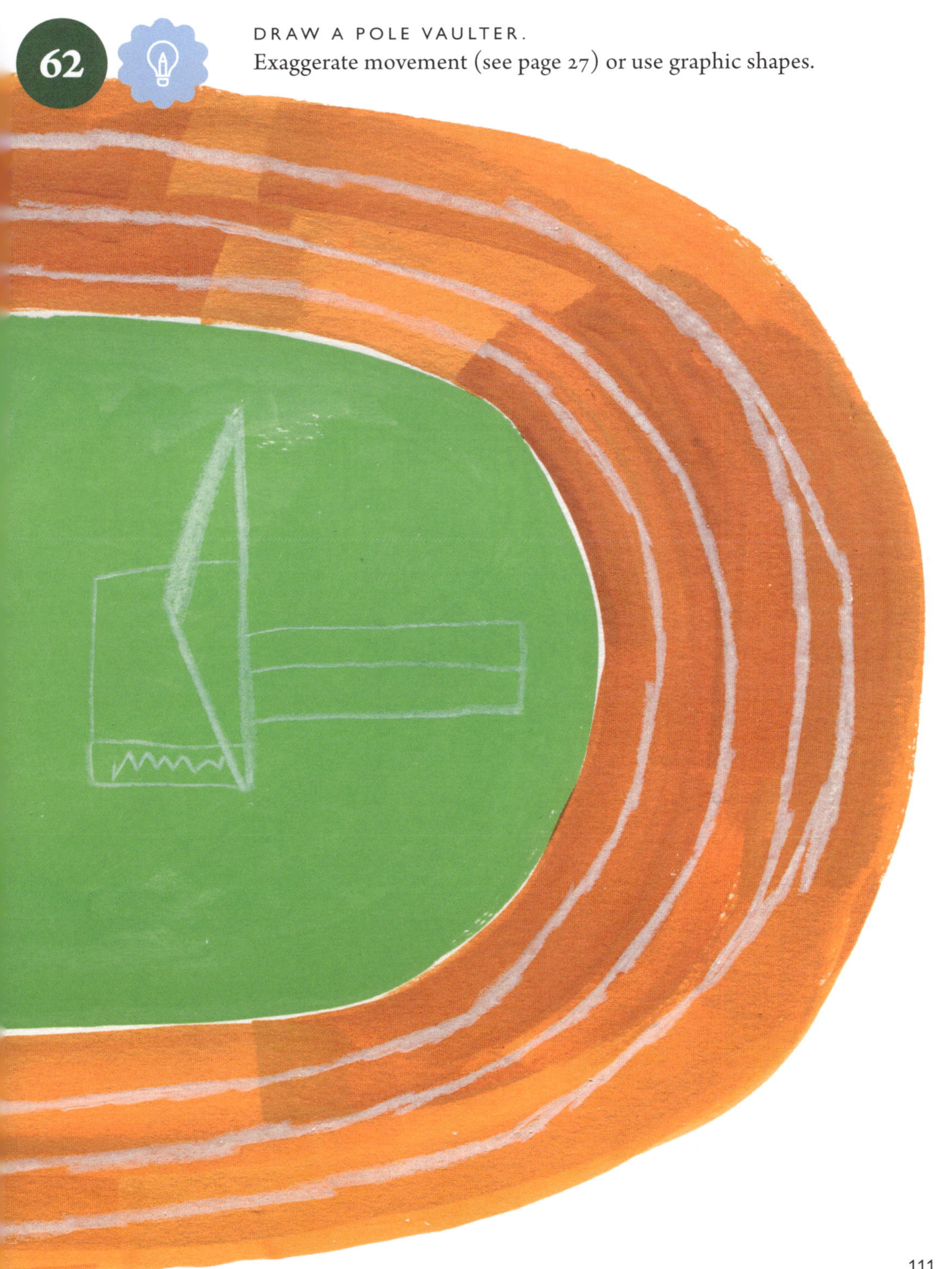

63

A cyclist, for example, can have a huge curvy back or big leg movements. Maybe a dancer moves their legs so fast they become two intertwined laces. You can exaggerate a feature or a movement or a shape and pose.

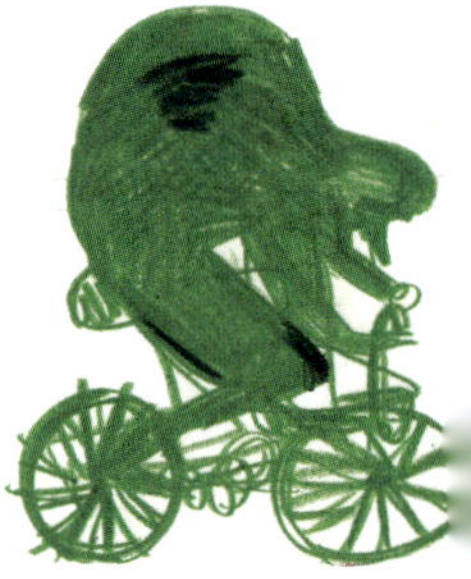

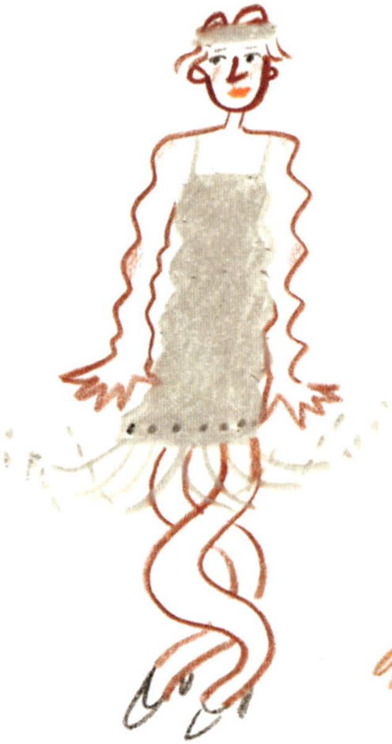

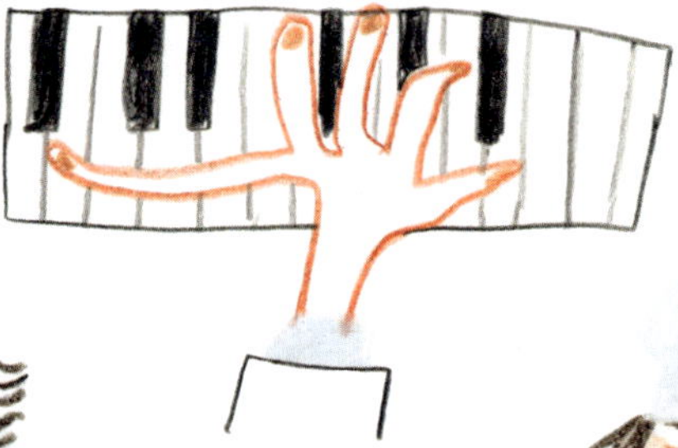

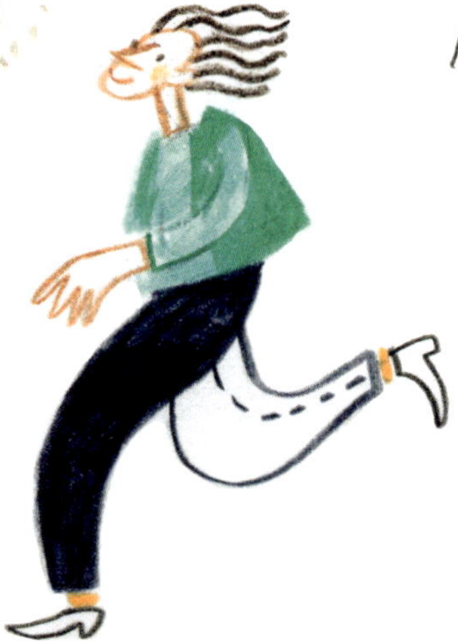

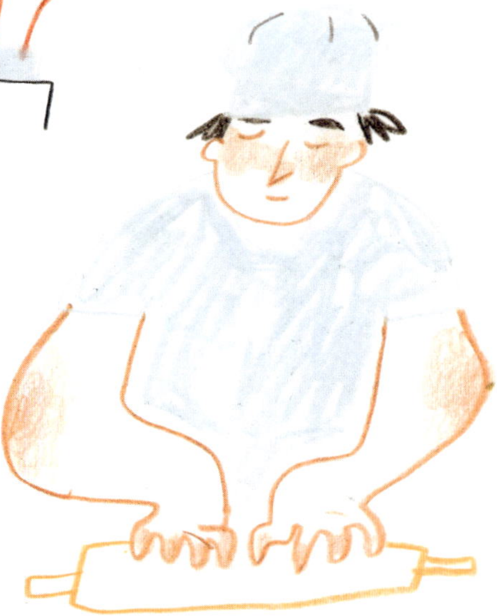

Let's practise here and keep in mind this tool for
your future drawing. Play around on this page and
exaggerate features, such as long legs, arms and face.

Try drawing exaggerated movements and draw
the quality of that movement, too.

64

DRAW AN ORCHESTRA PERFORMING.
Add in the people playing the instruments below.

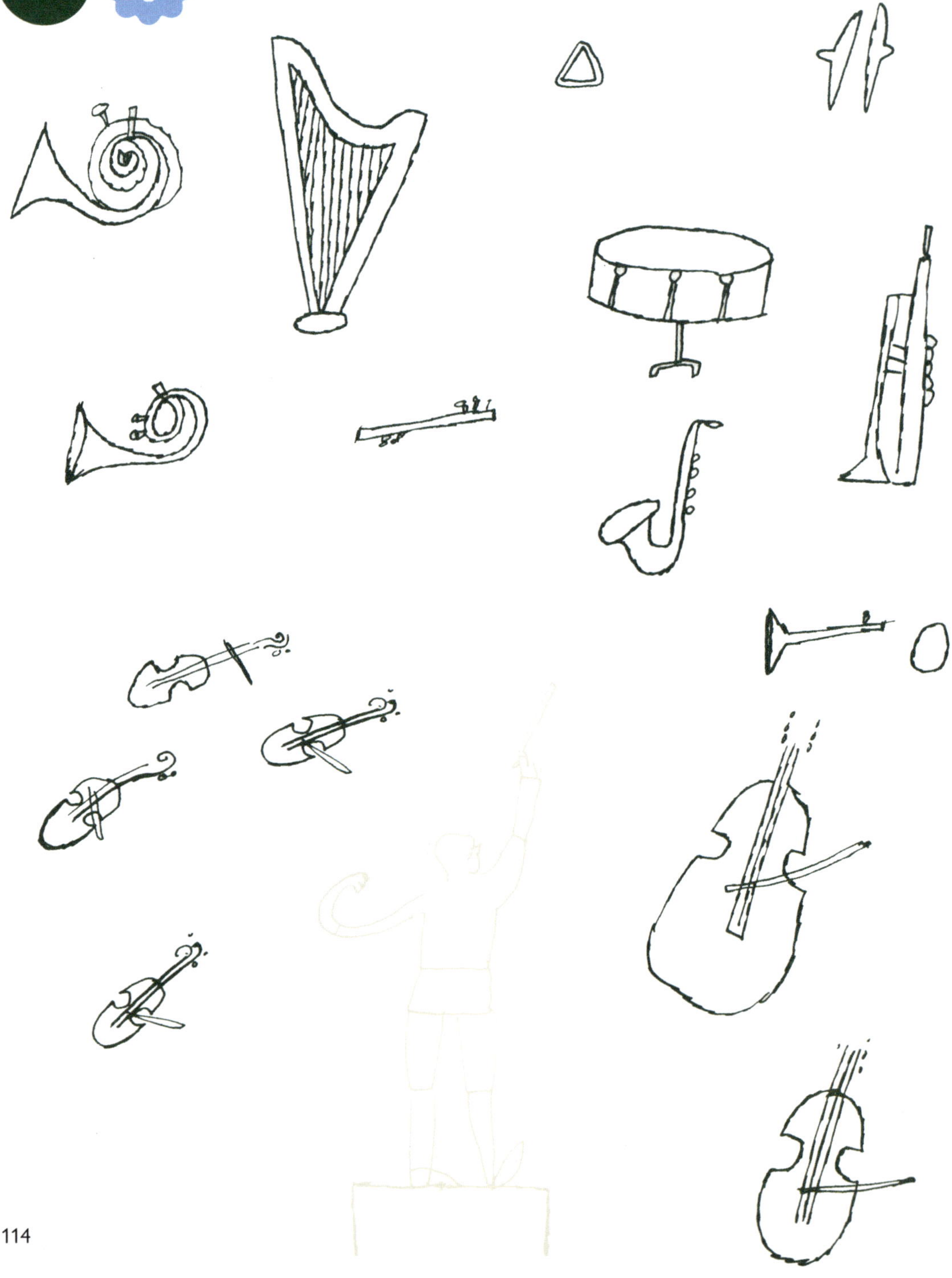

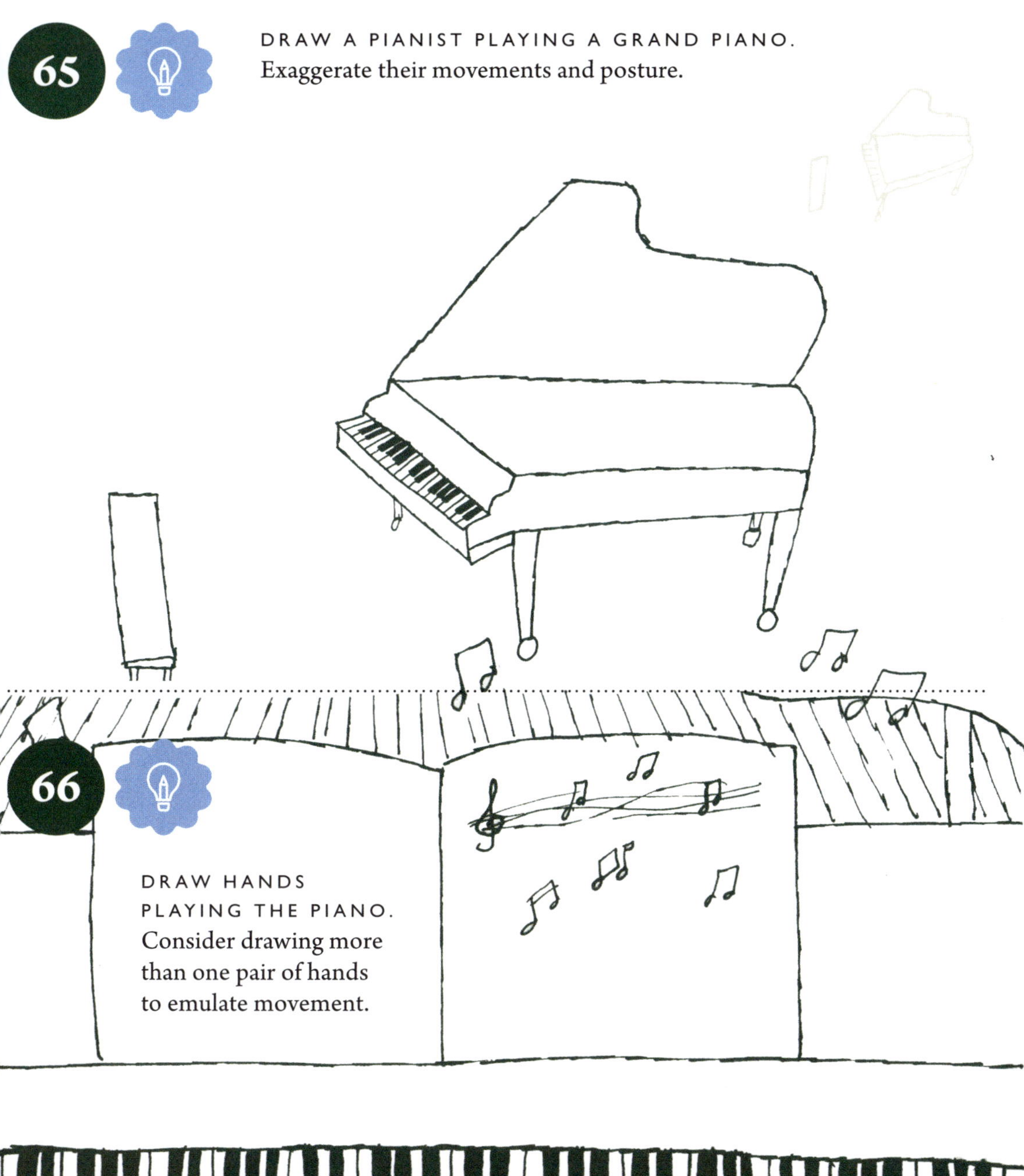

65 DRAW A PIANIST PLAYING A GRAND PIANO.
Exaggerate their movements and posture.

66 DRAW HANDS PLAYING THE PIANO. Consider drawing more than one pair of hands to emulate movement.

SHADING STEP-BY-STEP.

Shading helps us to place a person in an environment and to create depth and dimension. In this exercise, we will add shadows that are quite neutral, which show the shape and dimension of the face.

> **TIP:** *Imagine the head as a collection of geometric areas. This will help to place the shadows. Use a lamp and a mirror and change the angle of the lamp to create different shadows. Sketch them to see how they change the face and the atmosphere.*

STEP 1

Lightly sketch a head and shoulders, face and eyes. Feel free to draw based on my drawing, choose your own or use a mirror for reference to draw yourself!

Use your medium of choice to fill in the face and neck area. I'm using gouache here but you can use markers, watercolours or pencils.

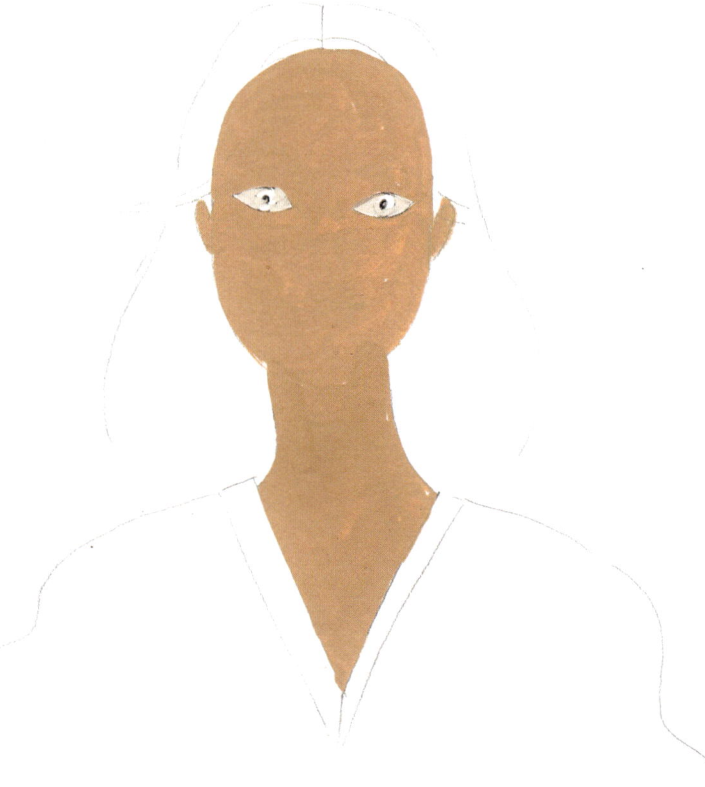

Colour in the hair and the top. I used orange with some burnt sienna for both, and burnt sienna for her eyes. Add a bit of detail to the hair using a slightly darker shade to create body.

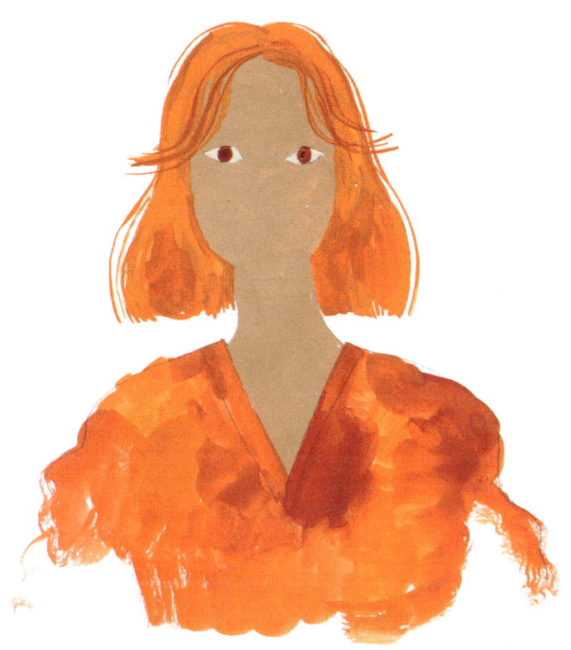

STEP 3

Using a dry medium, such as pencil, pastel, or even marker, make some lines around the eyes, nose and hair to add movement. Add pattern to the shirt. Using a bright colour, add eyeshadow. I've used dark brown to highlight the nose, eyebrows and shirt and light brown for the lips and to outline the face against the neck as well as the addition of freckles. It's up to you how many details you'd like to add and in what colour.

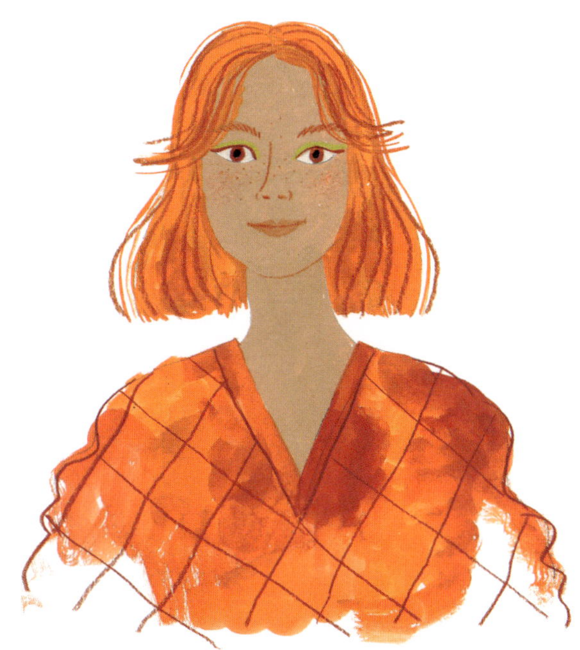

Now we start shading using a pencil to gently overlay the areas you want to address. Add shadows under and above the eyes, under the nose, under the chin, under the lips and under the hair. As you see it instantly creates depth and dimension. You can create shadows by making a pattern of dots, lines or squiggles and they can be dark blue, dark brown, purple, green or grey.

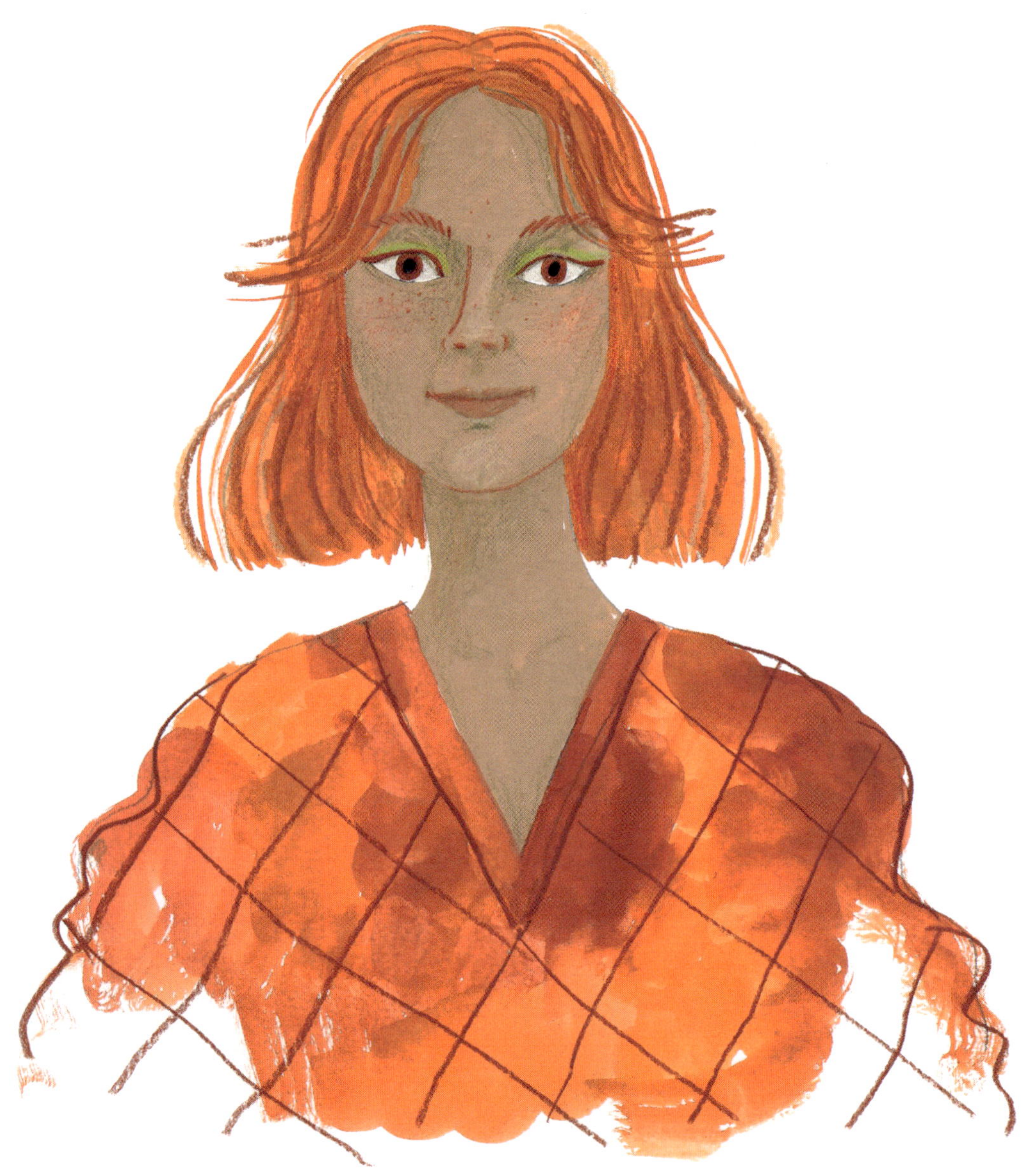

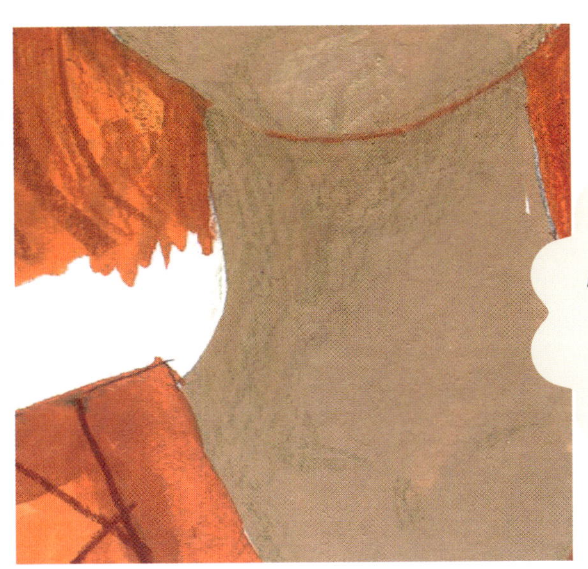
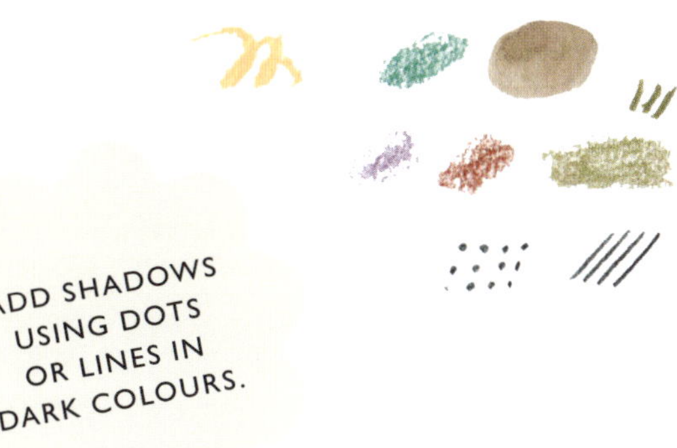
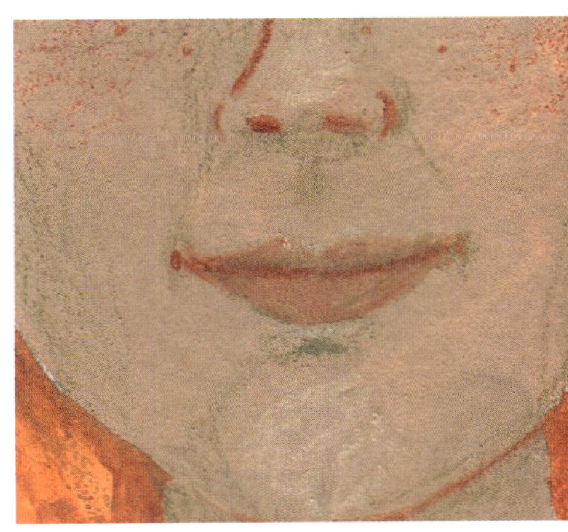

ADD SHADOWS
USING DOTS
OR LINES IN
DARK COLOURS.

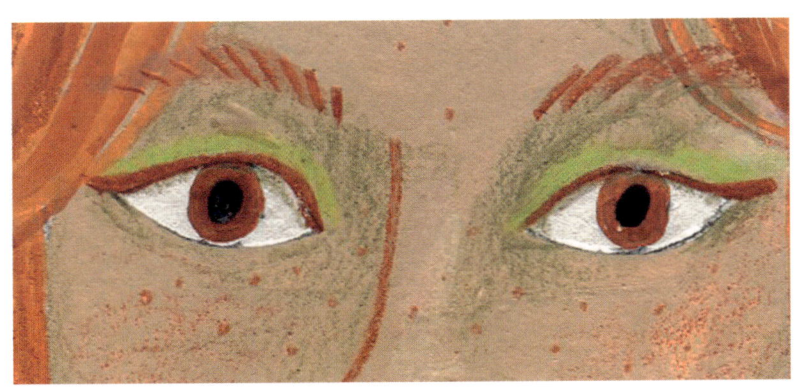

68 DRAW A DIARY
OF YOUR WEEKEND.
Draw the people you saw
and in what setting.

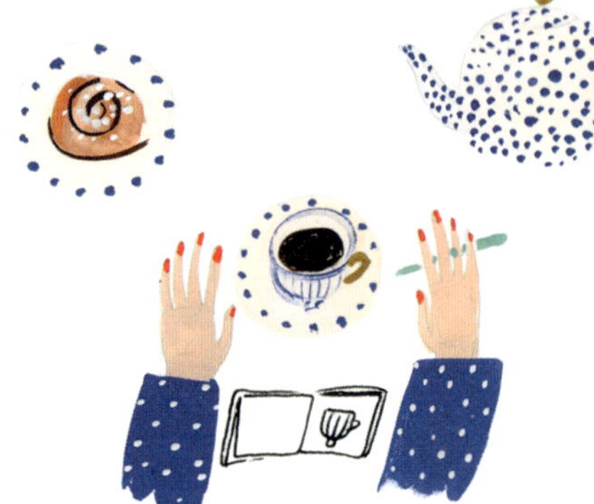

LET'S PLAY WITH MARK MAKING AGAIN.

It's good to bring focus to the mediums we use in our drawings and experiment with them. What happens if you use paint or marker to create texture and pattern? What if you play around with your pencil, applying different pressure? Draw a self-portrait and experiment with different marks!

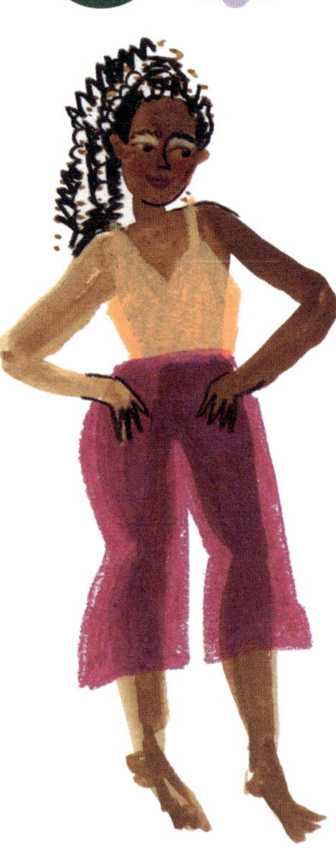

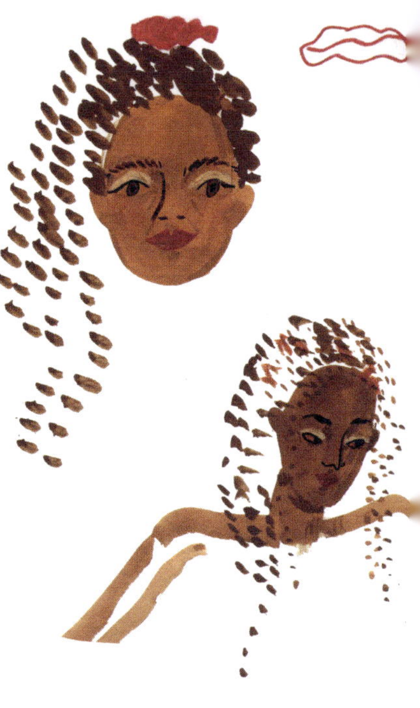

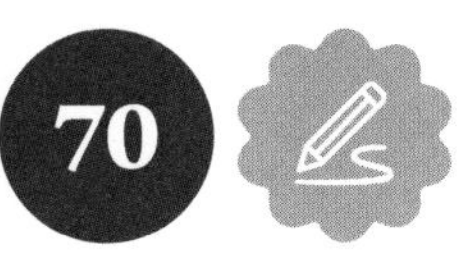

DRAW A COMIC FEATURING YOU AS THE MAIN CHARACTER.

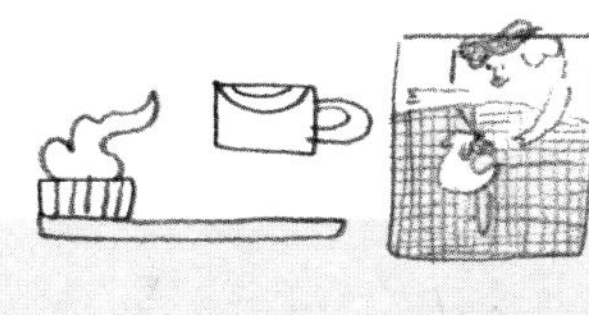

DRAW PEOPLE IN THE POOL.
They can be sunbathing or jumping in!
Add fun accessories and water floats and splashes.

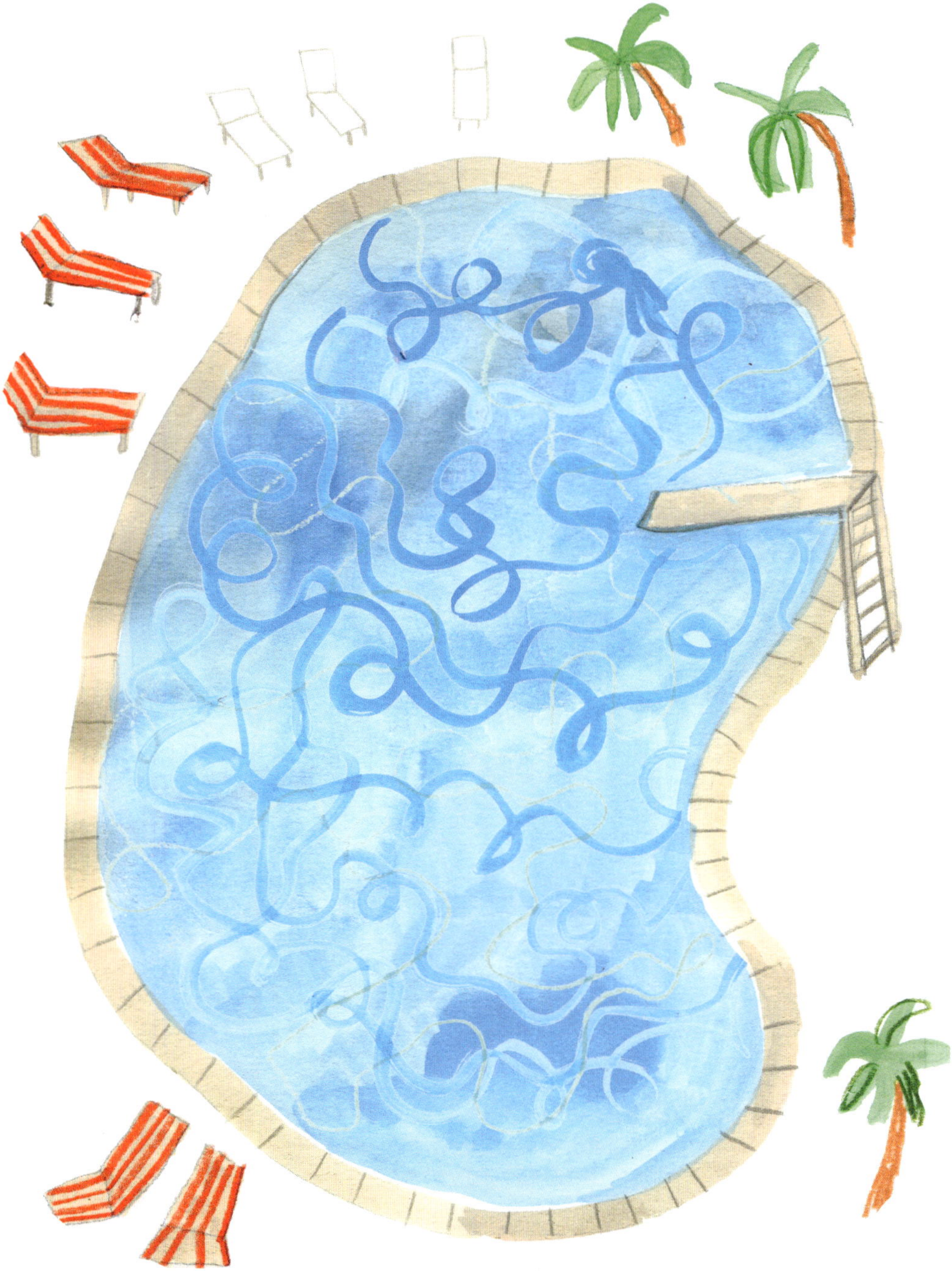

ADD FIGURES TO THESE SHAPES.
Match the emotions of the people to the shapes and colours.

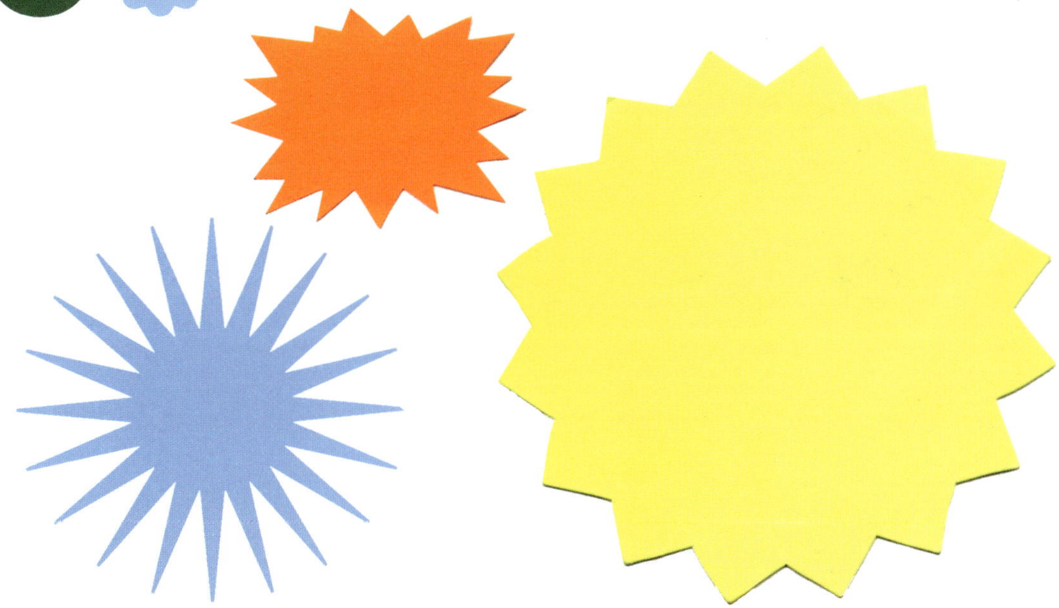

DRAW PEOPLE DANCING.
Use the abstract shapes to communicate the mood of the dancers.

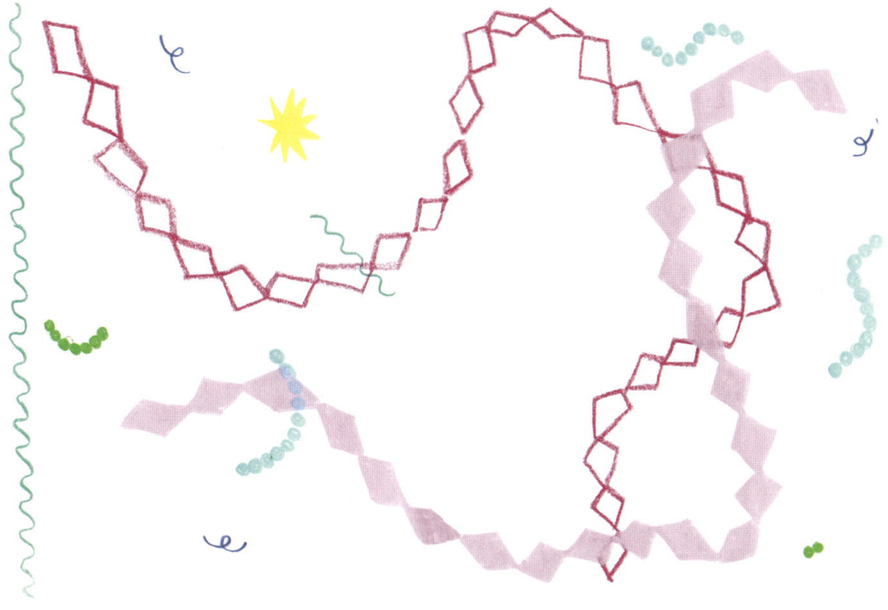

74

Let's try now. Draw a self-portrait. Be kind to yourself and use a mirror for reference.

DRAW YOUR LOVED ONE OR A FRIEND.

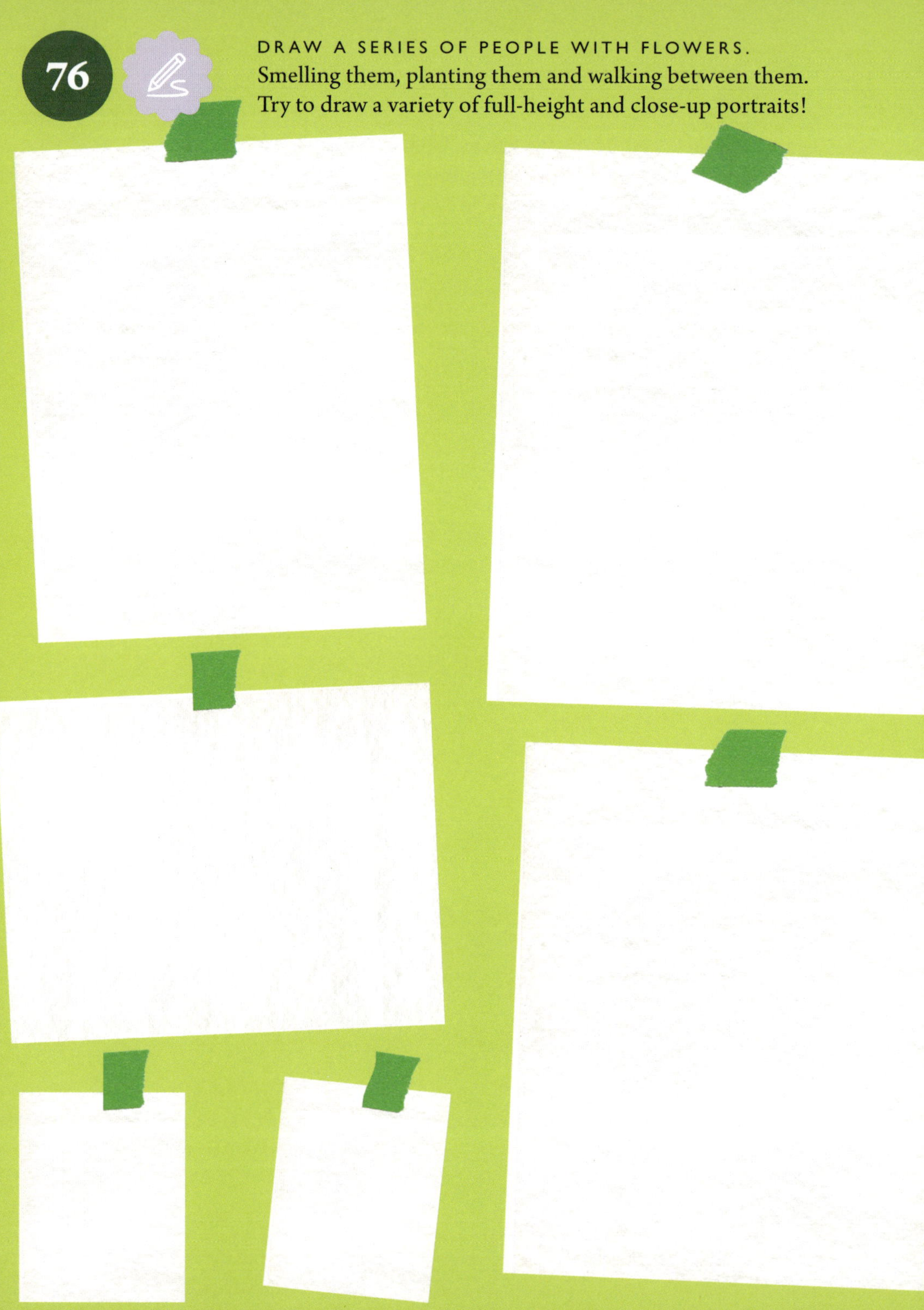

76
DRAW A SERIES OF PEOPLE WITH FLOWERS.
Smelling them, planting them and walking between them.
Try to draw a variety of full-height and close-up portraits!

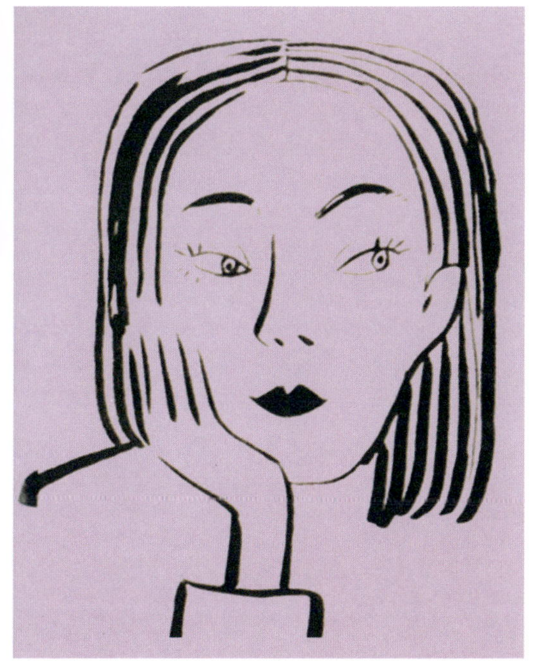

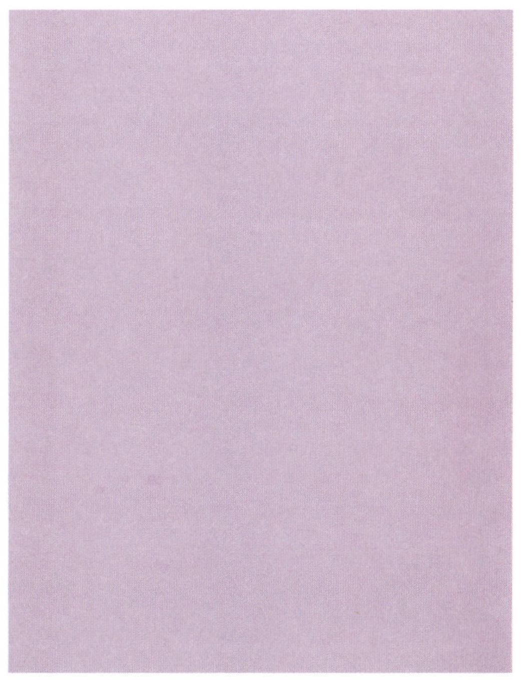

DRAW PEOPLE SITTING AND ENJOYING NICE WEATHER IN THE MUSEUM COURTYARD.

Practise drawing people in different seated positions and add a few more on the way to meet friends, bringing scale into your drawings, too.

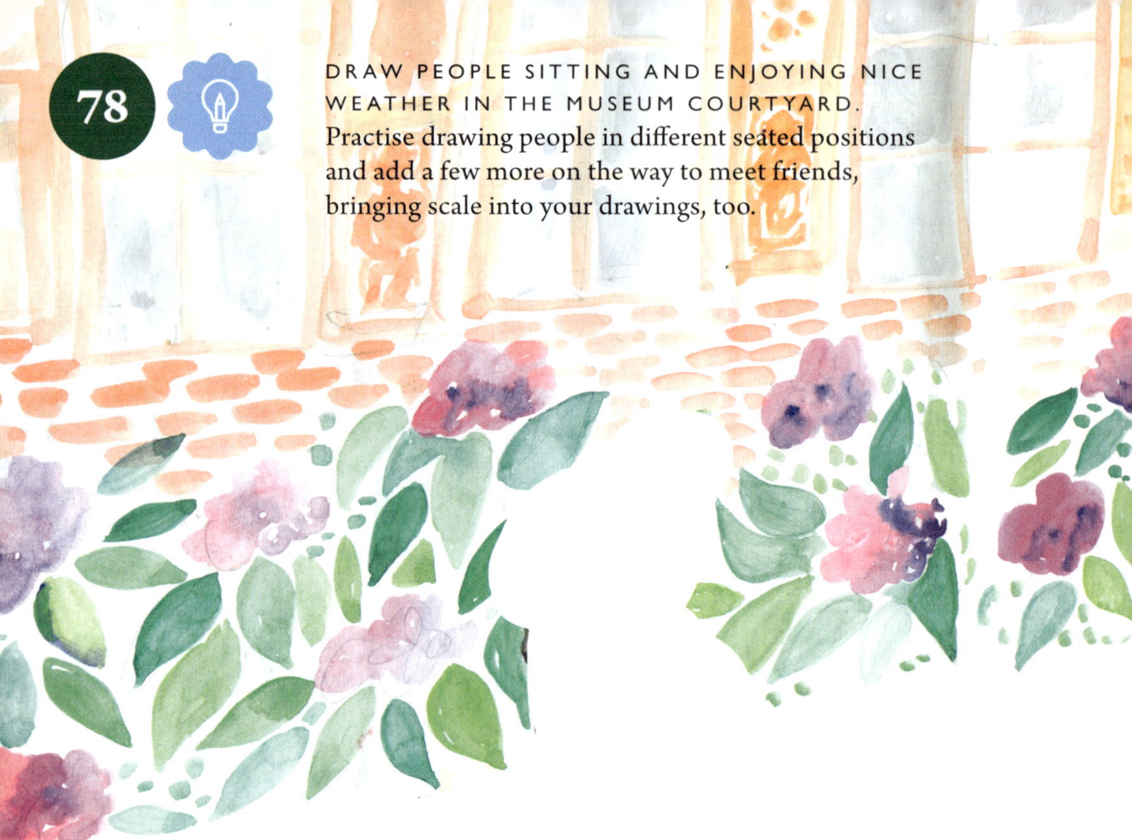

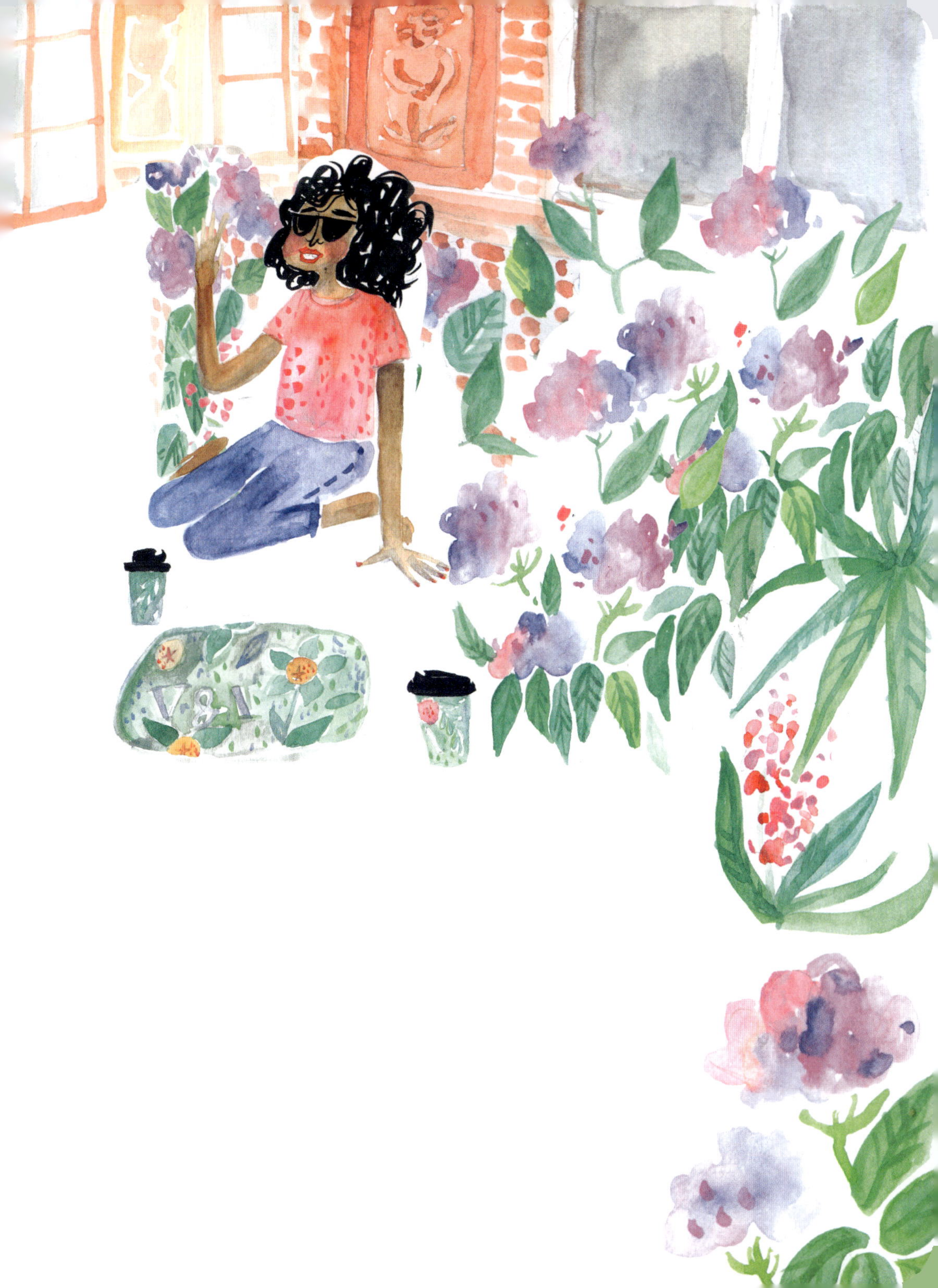

DRAWING MOVEMENT STEP-BY-STEP.

Capturing movement works best if you want to communicate energy and action or are drawing from observation. It is especially effective if you are capturing fast and energetic action. And that is what we will be doing in this project!

Think what kind of energy there is. Look at the person you are drawing and start your sketch by creating a symbol or outline of the movement they are making. What jumps out at you? Their posture? Hands? Is it slow and gentle movement? Fast? Strong? Chaotic? Channel the feeling and energy into the lines.

Now let's try to draw dancers! Dancers exaggerate their movements, and make everything expressive.

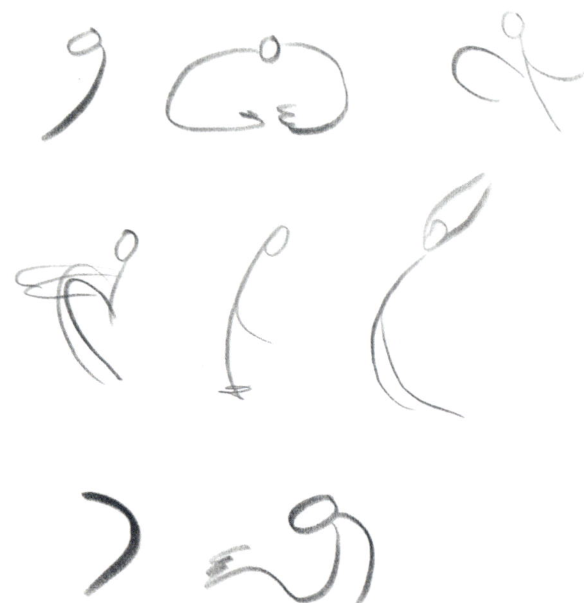

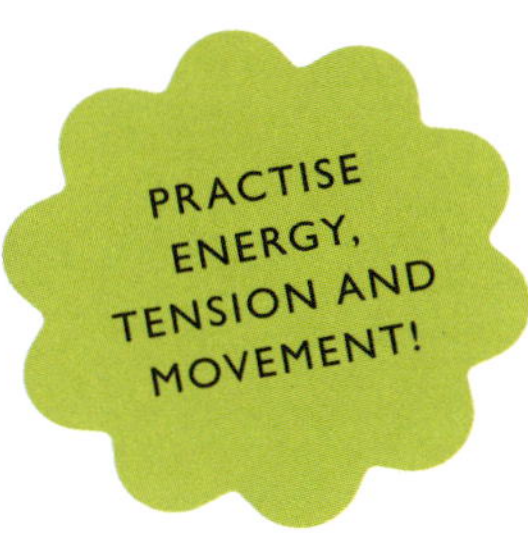

STEP 1

Using graphite pencil add two main marks
to communicate two figures in dance.
I'm drawing a figure on the left, paused
in motion, and another holding a lot of
tension with arched back and tensed hands.

STEP 2

Add more details, such as heads,
feet and arms – anything which helps
to communicate movement.

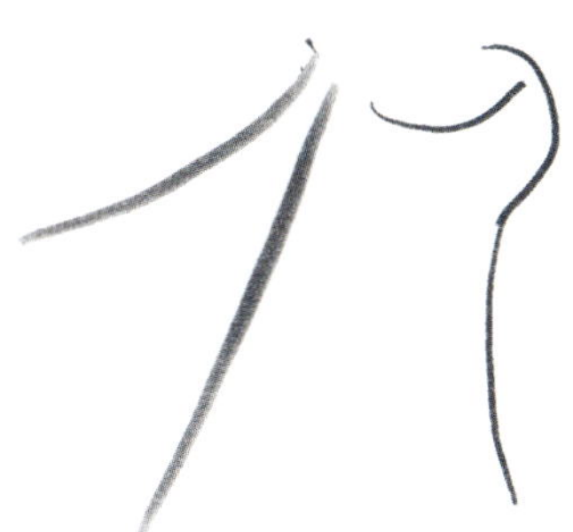

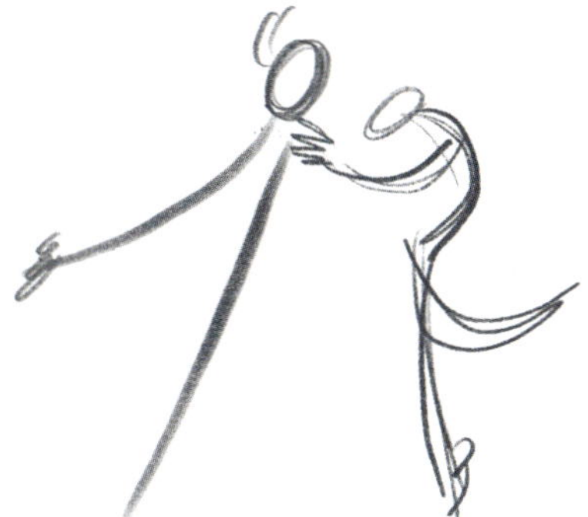

Now let's start adding more definition
and dimension to the figures. Don't
think about proportions or making them
anatomically correct. Keep the lines of the
movement and don't add too many angles.
Add any details which will help to accentuate
the movement, like hair and items of
clothing, such as tassels on the lady's dress.

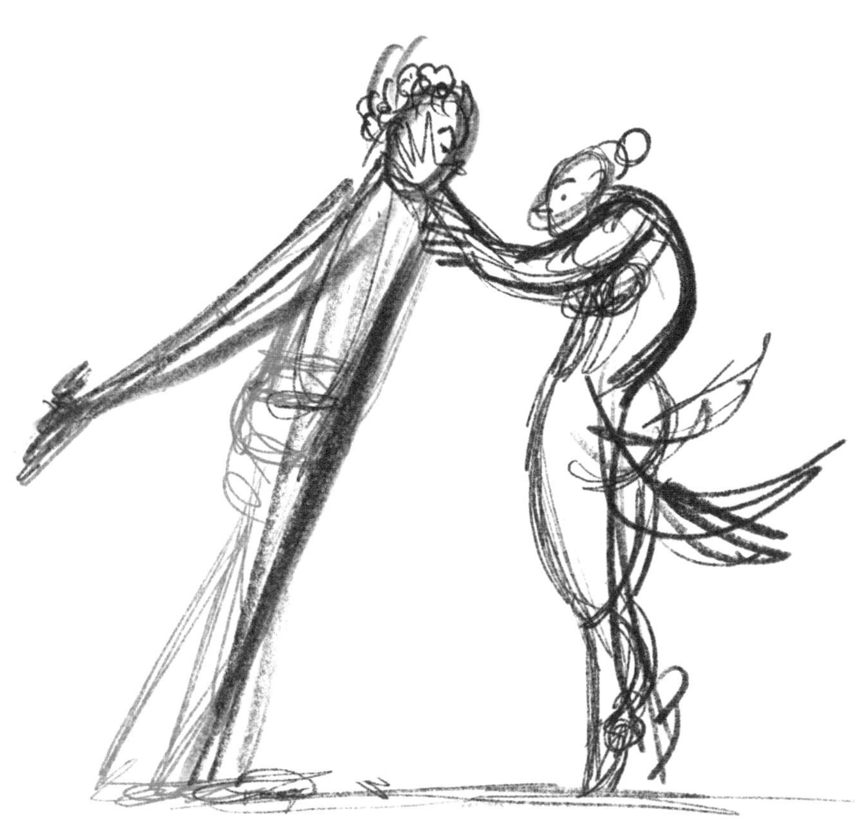

At this stage you can either go over your sketch with a marker or ink and erase the initial marks you have made, or start a new drawing entirely, using the sketch as a preliminary study.

Think about the medium you would like to use. Which material will communicate movement the most? What do you enjoy working with?

I started a new drawing with ink because I wanted the lines to be more spontaneous and quick. I focused on making the lines round and expressive for the bodies and straight and angular for the faces and hands to communicate tension. I also made some expressive marks to add even more movement and energy.

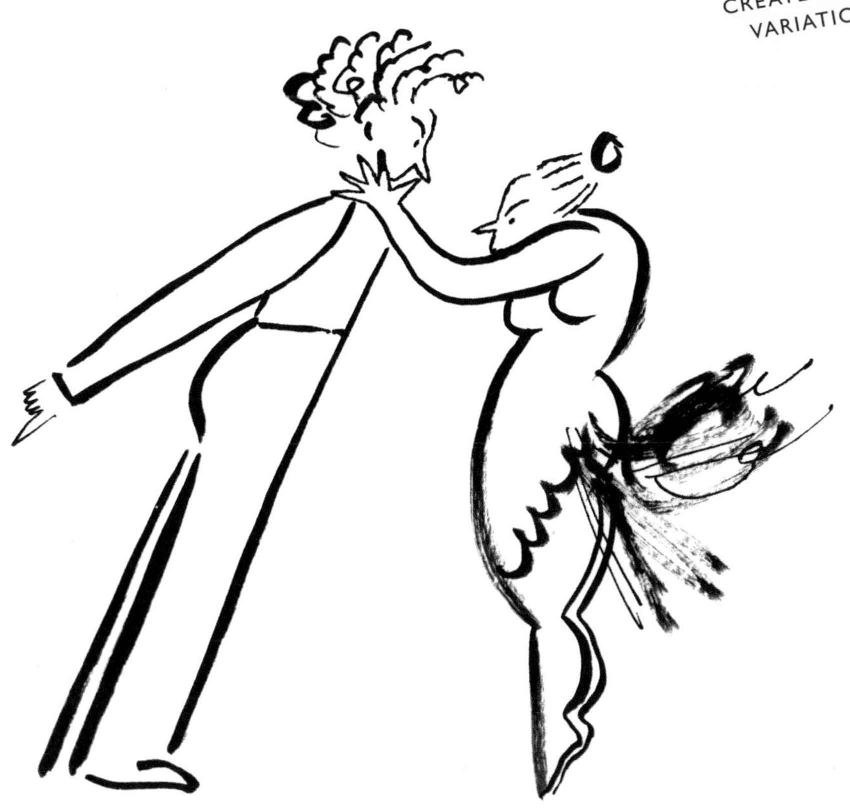

DRAW AN ARTIST AT WORK.
Add energy to their movement.
Most importantly, draw their artwork.

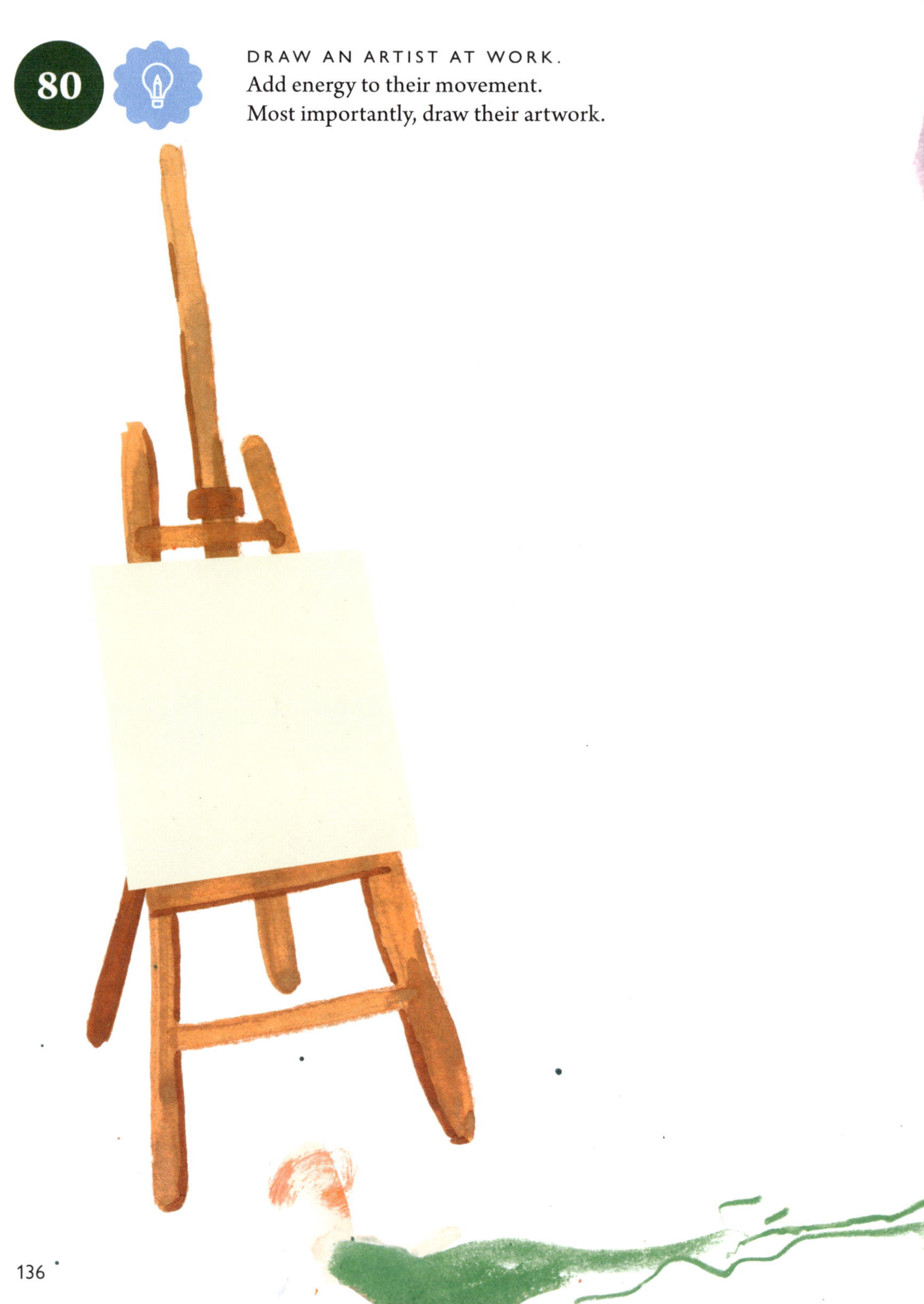

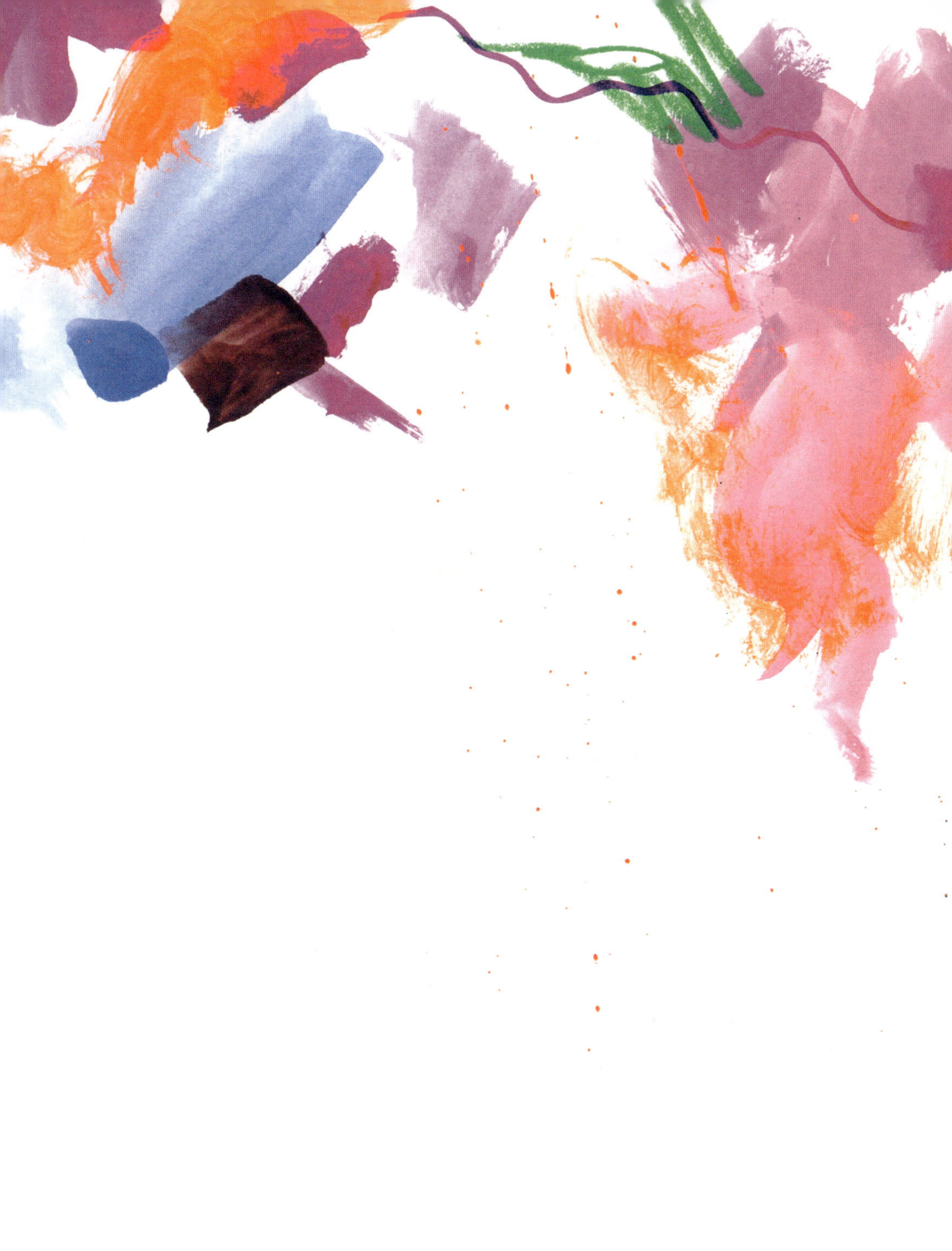

DRAW PEOPLE INTERACTING WITH THE BLOCKS.
It's a fun exercise to start you thinking about drawing outside the box!
Think about a character who peeks around from behind a block or
someone hanging onto it, pushing it, jumping out of it or running into it.

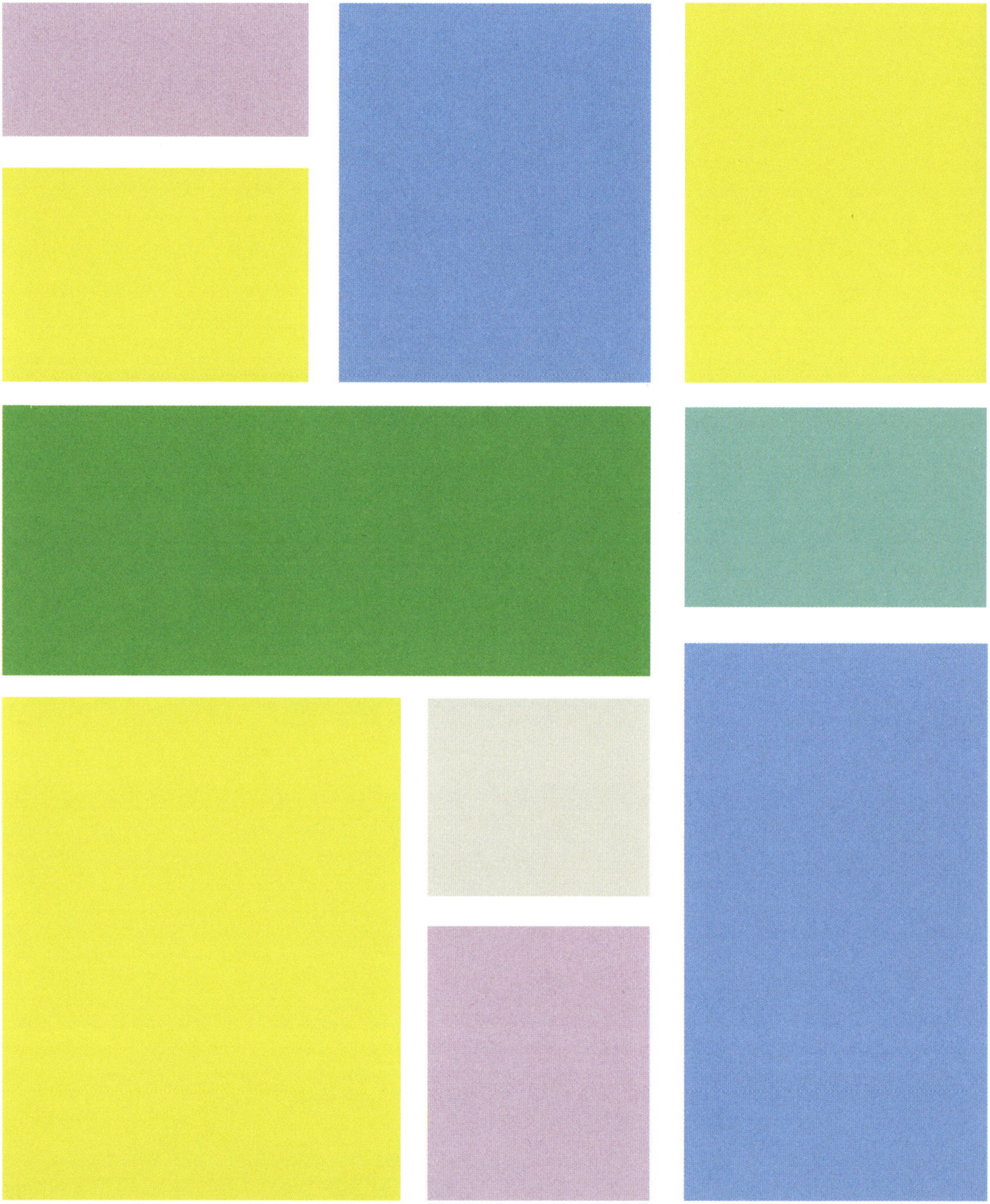

DRAW KIDS CARRYING ANIMALS.
It's always a pleasure to draw cute things and it really can boost your mood.

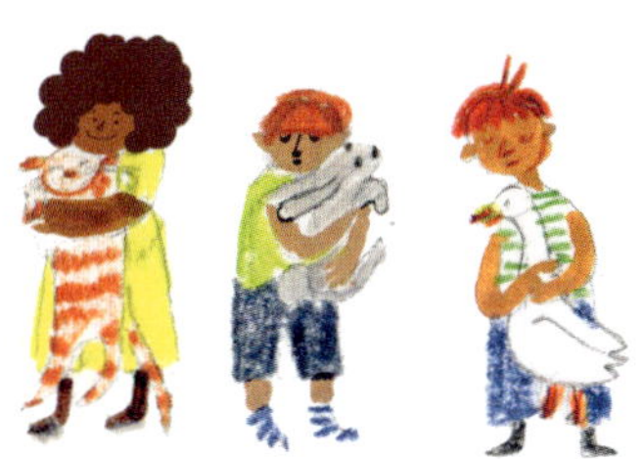

DRAW CHILDREN AT A PLAYGROUND.
Be as silly as you like! Remember kids' proportions, too (see page 25).

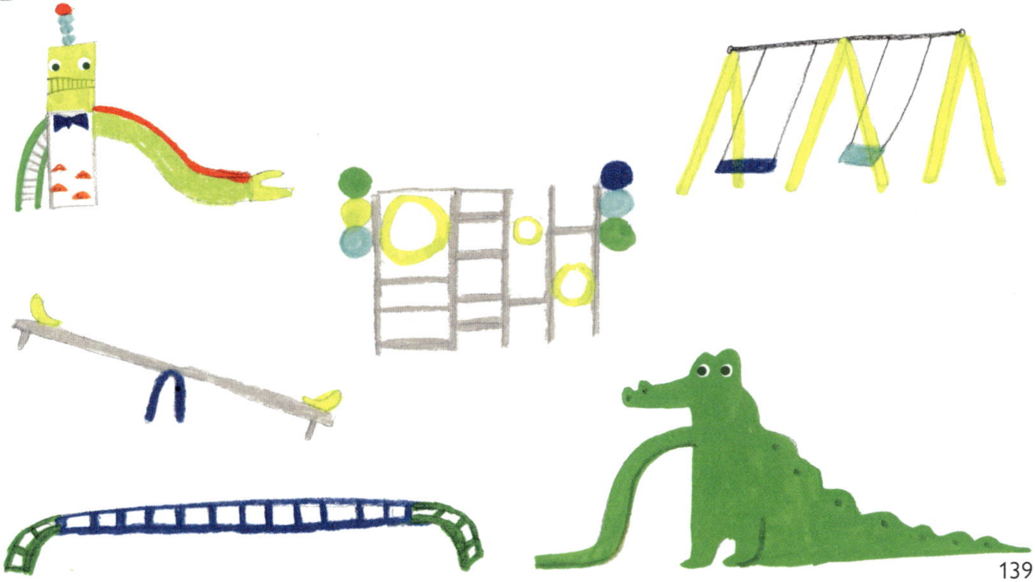

DRAWING PROFILES,
Try to draw as many profiles as you can of children
and adults with different chins, noses and foreheads.

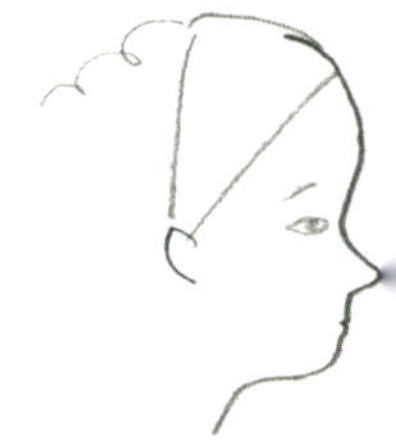

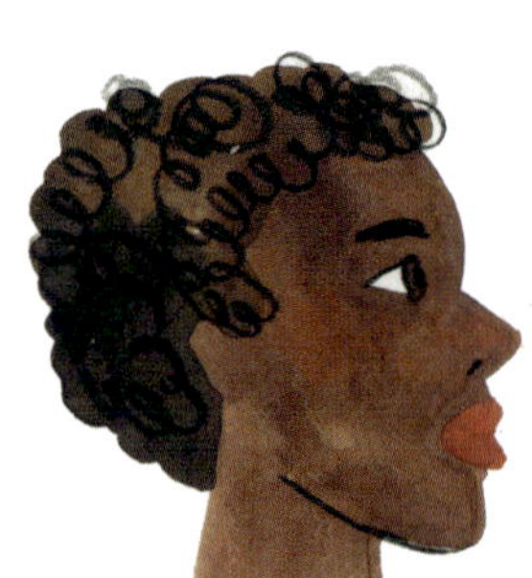

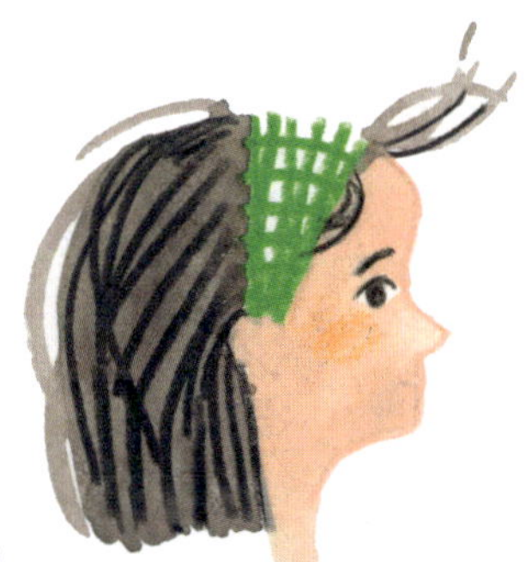

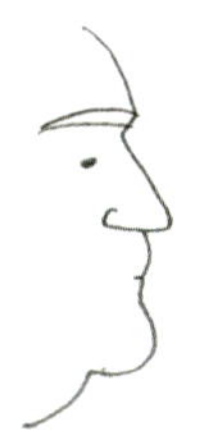

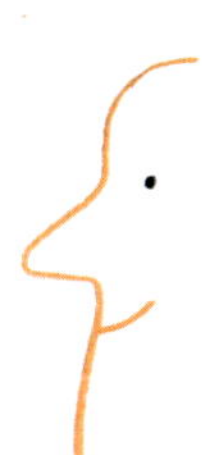

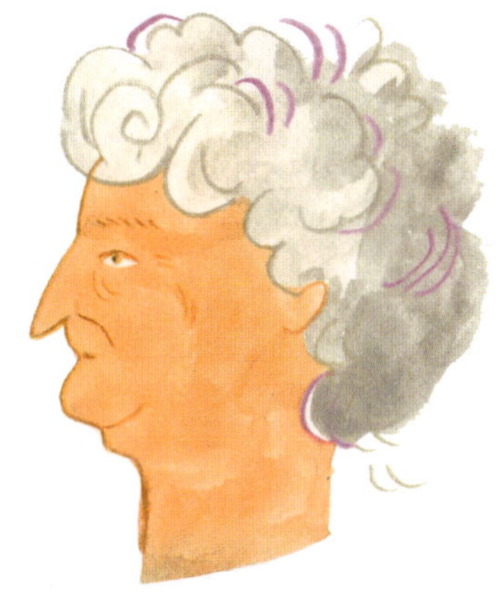

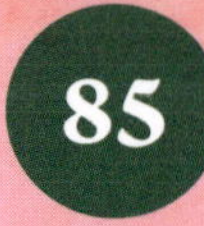

85 DRAW PEOPLE AS SILHOUETTES AGAINST THE SUNSET.
Think about shapes, be playful and loose. Draw people from different angles, in profile, from the back and so on and play with different sizes to create depth, with some figures smaller (appearing further away) and others bigger (closer to you).

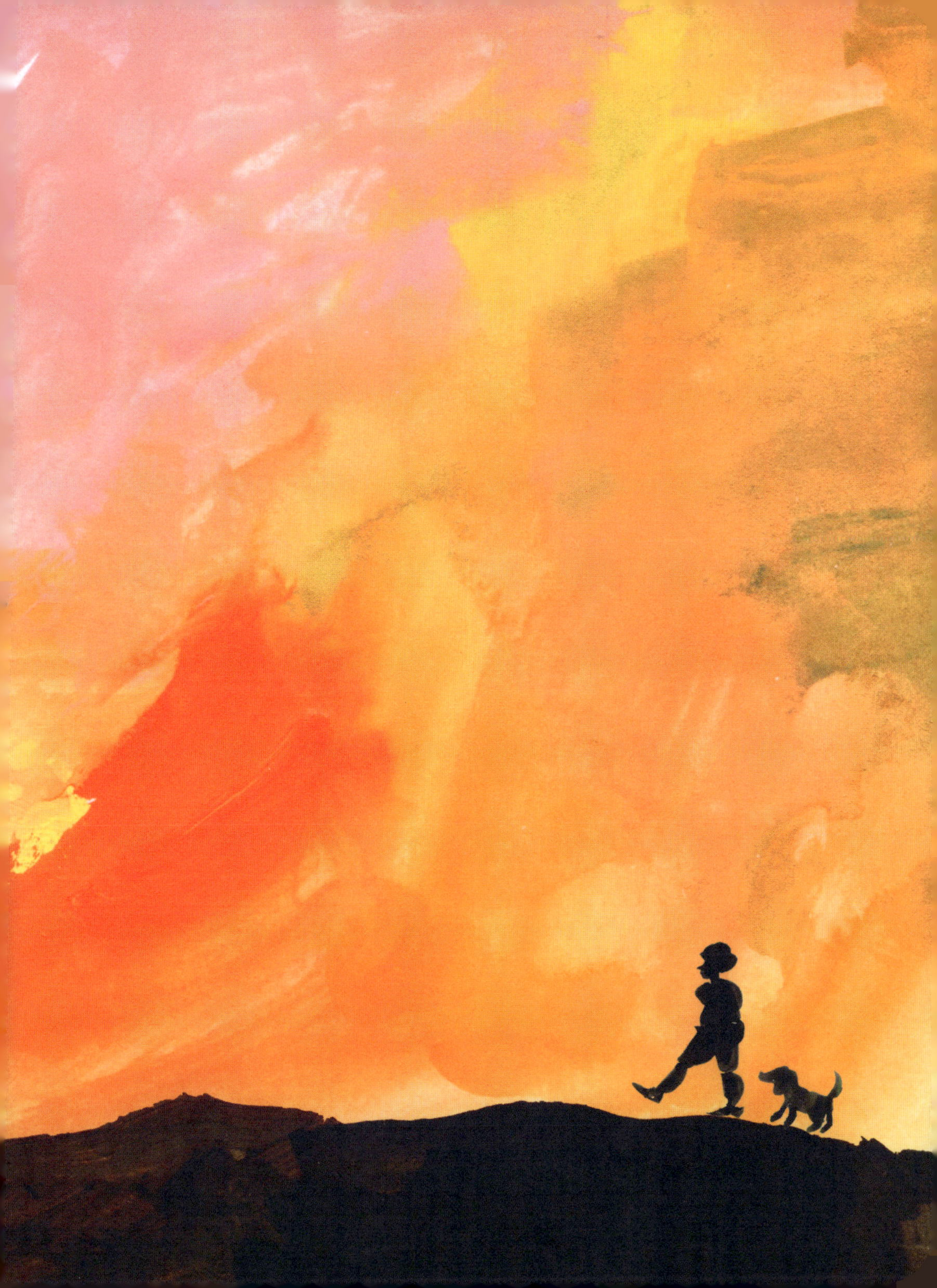

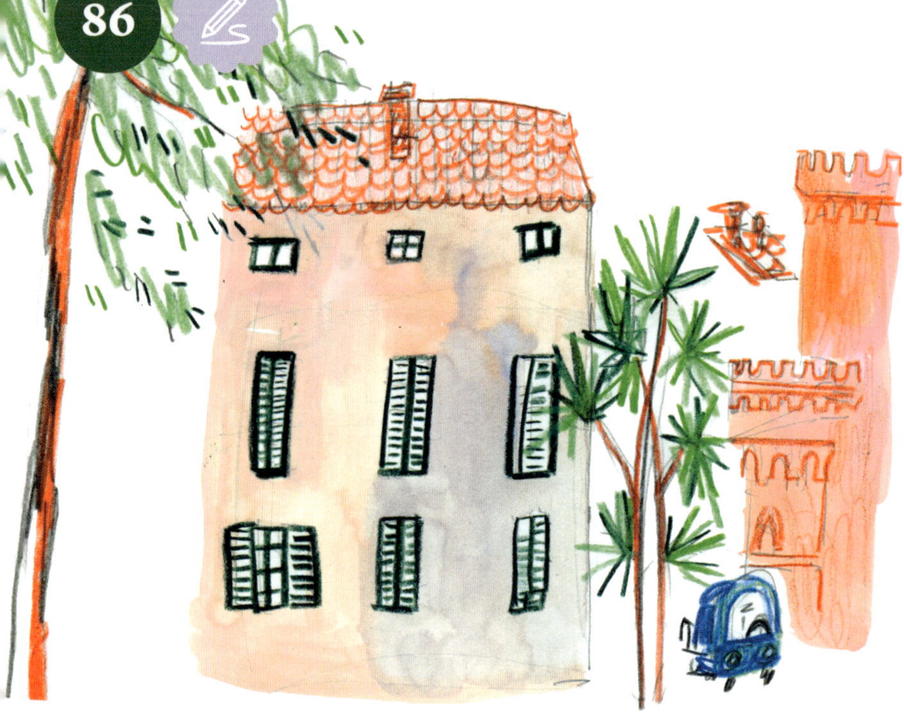

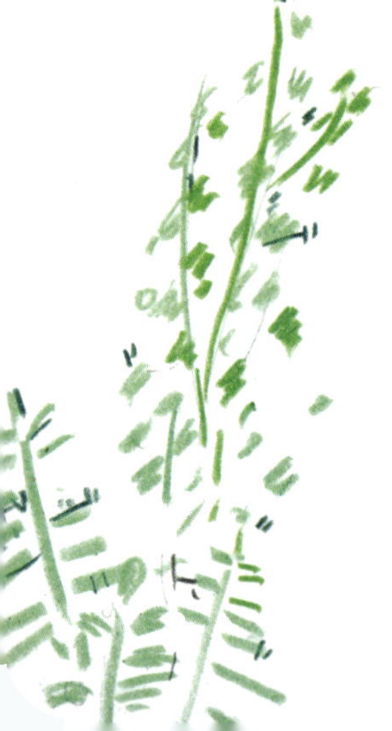

Remember that as we get older our bodies change and we have different postures and mannerisms and our faces will alter with potentially more wrinkles (see page 25). Draw as many shapes and people as you can imagine, and play with scale.

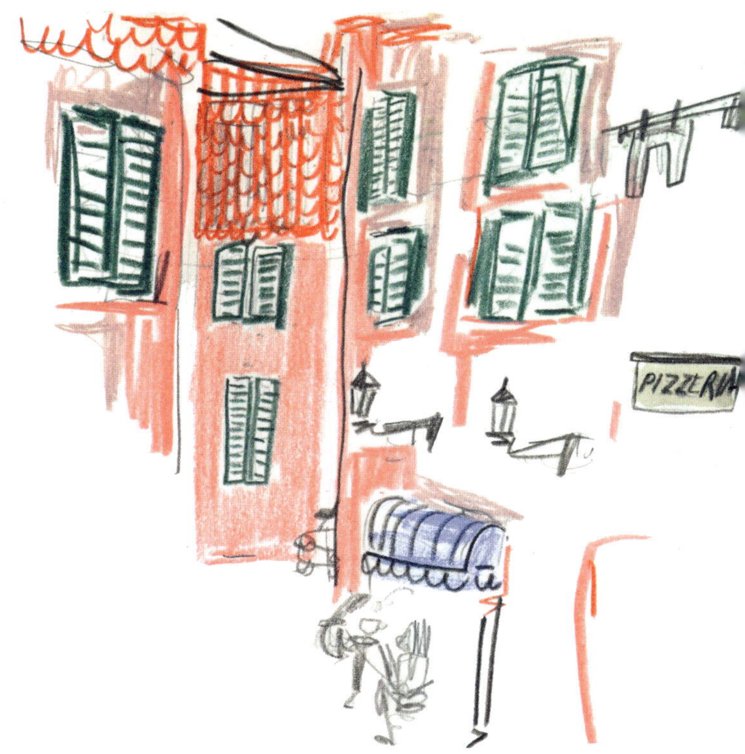

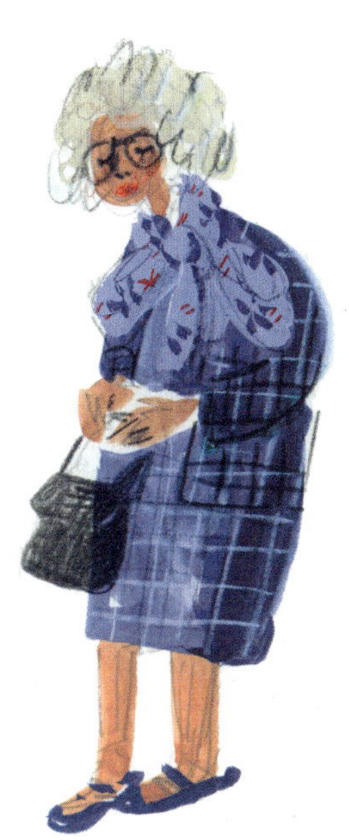

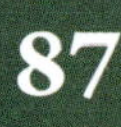

DRAW PEOPLE LOOKING AT SCULPTURES.

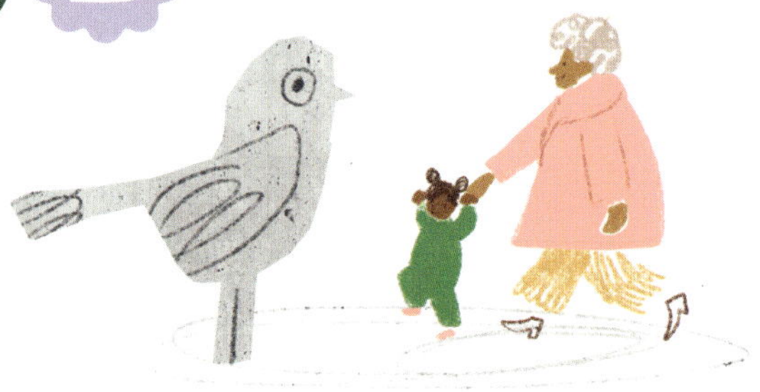

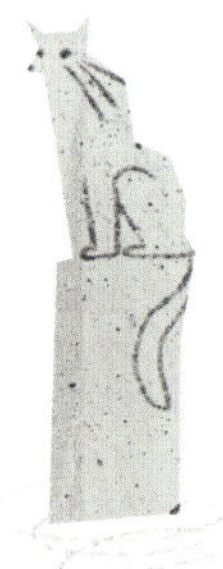

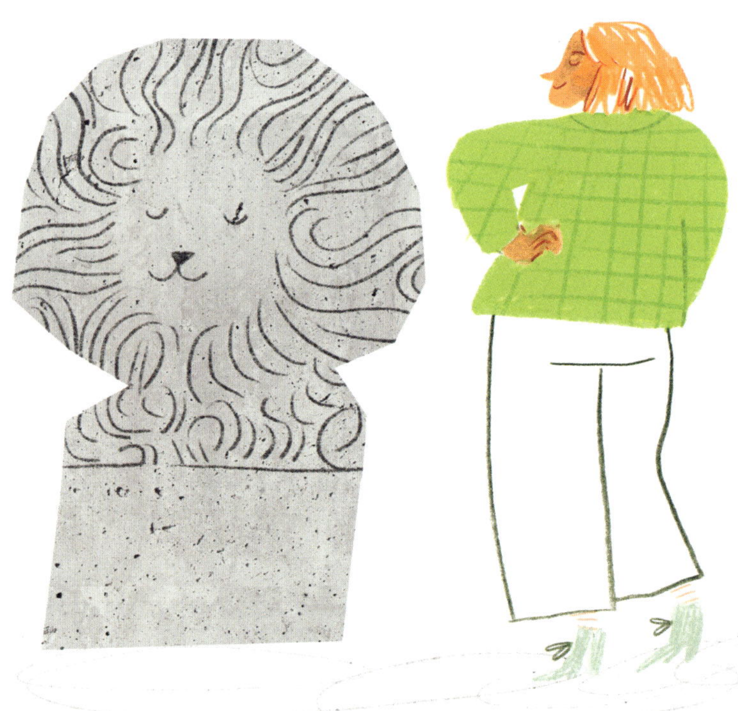

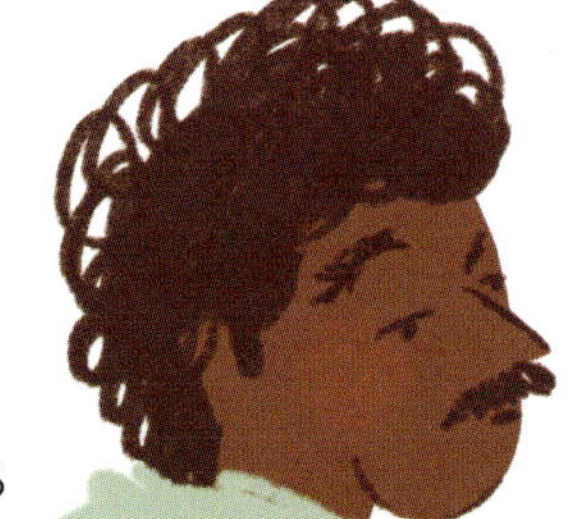

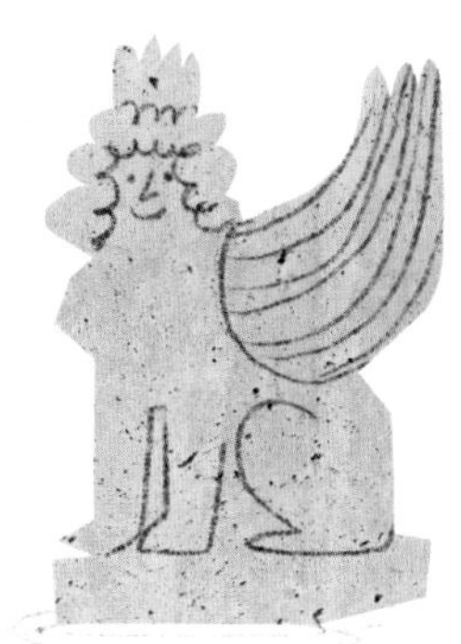
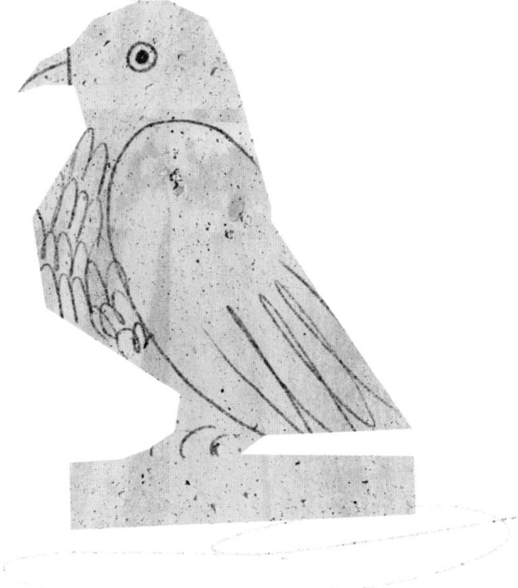
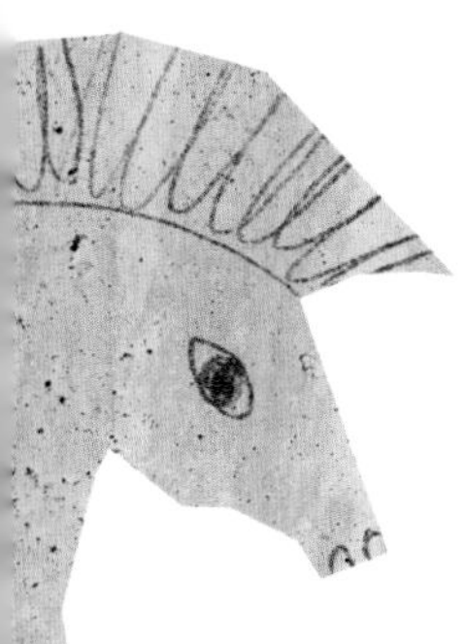
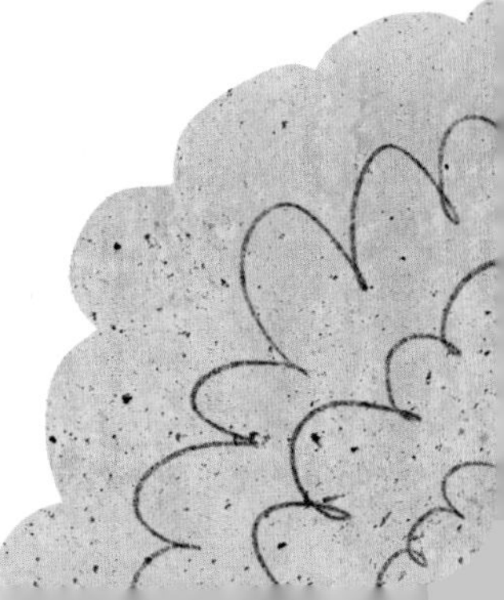

USE YOUR GRAPHITE PENCIL AND FILL IN THESE RECTANGLES WITH PEOPLE. Make them fit each shape and don't be afraid to go crazy with proportions!

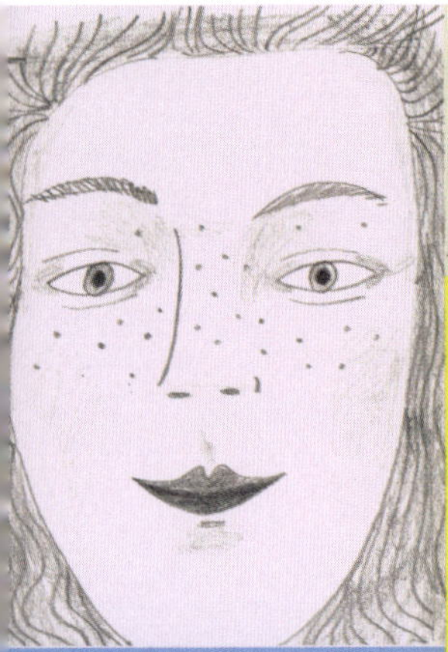

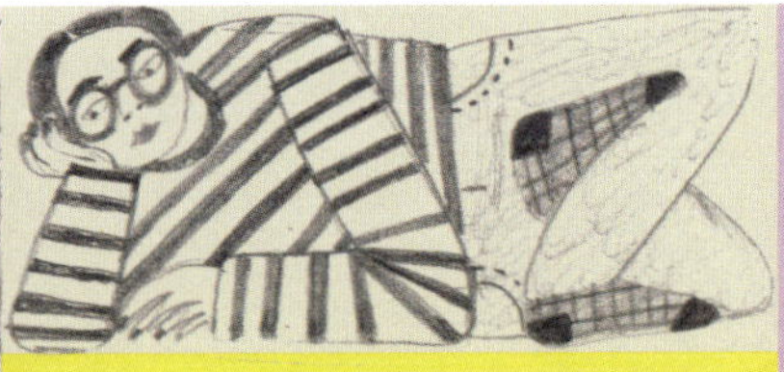

DRAW A PORTRAIT USING UNEXPECTED COLOURS. Maybe the skin is green, purple or yellow, go for the wildest and weirdest colour!

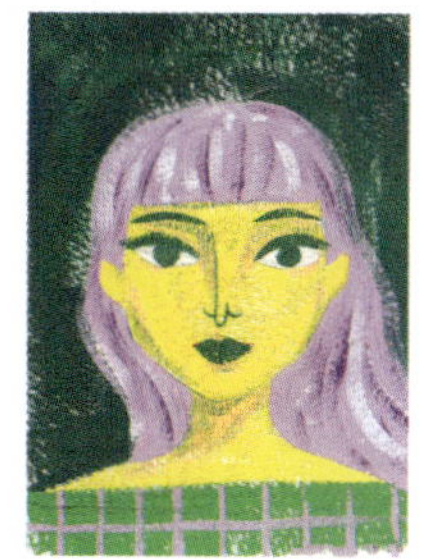
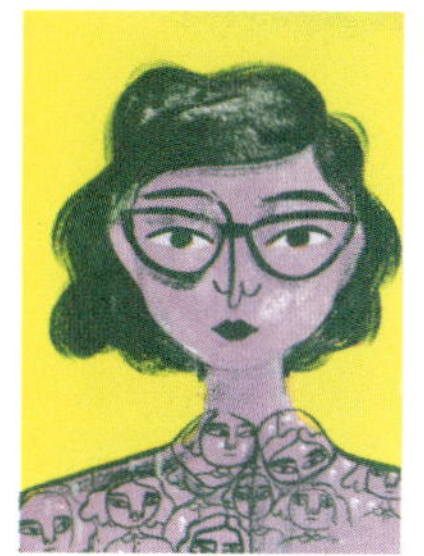

SET A TIME LIMIT OF THREE MINUTES
AND DRAW TWO PEOPLE.
One head and shoulders, close-up, and
one full body. Work fast and enjoy it!

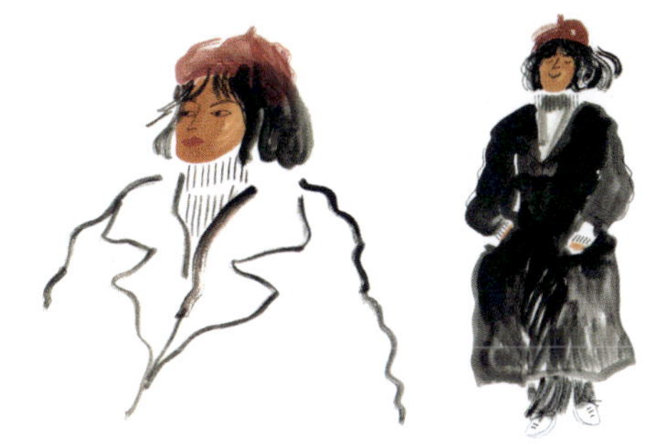

DRAW PEOPLE HAVING DINNER.

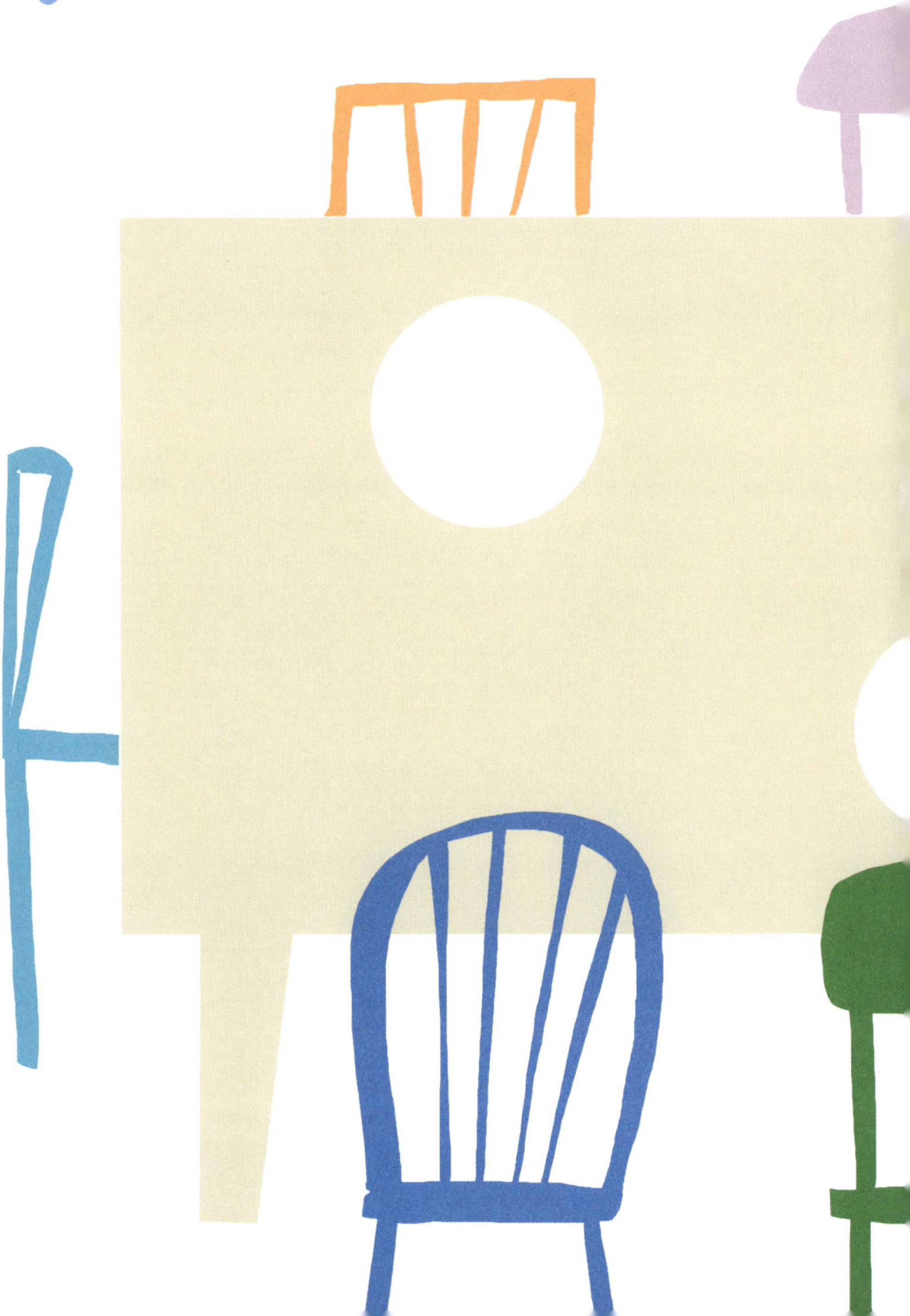

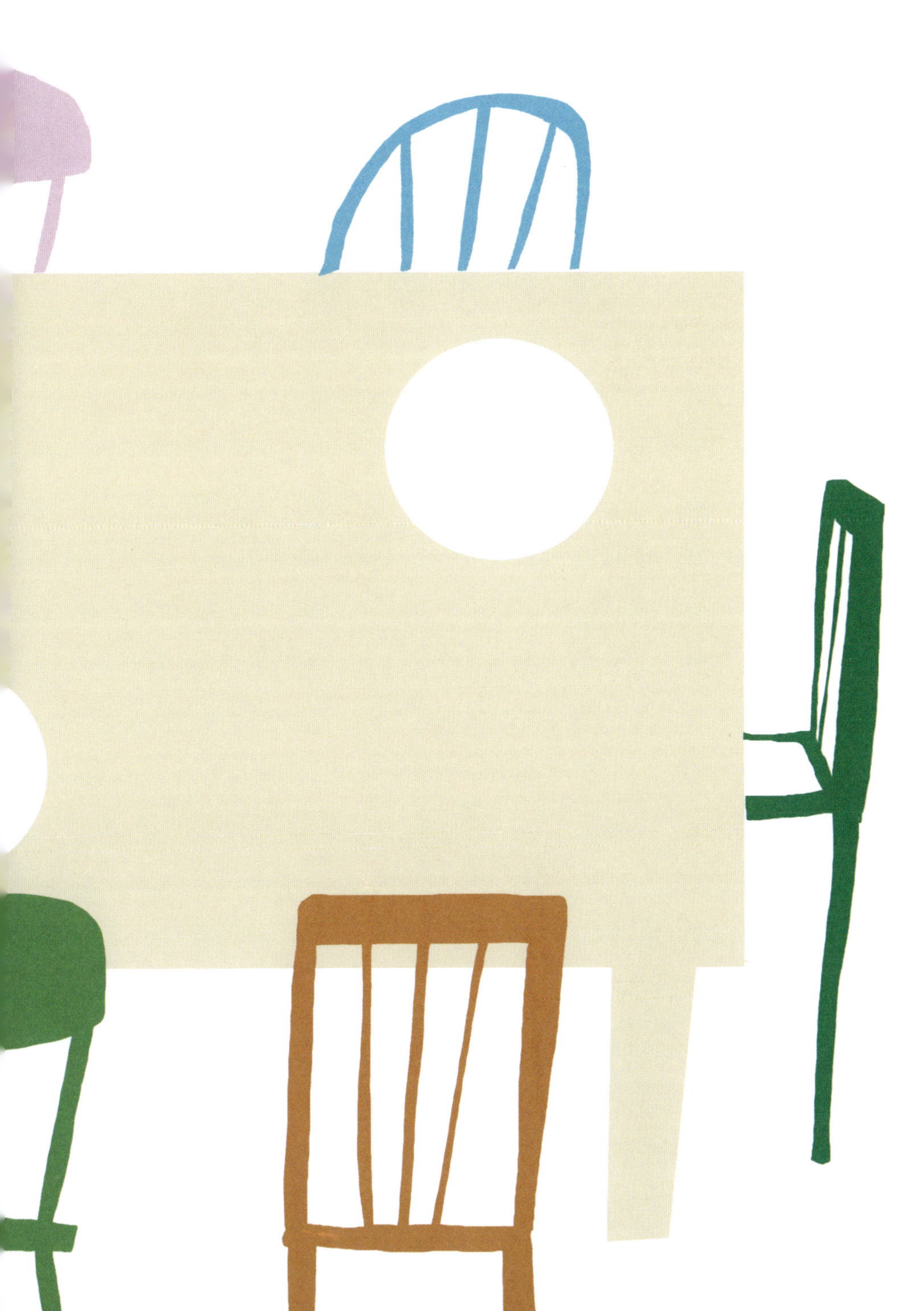

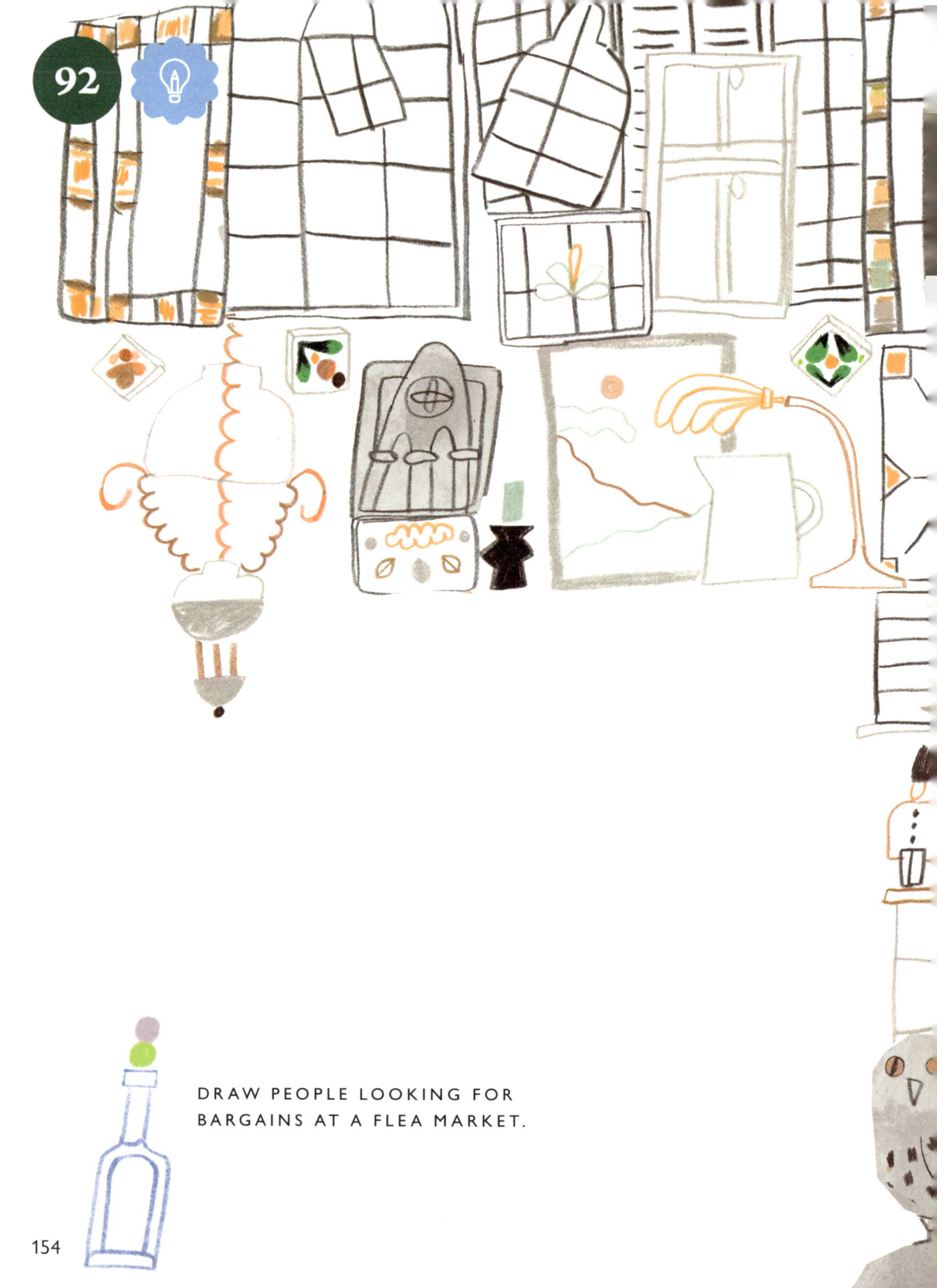

DRAW PEOPLE LOOKING FOR
BARGAINS AT A FLEA MARKET.

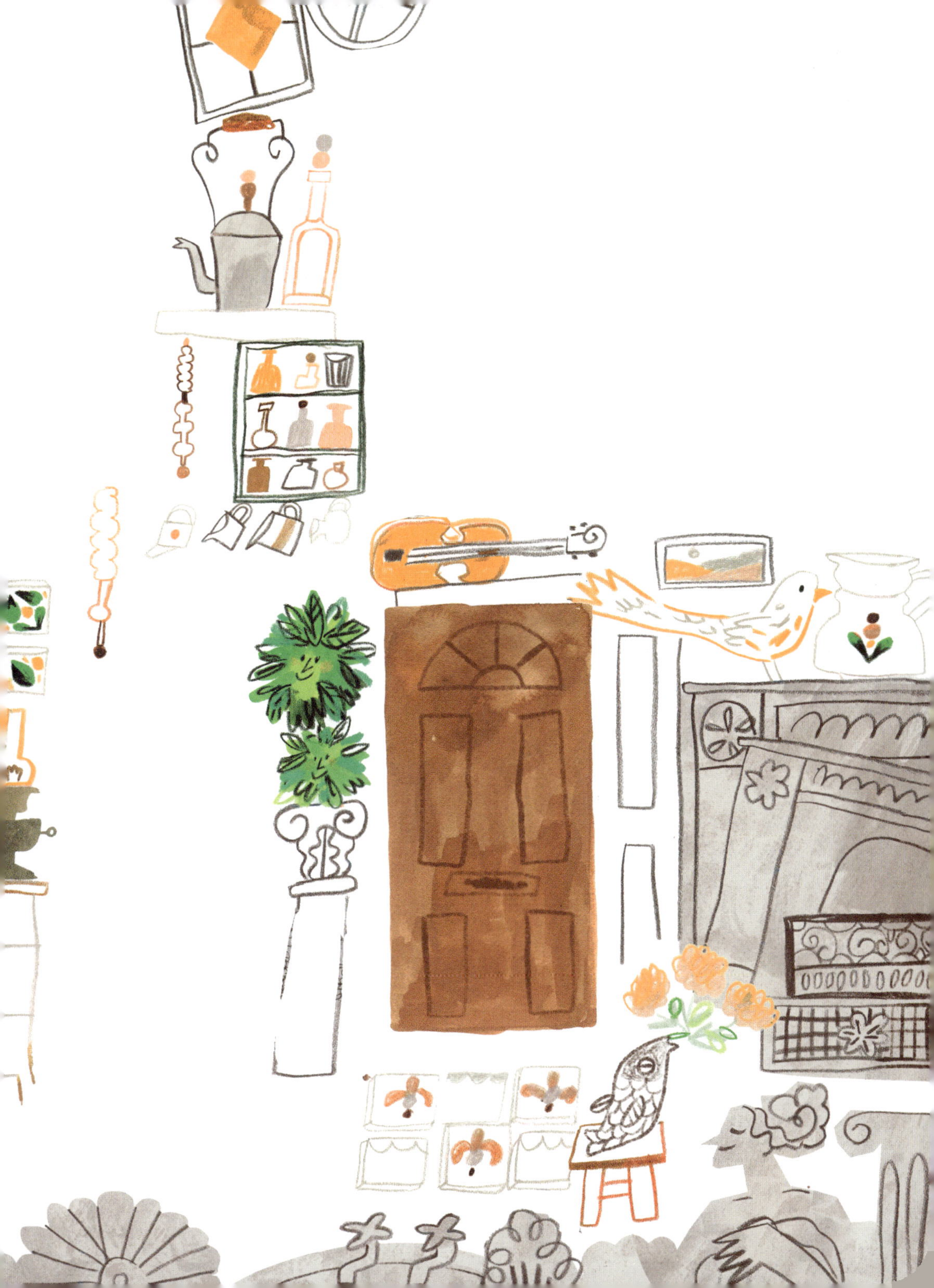

93

DRAW A FAMILY PORTRAIT.
Body or head and shoulders only. Create a limited colour scheme and once you have decided on composition and colours draw the portrait on the opposite page.

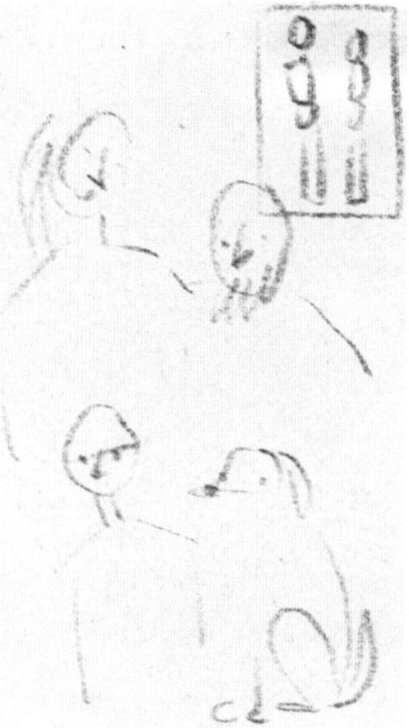

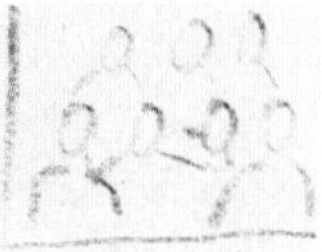

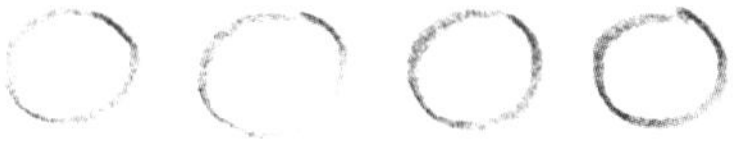

94

CREATE AN INTERESTING AND DYNAMIC COMPOSITION BY PLAYING WITH SCALE. Draw two people, one close-up (head and shoulders) and another full height. Use my sketchbook drawing as inspiration or draw your own. Try choosing subjects that are new and exciting to you. If you mostly draw women, draw men of different ages and body shapes.

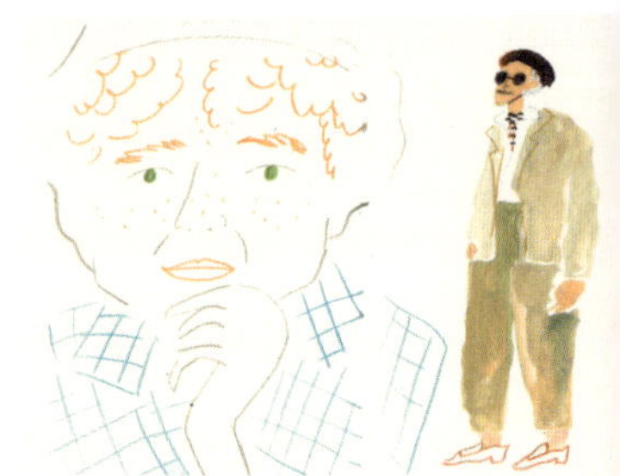

EACH PICTURE YOU DRAW IN THIS BOOK HAS COMPOSITION
That means we can copy it to create our own new drawing.
Below are four compositions and people I drew using them.
Come up with your own drawings on the page opposite based
on the fun compositions I have worked up for you.

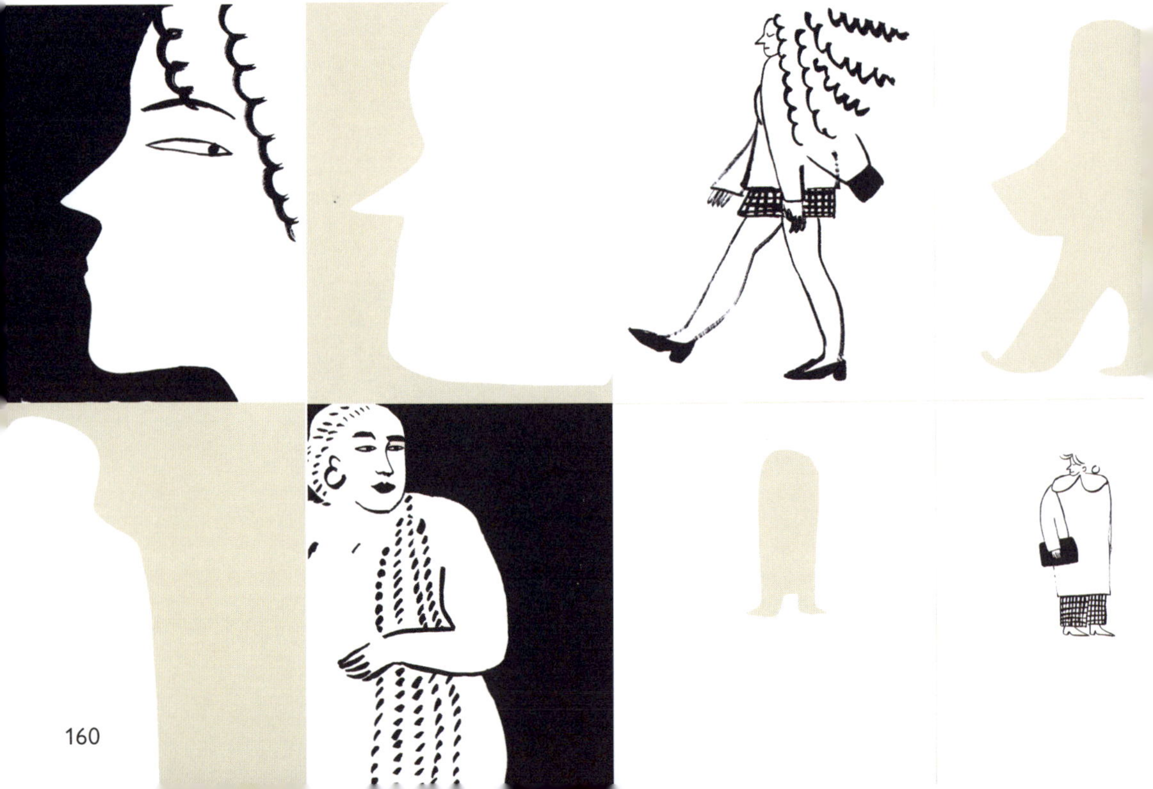

MAKING A COLLAGE PERSON IS SO CREATIVE. Collage is made by combining different materials – such as photographs, pieces of paper or fabric – to make a new piece of artwork. Use collage to make a head and shoulders portrait.

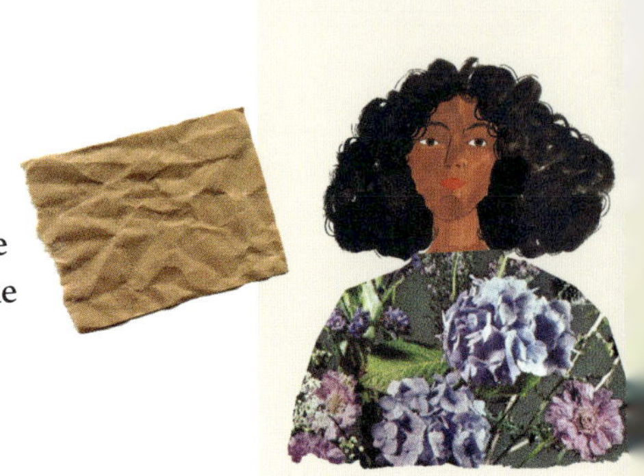

DRAW A FULL-BODY PORTRAIT, THEN ADD DETAILS USING COLLAGE. You can use collage elements for the hair, facial features and clothes.

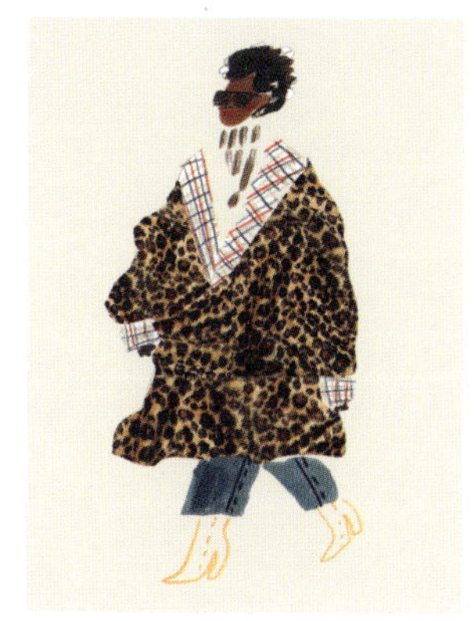

Draw a person in black and white with their clothes in colour. The contrast between the monochromatic and full colour will create a fun and graphic result. Colour in your frame in any matching shade.

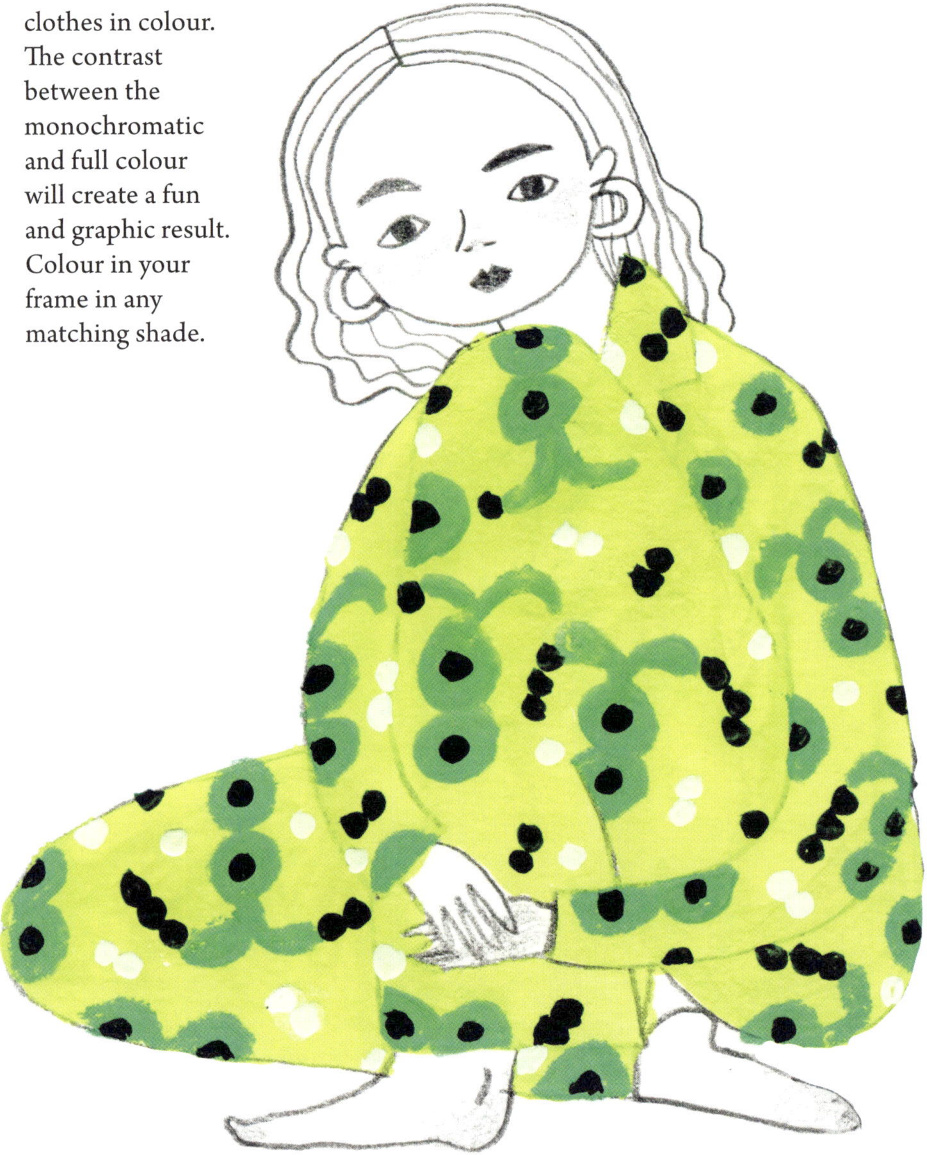

99

If you have the chance, go to a life drawing class and fill in this page with different poses and people! And if it's not for you, draw dressed people (feel free to add clothes to this model too).

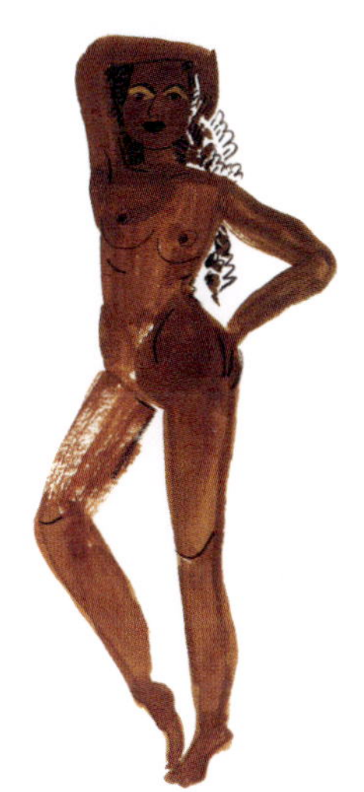

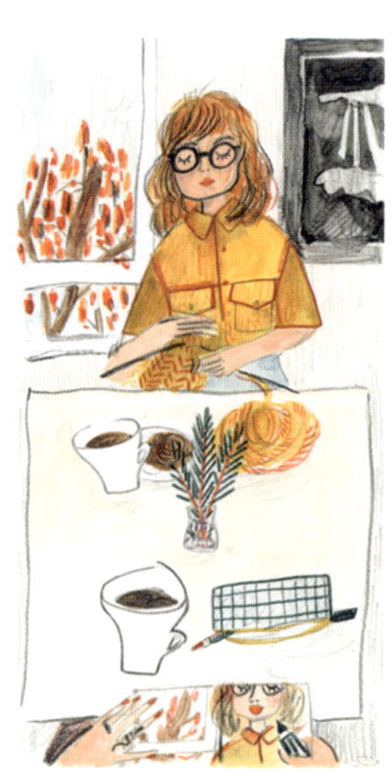

TAKE YOUR SKETCHBOOK OUT WITH
YOU FOR OBSERVATIONAL DRAWING.
Draw a scene of the people around you.

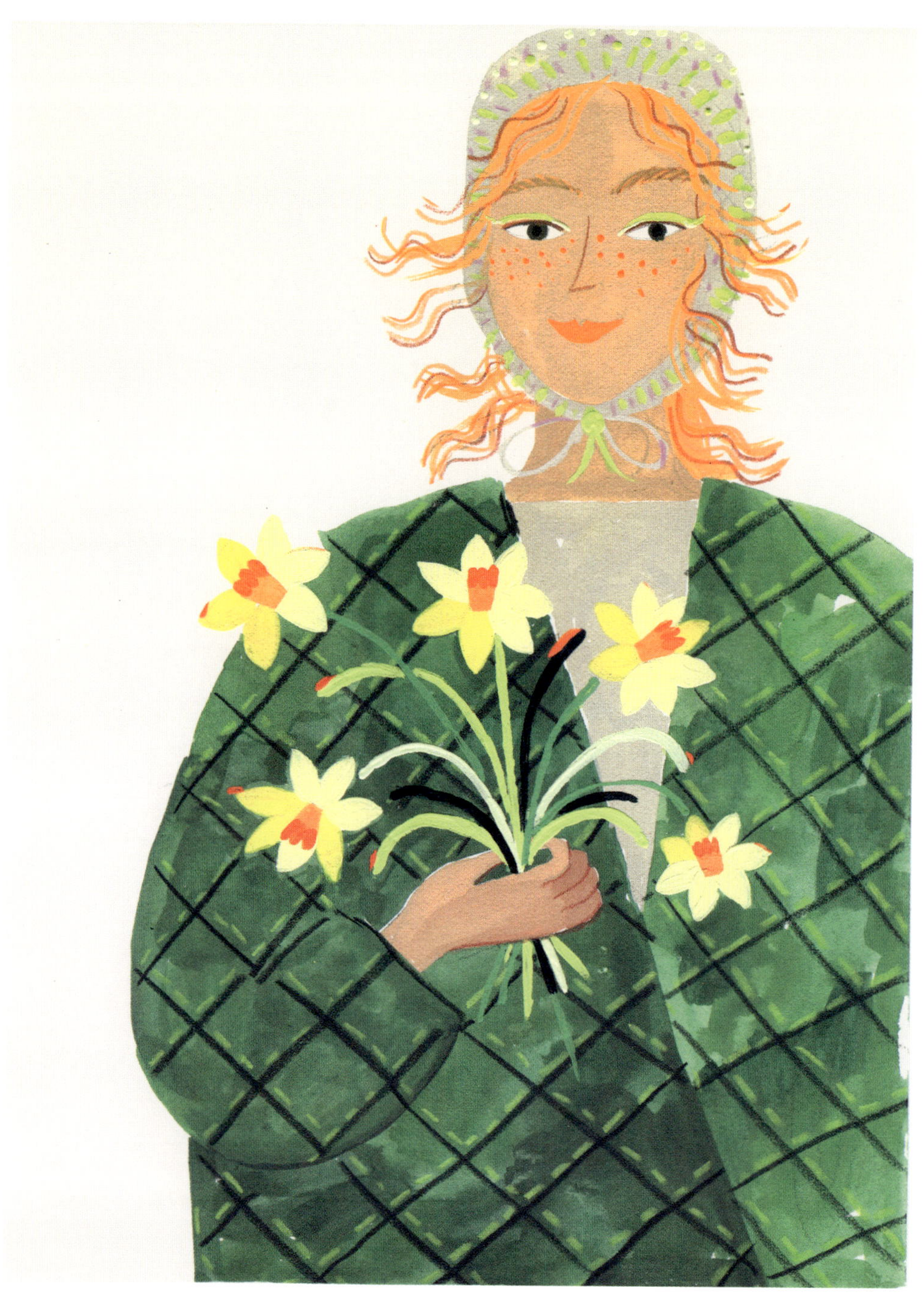

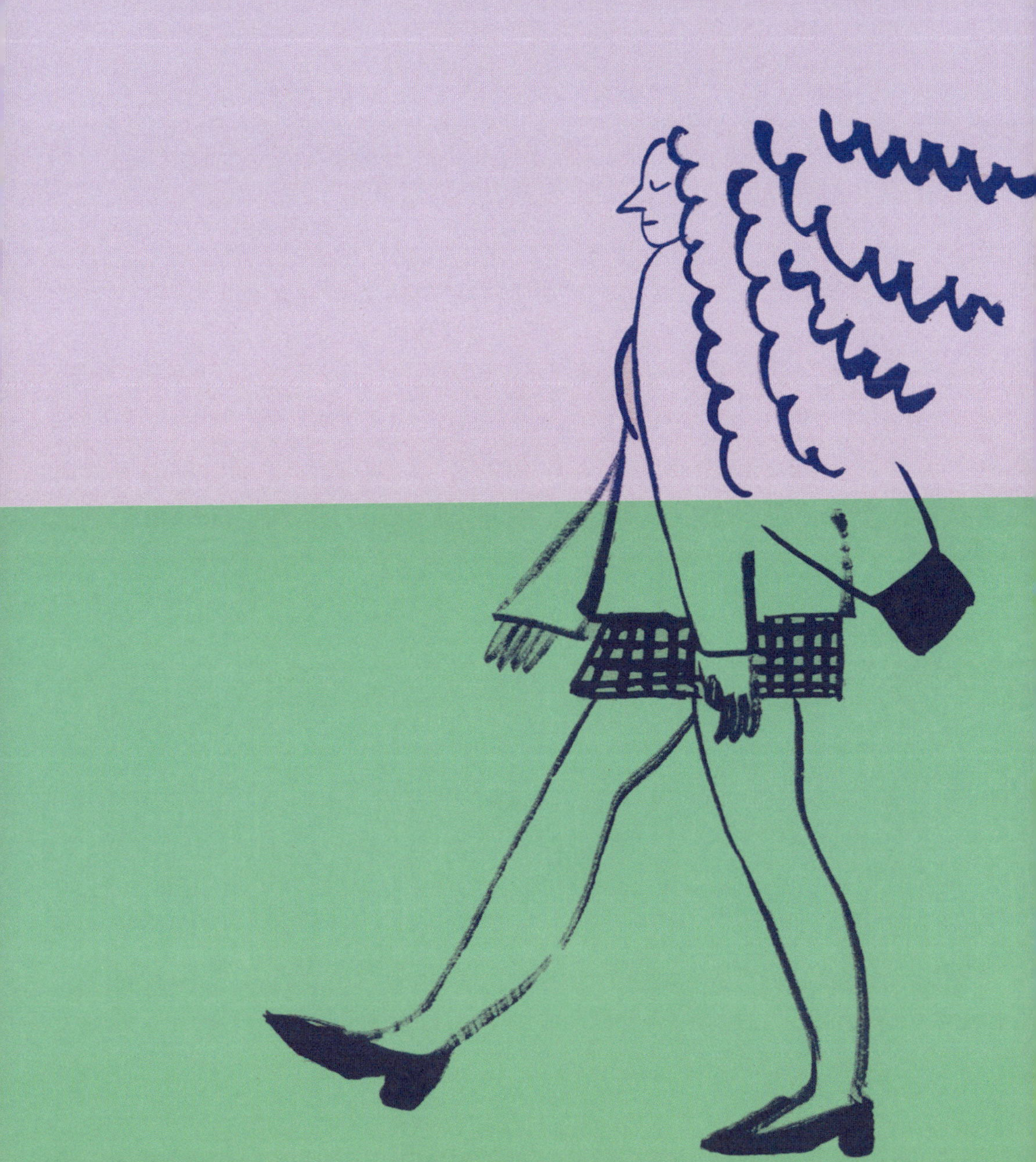

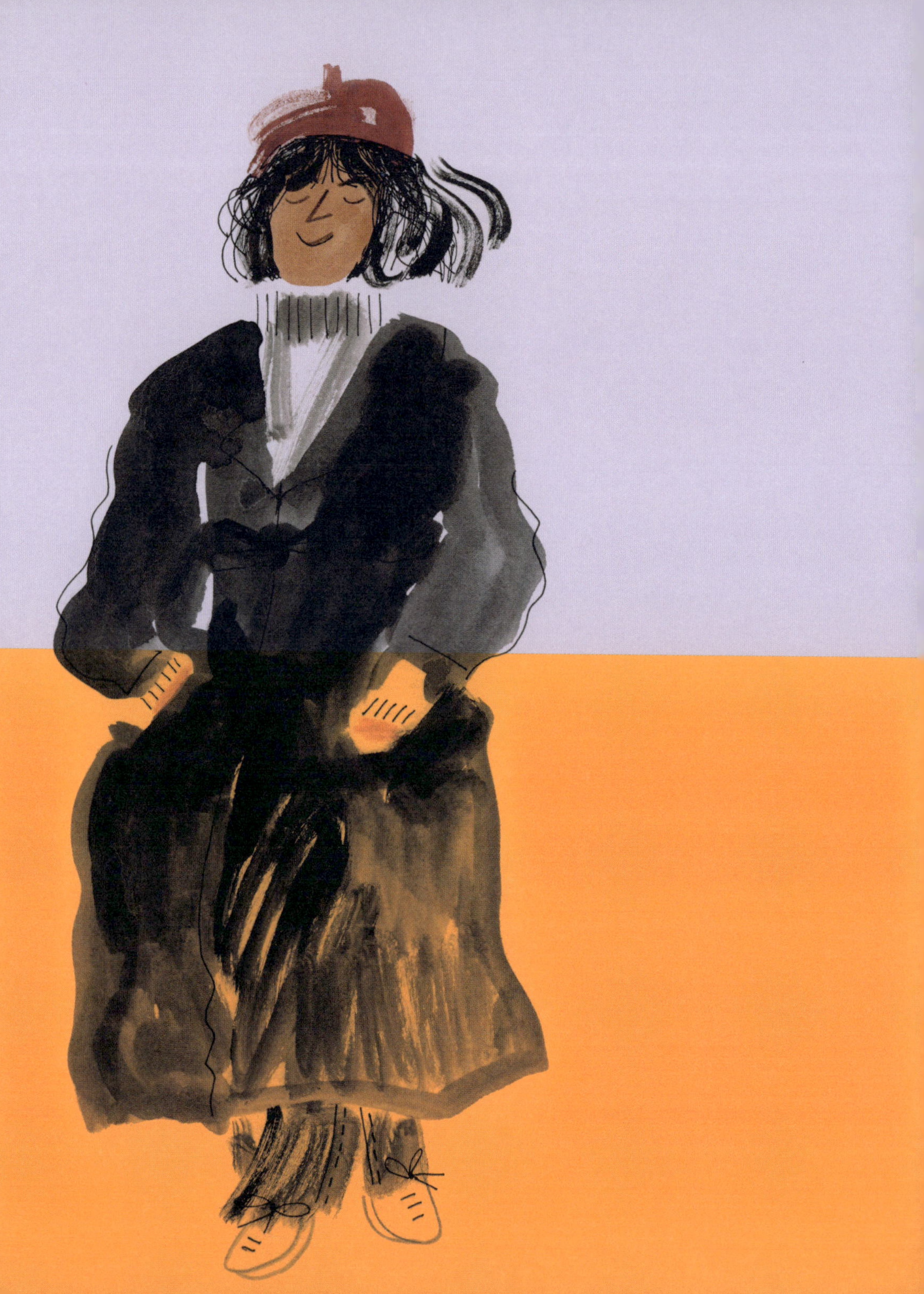

Acknowledgements

THANK YOU SO MUCH TO...

My editor Kate, for believing in this book and my work, for the generous words of encouragement and enthusiasm. To Claire for elevating my work into an inspiring journal for people to use, thank you for making it all look so so good!

Thank you to Hardie Grant for making this project a reality.

Tusen takk to my partner Ole for coffee, excellent jokes and being a great support.

To my grandfather Viktar and grandmother Liudmila, for unconditional love and generous advice that I don't always listen to but absolutely should. Here it is so you don't repeat the same mistake I did: meet deadlines early and enjoy time in nature.

Thank you to my parents and my sister, you are my inspiration! And to my friends and colleagues for all the pep talks and support.

And to you my dear to readers, you who support my work, leave reviews and send messages. Without you none of this would be possible. Thank you so much!

VIKTORIJA SEMJONOVA

Viktorija is a Latvian illustrator and designer, now based in Bergen, Norway.

Having studied and lived in London, UK, Viktorija draws inspiration from diverse artistic influences.

With a passion for drawing from observation, she specialises in creating illustrations for publications and products using traditional materials such as gouache, pencils and pastels.

She has taught workshops at the Victoria and Albert Museum and shared her knowledge of drawing people both in person and online. She is passionate about encouraging everyone to get drawing and be creative without limits.

Viktorija has created illustrations and worked on a range of creative projects with Pinterest, Ovarian Cancer Action, Global Citizen, YouTube, Swatch, Tombow, Kikki.K and various book publishers.

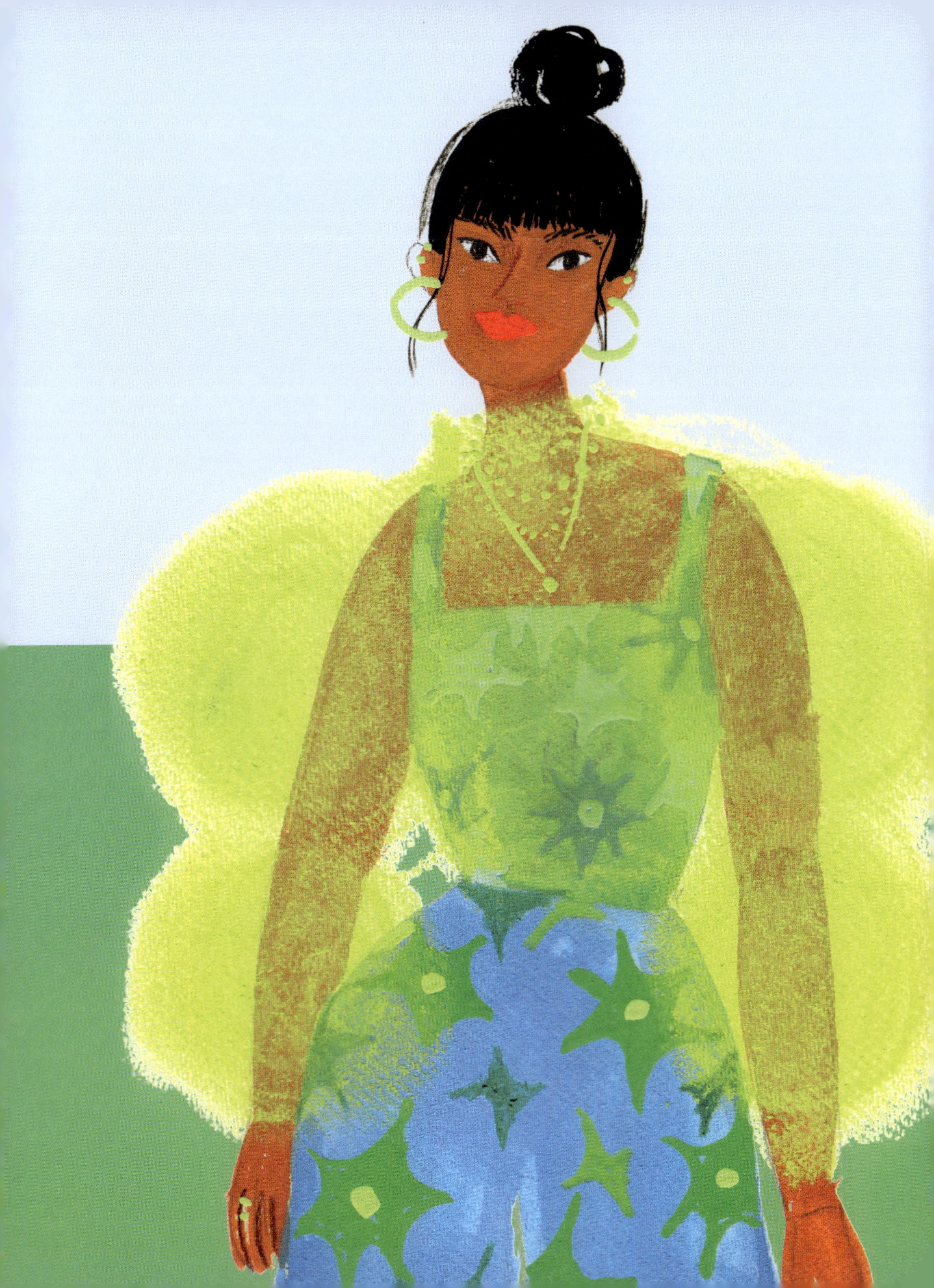

Quadrille, Penguin Random House UK, One Embassy Gardens, 8 Viaduct Gardens,
London SW11 7BW

Quadrille Publishing Limited is part of the Penguin Random House group of companies
whose addresses can be found at global.penguinrandomhouse.com

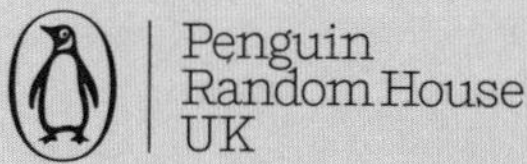

First published by Hardie Grant Books in 2023

www.penguin.co.uk

A CIP catalogue record for this book is available from the British Library

ISBN: 9781784886417
10 9 8 7 6 5 4

Publishing Director: Kajal Mistry
Commissioning Editor: Kate Burkett
Design: Claire Warner Studio
Photography: Maryna Kolpakova
Copy Editor and Proofreader: Clare Double
Production Controller: Martina Georgieva

Printed in China by C&C Offset Printing Co., Ltd.

The authorised representative in the EEA is Penguin Random House Ireland,
Morrison Chambers, 32 Nassau Street, Dublin D02 YH68.

Penguin Random House is committed to a sustainable future for our business, our readers
and our planet. This book is made from Forest Stewardship Council® certified paper.